TWO DOT RANCH
A Biography of Place

NANCY HEYL RUSKOWSKY

Copyright © 2008   Nancy Ruskowsky
ISBN# 978-1-932636-47-5 Softcover

Library of Congress Control Number: 2009904818

Cover Design: Antelope Design
Cover Photo: Annette Chaudet

Library of Congress Cataloging-in-Publication Data

Ruskowsky, Nancy, Heyl, 1940-
Two Dot Ranch : a biography of place /
Nancy Heyl Ruskowsky.

p. cm.

www.pronghornpress.org

This book is dedicated to every Two Dot pioneer,
from the first to the most recent;
to each owner, manager, and foreman;
and to every hired hand
who ever pushed a Two Dot cow up the trail
or kept a cowboy fed.

C O N T E N T S

PART FOUR
THE ERA OF EXPANSION
1933-1975

Yves Burrus and his daughter Geraldine with cowdog puppies in 1995.
(Courtesy Yves Burrus)

FOREWORD

A VISIT TO Wyoming has a romantic and nostalgic appeal for many Europeans. The Far West still evokes visions of rugged mountains and green pastures, remote, idyllic surroundings, memories of Indian legends, wild stories of buffalo chases. The art of Frederic Remington, Albert Bierstadt, and Karl Bodmer among others—many found in Cody's Buffalo Bill Historical Center— remind us of the Wild West past, which still lingers through nature into the present.

Many friends joined me at the Two Dot Ranch while I lived there, intermittently, between 1978 and 1999. For many it was the fulfillment of a child's dream. Visitors are greeted by a valley through which a tree-lined stream splashes. On top of the hill, the beautiful log house ovelooks the ranch grounds with an endless view of meadows, forest, and mountains reaching up into the sky.

Early in the morning, around six, the cowboys would come up to the house for coffee. Their boots lined the kitchen entrance, but most of the time their hats were kept on, tilted slightly backward, which gave them an eccentric look. Around the table the day was planned: entertainment for the guests at the ranch—who was getting which horse, which saddle, which bridle; where elk, mule deer and more wildlife had been spotted; tips for the enthusiastic hunters, freshly arrived from all over—and how to allot the hunting permits. Guests examined the rifles and cartridges displayed in a glass cabinet.

The cowboys, who definitely were an attraction, sported beards during the colder months and were clean-shaven in the hot, dusty summer. They really looked like the Marlboro Man as dressed by Ralph Lauren: chaps over faded jeans, fringed elkhide gloves, bandanas, silver trinkets around the neck. The authentic cowboy look was there, worn and weatherproof.

There was lots to do, depending on the season: hunting, trout fishing, roundups, and brandings fragrant with charred cowhide. There was also the occasional cattle auction with serious-looking out-of-towners loading up, stampeding cows into huge trucks—destiny: the American hamburger.

There were wonderful excursions, as long as you dared jump on the back of a horse. This is definitely the best way to take in all the magic of the place: to ride up into the mountains, visit the mares with their foals on the way, picnic on a ridge overlooking half of the world, ride through sagebrush and wild irises, through steep canyons lined with majestic coral-red ramparts—silent reminders that dinosaurs and other monsters were at home here thousands of moons ago. Riding through thick pine forests, the cowboys might point out a badly scratched trunk and recount hair-raising tales of grizzlies and wolves.

But higher up, gentle and shy mountain goats and elusive bighorn sheep were grazing on the slopes, and if you were lucky, you could spot them on a summer's day. At the end of the trail was a deep blue mountain lake for those who liked to fish for trout. Later they might grill the catch over an open fire under the first glimmer of the stars.

Back at the ranch at dinnertime, guests might see herds of deer in the fields below. Now everyone related that day's adventures: who had shot an elk, who had lost the track of a deer in the woods, who had roped a runaway cow, who had fished the biggest trout, who had spotted a bear in the creek picking berries, and who had been lucky enough to see the newly introduced wild turkeys. Sometimes late at night the coyotes' laments could be heard.

On the last evening, we gathered at ranch headquarters with its residents, the cowboys, and their families for a farewell barbecue. Everyone now knew one another. If a guest sat down at the piano we would sing happily, yet with a trace of sadness. The wonderful days at the Two Dot had come to an end, yet everyone took a piece of the ranch with them in their hearts.

YVES BURRUS

INTRODUCTION

Ranch in Crisis, Tragedy, and Celebration

A Biography of Place

An early Cody Fourth of July parade headed down main street.
(Courtesy Beth Jobe Spears)

People afford the clearest window for looking on the world of yesterday. *

—Robert Utley

THIS IS THE HISTORY of the Two Dot, at one time recognized by many as the largest ranch in the world, set in the northwest corner of Wyoming, its vast acreage tipping over the edge of the Big Horn Basin and spilling into the Clarks Fork Valley. More importantly, it is the story of the people who settled, homesteaded, managed, expanded—and sometimes lost—the parcels of land that have gradually been merged, piece by piece, into today's Two Dot Ranch.

Since 1878 when John Chapman discovered the valley nourished by Pat O'Hara Creek, many have passed through the ranch's gates as owners, managers, horse trainers, cowboys and sheepherders, blacksmiths and mechanics, irrigators, teachers, cooks, foremen, and farmers. Some even came with moonshine on their minds, thievery in their hearts, or poaching in their plans. The Two Dot has always been home to colorful characters, major players in the livestock industry as well as short-term wannabes. Whatever their tenure, each of them, cowboy, farm manager, visitor, or hunter, seems to have come away changed in some positive way, no matter the source of their experiences.

In the beginning these lands had sustained Indian families for centuries. The Bannocks came from what is now Idaho, the Crow and Blackfeet from Montana, the Shoshone and Arapaho from farther south. Their stories tell of a wildlife paradise: buffalo, elk, deer, antelope, fish, and game birds provided their food, clothing, shelter, and tools. On Two Dot Flats one can still see traces of a drive line Indian hunters used to herd their prey.

The first white men to follow the trails and tributaries into the region were explorers and fur traders. John Colter is often credited as being the first white man in the Big Horn Basin; certainly he initiated the mountain man era when he left the Lewis and Clark Expedition in 1806 to return to the mountains. Documented mostly by others, Colter's travels brought him to some of the West's key landmarks that we all recognize today.

In the next seventy years many others followed, but seldom left their stories. American Fur Company trapper Pat O'Hara was the exception; his eccentric behavior feeds folk tales still told today. If oral histories are correct, would-be rancher John Chapman spent just one day with O'Hara in that wilderness before laying claim to it in 1878. Later Chapman would name the creek that wandered past the trapper's cabin, and the mountain that loomed above, in his honor. The time of O'Hara's disappearance is not recorded but he did complain to Chapman that the area was becoming overpopulated. Chapman never saw him again.

On September 4, 1878, the very day that Chapman negotiated with O'Hara for ranching rights, a battle raged along the Clarks Fork

River just to the north. At the battle of Bennett Butte, Colonel Nelson A. Miles and his troops killed eleven Bannocks and captured thirty-one of some eighty Indians who were encamped there. Also among the dead were Captain Andrew S. Bennett, namesake of the butte and a nearby creek, and a Crow guide named Little Rocky.

Indians had long used the Bannock Trail, which leads across the mountains from Idaho and skirts the upper pastures of today's Two Dot, in their annual food-gathering cycles. But now the trail had evolved into an escape route for bands on the run from skirmishes with whites.

The year before the battle, Chief Joseph had led his Nez Perce people through the Clarks Fork Canyon. It was an impossible feat according to military strategists trying to keep up with him. Headed for freedom in Canada, Joseph's band of seven hundred warriors, women, and children—a party the size of many present-day towns in the area—moved on horseback at a speed that army officials found unbelievable. But it wasn't fast enough: they would be captured just a few miles from the Canadian border.

Although geographically the Two Dot is considered part of the Big Horn Basin, it lies well over its northern lip and in the Clarks Fork watershed. The ranch has long straddled the Wyoming-Montana border, and so have its residents' loyalties, their interests often split between investments and issues in both states. That was especially true before the town of Cody rose in 1901; until then the ranch's supply hub was Red Lodge, just north of the Montana line. At around the same time the hundred-mile trail from Red Lodge south to Meeteetse was improved into a real road for passengers, supplies, and freight. As a newcomer twenty years earlier, though, John Chapman had to travel three hundred miles to Green River in southwest Wyoming to register the patent on his first land claim; he picked up his mail once or twice a year in Bozeman, Montana, more than two hundred miles north.

The Chapman ranch became a community unto itself. Chapman's wife Affie saw no other woman in her first two and a half years there—the closest neighbors were Otto Franc of the Pitchfork Ranch nearly fifty miles south at Meeteetse, and the Dilworth Ranch to the northwest in Montana Territory.

But while Chapman laid claim to the open range as far as the eye could see, the Homestead Act of 1862 had given other land-seekers the right to nibble at the edges of his cattle and sheep operation. With the future becoming clearer each day, Chapman was the first to fence the property and register his ownership—piece by piece and acre by acre. Ironically, the very neighbors taking their bites from the Chapman pie often found work at the ranch as they scrambled for cash to prove up on their claims.

Many prominent ranches today are run by multi-generational families who stake their reputation and future upon the land they own. In the history of the Two Dot only one family fits that description of longevity. The Taggart brothers, whose construction business built roads into Yellowstone National Park in the late 1920s and early 1930s, purchased the heart of the Two Dot in 1933. The family operated the ranch for twenty-nine years over two generations, its longest era of expansion.

The Curtis family followed with the same multi-generational dream. Partnering with H.P. Skoglund, a Minnesota insurance executive, they were on the verge of realizing it when circumstances changed, and once again the ranch was up for sale. Indeed, what the Two Dot's most successful families seem to share is the ability to develop, expand, and pass it on to newcomers. The value of the ranch has increased with every sale. Even so, ownership has often changed suddenly, uprooting those who called it home.

The Two Dot's most profitable eras have been led by partnerships: an experienced manager teamed with a deep-pocketed investor with dreams and funds to outpace the costs of tough winters, drought, and fluctuating livestock prices. The first such partners were E. M. Bent, the working member, and J. P. Allison, a visionary known as one of the fathers of Sioux City, Iowa; next came sheepman Joseph Ganguet and August Barth, a hardworking Billings blacksmith turned investor; later the team of Charles Curtis and H. P. Skoglund. It was "Skog" who built the beautiful lodge, sited for enjoyment of the mountain landscape. He was an owner of the Minnesota Vikings football team at the time.

In other partnerships, skilled managers represented out-of-state ownership. While Mick McCarty, the most recent, has worked for more than twenty years with two owners, John and Martin Jobe were technically the first to fit the job description.

The Jobe brothers went to work for John Chapman before the turn of the last century. In fact John applied for and received a land grant for a piece of property literally in his boss's front yard. Later Chapman had to buy a piece of land he thought he already owned in order to keep his operation together. When Chapman moved to Red Lodge to start a banking business, the Jobes continued running the ranch for him. They went on to manage the operation for two more sets of owners as well.

But Martin Jobe eventually fell in with Prohibition-era bootleggers developing a line of moonshine stills along Pat O'Hara Creek. He was caught at a still on the North Fork of the Shoshone River, the route from Cody into Yellowstone. While Jack Spicer was the region's ringleader and master liquor maker, it was Martin Jobe who fell from respect to infamy, the area's only bootlegger sent to the "pen." Ironically, though, it was Spicer who was killed in a Hatfield-McCoy–style shooting the same month Prohibition was repealed.

Butch Cassidy, of course, was far better known for his criminal activities than was Martin Jobe. He and his gang, who reportedly hid out on the ranch's east edge, made the mistake of stealing horses from John Chapman. He soon discovered that he was no match for Chapman's wrath: the rancher tracked Cassidy down and with Otto Franc eventually saw him to prison. It was the only time the outlaw found himself behind bars.

Even before Cassidy's escapades in the late 1880s and early 1890s, cattle rustling gangs had developed an underground that moved livestock through a five-state territory and beyond. The Wyoming Stock Growers Association was born during this contentious era. While Chapman never belonged, perhaps due to his Montana leanings and his bent for taking matters into his own hands, many of the ranch's later owners provided leadership for the Association, including two generations of Taggarts.

Today, legal issues still concern the Two Dot's overseers. In the late 1970s new owner Yves Burrus, amazed by the number of poachers and trespassers taking advantage of the ranch, took steps to control illegal activities while providing fair hunting access according to season.

A Geneva investment banker and Two Dot owner from 1977 to 1999, Burrus has said, "I feel like I am a man of three countries –Switzerland, France, and Wyoming." If so, he has predecessors: Burrus, early on, discovered the Two Dot's "French Connection." Just as the Scotch supported the Swan Land and Cattle Company in southern Wyoming and the English invested heavily in other areas of the state, Frenchmen have steadily reappeared throughout the ranch's 125-year history.

Burrus's research indicates that the LaVerendrye brothers may have reached the region as early as 1742, coming down from Canada. Paul Breteche arrived in 1884 to manage earlier French investments involving the Trail Creek, Crown, and Shield ranches, all started by another Frenchmen, Victor Arland. Arland planned to sell his startup ranches to fellow countrymen.

Breteche and Chapman frequently worked together; they also co-invested in two Red Lodge enterprises, a butcher shop and the bank that started as Meyer, Chapman and Breteche. But by 1897

Breteche had returned to Nantes, France, having sold all his American investments. All that remain of his years in the West are a few photographs, some letters, and his name on a North Fork creek.

Another Frenchman who actually lived two lives in America, Joseph Ganguet, saved the ranch from extinction during the early twenties. A sheepman, Ganguet had immigrated to California as a sixteen year old herder. After five years of guarding his boss's flocks he came out of the hills to collect his wages, only to learn that the owner had no money. Ganguet returned to France to patch up his dream. When he boarded another ship bound for America several years later, he was determined to own his own livestock. Eventually, Ganguet would give the Two Dot Ranch its permanent name, based on the brand that marked his sheep. He held the operation together through some tough times in agriculture.

During the Two Dot's homestead era, which actually lasted from the 1870s through the 1950s, the ranch's owners multiplied, its lands worked by several families. Culminating in the 1920s and early 1930s, the era was—for some—an age of hope and celebration of dreams realized. But while today's dreamers may harken to those "good old days," in actuality many of those settlers were tragically smoked out, their efforts unrewarded. While millions of acres of rangeland sod were plowed under in the first years of land grant offerings, the lands of the Two Dot, like much of the West, were not intended to be broken into sections, half-sections, and quarters.

The dreams of some other owners, too, were short-lived. Timing was the trouble for Frank Hudson of Lander. When he bought the ranch from Ganguet and Barth's widow in 1919, climate and weather patterns that had provided perfect conditions for more than a decade were finally returning to "normal"— that is, less conducive to lush grazing and profit-taking. No longer could investors get rich overnight. It was Joseph Ganguet who put off his own dream of returning to France to stay on the ranch and protect it when Hudson was forced to walk away. James McKnight of Texas made his own stab at the Two Dot dream in 1924 when Ganguet finally sold. But McKnight, too, watched his dreams slashed into economic ruin, although he managed to hold on until 1930.

Ken Rogge's tenure was also brief. An Oregon lumberman, Rogge found himself on an environmental hot seat. He purchased the Two Dot, planning to use it in a land swap, just before public concern erupted for the spotted owl in the forests of his home state. Those concerns, and their economic fallout, altered his status from wealthy businessman to an owner backing out of his Two Dot deal just two years after the purchase. A powerful message for the future was being played out in Oregon, an environmental scenario that would affect the future of the Two Dot and ranches throughout the West—a call for management changes.

The environmental solution probably came easier for Burrus, who was raised with a European stewardship ethic. He had been hunting with his French grandfather since childhood, absorbing the lessons of stewardship, conservation, and preservation. His purchase of the ranch opened an era of environmental focus with broad-based stewardship projects in water management and species protection. Today the ranch provides protection for a number of endangered and threatened species including the mountain plover, prairie dog, and grizzly bear. In the last few years a wild turkey flock has been established near the headquarters.

The present-day operation incorporates four major properties: the headquarters; the George Heald Ranch, often referred to as the horse ranch and now known as the Lower Two Dot; the Daly Ranch which is the heart of the farming operation, and the River Ranch where Ernest Hemingway spent a summer noting his trout catches in the guest book.

Today's Two Dot, a collection of deeded, oral rentals, state and railroad lands, and Bureau of Land Management leases, starts just over the rim of Skull Creek Pass about fifteen miles north of Cody. Headquarters lies a few miles ahead, and the surrounding irrigated hay meadows nestle deep between the shoulders of Heart and Pat O'Hara Mountains.

A map of the ranch introduces the curious to many place names that trigger conversations, sometimes about the pioneer and homesteading families that started there: Daly, Yost, Hill, Kimball, Simpson, Hogan, Newmeyer, Blaine and Pat O'Hara. More often for those who know these lands, the places remembered are settings for hard luck situations, tales, and events—especially wrecks. Much folklore has developed though settlers' tangles with horses, bears, and rattlesnakes, and with the human dramas of childbirth and devastating illness.

There's Chapman Bench to the north of headquarters spilling its sagebrush pastures onto the badlands to the east, which are nourished so shallowly by Big and Little Sand Coulees. This wide strip of high desert creeps still farther east, finally narrowing to a neck before spreading out into a northeastern head that merges into oil fields and the dry winter country known as Polecat Bench.

While little actual farming is done today, hay is still produced on meadows to the northwest that were once part of Paint Creek Ranch and the Daly place. Other locales with names like the Ox Yoke and Skull Creek, Natural Corral, and Water Gap may be tougher to imagine but Heifer, Mare, Gas Well, Red Hill, Beef, Sheep Creek, and Willow Patch conjure up the pictures intended. Other pasturelands are named directionally, such as the North Badland and South Chapman.

Pat O'Hara Creek flows off the mountain it shares a name with, wending eastward, then bending north and snaking its way through the Two Dot until it reaches the Clarks Fork, quenching the thirst of land and animals along the way. Other water sources the ranch depends upon are Blaine, Dry, and Paint Creeks, all wandering across the lands of the Two Dot until through one means or another they dump into the Clarks Fork.

Bald Ridge—the range which figures so prominently in the stories of the Two Dot Ranch and the government lease ranch owners were so dependent upon—sprawls out to the northwest well away from headquarters and is centered above the Clarks Fork Canyon.

While Heart Mountain has been so named for as long as whites have traveled the area, Pat O'Hara is the more forbidding mountain—yet its intrigue and beauty leave one breathless. Its forested peaks and high mountain meadows invite from afar, beckoning cattle, cowboys, and dreamers in the summer and drawing hunters into the fall until the expiration of their licenses drives them home with December snows.

Today the ranch is once again under new ownership, but a loyal employee base remains; these skilled individuals see their positions as more than jobs. Their livelihoods call for the same emotional commitment that has served the land well over time.

As promoted by Burrus early in his tenure, wildlife abounds, water is managed carefully, and grass is recognized as a major natural resource. While environmental concerns are paramount, sound financial policy demands that the ranch succeed on its own. Fortunately, these goals can support one another. The Two Dot continues to foster a diversity of land and animal resources, sustaining profits while protecting the land as well.

While this is the first book to be written on the Two Dot, it is not to be considered the definitive work by any means. The final word on the ranch belongs to the people who have been a part of this landscape—they own the opportunity. The full story will come to light only gradually: around kitchen tables, at brandings, or in calving sheds—or maybe among those moving cattle on the mountain or hunting at camps throughout the region. It will be told in the hundreds of homes and gathering holes where tales like these are shared by those who have lived the Two Dot story.

Within the confines of these covers we attempt to celebrate the richness of the information so enthusiastically shared up to this point and look forward to learning much more.

*The introductory quote used in this section is taken from a speech the former chief historian for the National Park Service, Robert Utley, now retired, gave at the dedication symposium for the Buffalo Bill Historical Center Harold D. McCracken Library, Cody, Wyoming.

A Biography of Place

PART ONE

A Ranch Built on an Historical Stage
1800-1878

A Biography of Place

CHAPTER ONE

John Colter:
A Lewis and Clark Explorer
in Two Dot Country

Two Dot cowboy moving cattle.
(Courtesy Jane Riddle Thompson)

HUNKERED NAKED UNDER a tangle of brush in the icy waters of Montana's Madison River, John Colter pondered his plight. The young explorer had left the Lewis and Clark Corps of Discovery on its homeward journey two years earlier, drawn to stay in the Rocky Mountain wilderness. Here, north of the Big Horn Basin, he had developed friendships among the Crow, Shoshone, and Flathead tribes. It was the Blackfeet, though, who had him trapped among the driftwood snags, and their intentions were not friendly.

Actually, he must have been amazed to be alive. That was more than the Indians had planned for. If he kept his wits about him, he might still make his way back to Fort Raymond, two hundred miles away at the confluence of the Yellowstone and Big Horn Rivers. His plan called for a great deal of patience, something fairly new to Colter's nature.

The Blackfeet had captured Colter on the banks of the Jefferson Fork, five miles south of the Madison, after shooting his partner. More than once they had turned their guns on him. That was just yesterday. But if, during this nightmare, Colter had any misgivings about the life he had chosen, he would soon dismiss them.

As he clung to the underside of a driftwood raft snagged on

Aerial view of the basin called Big Horn that sits between the Bighorn Mountains and the Rockies. The Two Dot continues over the far northwest lip.

cottonwood roots along a sandbar, it took all his patience to outwait the warriors searching for him. His feet throbbed, studded with prickly pear spines. Clotted blood stained his cheeks and chin where vessels had burst during his running escape from the fleet Indians. It had been a game planned by the chief, much as a cat plays with its prey—a chase to delay Colter's certain death. They underestimated their enemy.

The man hiding in the river on that spring day in 1808 was scarcely the same person who had signed on when Meriwether Lewis stopped for recruits at Pittsburgh five years earlier. Army Private Colter was ready for adventure as he climbed aboard the keelboat. But his job offer would remain tentative until William Clark, waiting downstream, met him and agreed. Neither leader was to engage anyone without the other's approval.

With the rest of the party, Colter floated down the Ohio River to winter camp above St. Louis, counting his days in mischief until the spring launch of 1804. The patience he called for this day had eluded him that winter. The rowdy, whiskey–drinking kid, who seemed much younger than his late twenties, caused Lewis and Clark much trouble at Camp Dubois as the team waited out the cold on the banks of the Mississippi.

Today patience would make or break him as he bobbed up periodically to scan the banks and waters, then back down under the jumble of branches, determined not to disclose his hiding place.

Actually, Colter had been an easy pick for Lewis. He was a wily specimen with the mind of a survivor and the skills of an expert wilderness traveler. He absorbed much more on the trek, both from the natural world and from the Indians he met who dealt with that world so differently.

• •

Colter, familiar with the attitude of the Blackfeet, had started exploring this region in the fall of 1807, while his Corps of Discovery comrades were safely back home. The next year John Potts, another Lewis and Clark veteran, had suggested this trip back to the Three Forks area—where the Jefferson, Madison, and Gallatin rivers join to form the headwaters of the Missouri.

As they paddled up the Jefferson River in separate boats, a large contingent of Blackfeet suddenly appeared on the bank. They ordered the two trappers to come ashore. While Potts insisted they remain in their boats, Colter's instinct was to do as the Blackfeet ordered. Realizing that the Indians were intent on detaining the men, he dropped his traps in the water, hoping to find them again later, then obeyed their orders. Potts refused.

As Colter neared the bank the Blackfeet surrounded his boat, then dragged him ashore and stripped him. Potts was determined to paddle away, but first raised his weapon to fire. The ensuing gun battle left his body and boat riddled with bullets, his traps in the Indians' hands, and Colter awaiting his fate, all in just a few minutes.

Thoroughly convinced he would be executed, Colter listened in amazement to the debate between the warriors and their chief. Although familiar with their language, he was not sure he had understood. Finally the chief turned toward him and, swinging his arm, signaled Colter to move out into the open, away from camp. He kept motioning him to go, to move ahead—farther, farther.

Colter had heard right. He was the game. They were the hunters. He turned his head to scan the open upland desert filled with prickly pear cactus. At least it was a chance. Naked though he was, here was opportunity.

Thinking fast, Colter estimated the distance to the Madison River at five miles. If he could make it to the water he had a chance. He leaped forward.

Expecting to chase him to his death, the warriors apparently had not recognized him from an earlier skirmish, when he had fought valiantly to reach freedom, displaying speed and endurance, strength and courage. Even so, Colter knew his body had never been tested to its limits. The Indians came on. He ran harder. He sensed he was pulling away but this was no time to look back to assess his advantages. He pushed harder. Something popped, cracked inside himself. He was breaking down.

Colter felt the rush of blood spurting from his nose, his mouth. He couldn't resist a quick glance over his shoulder. A lone warrior with a spear was bearing down on him. Without even a conscious decision, Colter stopped—suddenly. Taken by surprise, the Indian failed to check his own run. As he stumbled past, Colter grabbed his spear, which snapped as he jerked it away. Lashing out with the shortened weapon, he spun around to the Indian, killing him.

Though the action took only seconds, it decreased the

distance between Colter and the rest of his enemies to a minimum for survival. He was still more than a mile from the cottonwoods lining the Madison, his only chance for protection. He ran on. Finally, his feet splashed through a shallow pool. Then a diving leap took him into the deeper channel where he swam underwater until he was well ahead of his pursuers. At that point he discovered the driftwood raft caught at a tilt on the edge of a brushy sandbar midstream. Colter grabbed the underside of the raft and remained there all day as the Indians searched around him, even stepping onto the raft itself periodically, using it as a lookout.

The warriors took advantage of the very last shaft of light before leaving. Despite his swollen feet, lack of clothing, and the broken spear as his only defense, when dusk finally settled over the landscape, the waterlogged explorer could wait no longer.

Colter slipped from the river's edge into the tall willow brush and out into the border of cottonwoods. At first he edged from tree to tree. Finally, his patience drained, he darted from the trees and lit out cross-country for Fort Raymond.

• •

There is a direct link from the Lewis and Clark Expedition to the lands of the Two Dot, and that link is John Colter. But while the Corps of Discovery was Colter's ticket to the West, it was his own hunger for adventure that kept him there. The Rocky Mountains exerted their own gravity on the soul of John Colter, pulling him to vistas never before seen by a white man—including the magnificent lands that would become the Two Dot.

Interestingly, when President Thomas Jefferson began planning this journey up the Missouri, his main concern was the value of New Orleans to his country. He had been tempted to purchase the vast tract of land called Louisiana only after reading

Canadian explorer Alexander Mackenzie's proposal to open a trade route to the Pacific. Jefferson thought it an excellent concept, but it should be the United States that opened that trade route to Asia.

Forming his own vision for the exploration, Jefferson spoke to representatives of the Spanish Louisiana envoy about a scientific journey. Little did he know that Spain would soon sell Louisiana back to France, and France would sell it to the United States, before the Voyage of Discovery even shoved off from St. Louis.

In fact it was on March 9, 1804, that the Spanish flag came down and the French flag rose to the top of the staff. There it remained for a mere twenty-four hours. As it was lowered again, there was much murmuring of disappointment among the locals, most of whom were French. They had dreamed of living once again under their own flag as they had when France claimed the vast land called Louisiana forty years before. But they could only stand by as the Louisiana Purchase became real; Meriwether Lewis signing the transaction as a representative of the President of the United States.

Once the Lewis and Clark troop turned their boats into the Missouri River, Colter, who had drained his officers' patience along with his own, ceased to cause trouble. Some credited the change to maturity, others to the influence of George Drouillard, a French Canadian–Shawnee Indian civilian with heroic potential.

Drouillard knew how to sign, a valued form of communication with Indian tribes. He was intelligent, an outstanding marksman, skilled hunter and trapper, and would prove invaluable to the expedition. Much later Drouillard would also follow Colter into the Big Horn Basin, and may have crossed Two Dot lands himself.

Both men claimed to be twenty-seven years of age at the beginning of the trip; both would lead with conviction and handle every assignment with accuracy. Lewis and Clark had no doubt that Colter and Drouillard would protect the troop to the death.

The often-harrowing trip climaxed with the exhilaration of

reaching the Pacific followed by a catastrophic winter at Fort Clatsop near the mouth of the Columbia. The leaders were disappointed not to find the envisioned waterway between the headwaters of the Missouri and another river to take them to the coast. Still, they had opened the whole northwest region of the country.

Colter's story, for purposes of the Two Dot, starts halfway home. By the summer of 1806, the expedition had returned to the Mandan villages, in today's North Dakota, where they had spent their first winter. Here Colter found his excuse to again head west. He accepted the invitation of two beaver trappers working their way up the Missouri, Forrest Hancock and Joseph Dickson. Lewis and Clark discharged Private Colter with compliments for a job well done and orders to return to St. Louis with further reports.

The trio likely wintered at the mouth of the Clarks Fork Canyon just northwest of present-day Two Dot lands. They were certainly the first whites to explore the upper reaches of the Yellowstone. Colter may also have gone up the Clarks Fork River into the Sunlight Basin west of the canyon, gaining his bearings for his next winter of exploration—throughout the Big Horn Basin.

When the partnership failed, Colter thought of home, a longing he would suffer periodically throughout the next four years. But the emotion was fleeting. As he paddled down the Missouri he was surprised to find keelboats tied up at the mouth of the Powder River. Manuel Lisa, a Spanish trader and explorer who had already heard stories of the returning expedition, was on his way upriver to establish a fort for trade. Colter joined him.

In fact Colter guided Lisa's large party up the mighty Missouri, then on up the Yellowstone to the mouth of the Bighorn River. The log cabin Lisa built there was the first structure of its kind in the region. He named it Fort Raymond for his son, although most knew it as Fort Manuel Lisa or Manuel's Fort. From 1811 to 1824 it would be called Fort Benton, and later, from 1832 to 1835, the name was again changed to Fort Cass.

The trip had been rough, slowed by Indian conflicts and the logistics of such a large contingent. But the beaver filled the travelers' minds with money; all intended to go home rich men. They would live out their lives as landed members of American society for sure.

Almost immediately Colter received his first orders from Lisa: make contact with Indian tribes throughout the region. Although it was too late for fall hunting, Colter was to mingle with the Crow, the Shoshone, and the Flathead to encourage them to bring their furs and pelts to the fort. In essence, Colter was the marketing man. He was also expected to search out good beaver streams where trappers could be directed.

With Lisa's invitation in his mind, a thirty-pound pack on his back, and a rifle in his hand, Colter left the fort on a journey of some six hundred miles. It would be a history-making trek, launching the era of the mountain man in the American West.

George Drouillard, who had also joined Lisa after completing a map-making project with Lewis and Clark, had the same assignment, heading in a different direction. Splitting his winter into two shorter trips, Colter finally reappeared at the fort late that spring of 1808.

Colter did not blaze trails that winter, but struggled across snow-packed Indian and wildlife trails, finding food and shelter at Indian camps. While his exact route is uncertain, it is clear that he either entered or left the Big Horn Basin through the Two Dot lands at the far northwest corner, according to the map he directed Clark to make upon his return to St. Louis.

He probably paddled up the Big Horn River from the fort, then up the Stinking Water (now called the Shoshone) to "Colter's Hell." Here at the confluence of the North and South Forks he discovered a boiling tar springs, now buried under the Buffalo Bill Reservoir. Then he headed southwest, visiting Crow villages wintering along the river. Later he would describe the tall formation known today as Castle Rock. At the head of the South Fork he continued westward on the Indian trails recommended by the Crow. He climbed to the headwaters of the Wind River. After finding a passage through the mountains he dropped down into Jackson Hole where he surely rubbed his eyes in amazement at the glory of the Tetons.

He was clearly the first white man to visit that area. Many years later farmers near the border of Wyoming and Idaho found a head-shaped stone carved with "John Colter 1808," which National Park Service officials believe to be authentic.

Turning north, he explored the wonders of today's Yellowstone Park. He likely picked up the Bannock Trail, used by a number of Indian tribes on annual hunting trips into the Two Dot region. The trail brought him into Sunlight, the deep valley west of the ranch, then paralleled what is now its western border. Later he would describe landmarks to Lewis and Clark, particularly Hart Butte, now called Heart Mountain, which is visible from nearly every location on the Two Dot today.

Those verbal descriptions to friends and fellow trappers, and his help in documenting the Lewis and Clark maps, expanded the nation's mental visions of the lands northwest of the Mississippi.

• •

After his ordeal at the Madison River, Colter walked back through the gates of Fort Raymond in the spring of 1808, bringing all these stories to share. Some estimate that his trek from the river took about eleven days, others guess as few as five. But Lisa left him little time to recover, immediately sending him out again. This time Colter angled northwest toward the area that would nearly do him in. He crossed Bozeman Pass to the Gallatin River. About twenty miles north of Three Forks he met more Flathead Indians on their way to the annual buffalo hunt. He offered to take them directly back to the fort, but before they could get underway they were suddenly attacked by a band of Blackfeet.

For a while it looked like a losing battle. Colter was struck by a bullet, which lodged in his hip. Then from behind him a band of Crow seemed to come out of nowhere and everywhere, joining the fray. Badly outnumbered, the Blackfeet turned away. In the end the Indians on both sides of the battle recognized a ferocious warrior in the person of Colter.

The Blackfeet's hatred of the whites was heating to a firestorm and should have been an early warning to Colter and the others. It would not bode well for future meetings, by chance or planned.

Never one to dwell on his wounds, Colter couldn't resist a trip back to Three Forks. He wanted his traps back, the ones so hurriedly dropped into the water. By late fall, sure that the Blackfeet would be settled into winter camp, he went to retrieve them. Once again he miscalculated the tribe's determination to stop the trappers from depleting their beaver and, just as importantly, from distributing guns and ammunition to their enemies.

Once again he was attacked far short of the goal. Wounded again, this time with a ball in his leg, Colter promised God Almighty that he would never return to that region again if he were only permitted to escape with his life.

True to his word he packed up the following spring, encouraging Vasquez, who was overseeing the fort for Lisa, to do the same. Vasquez agreed that the Blackfeet were bent on annihilating them, so he locked up the fort and joined Colter. On the trip back to the Mandan villages the group carried only a paltry number of beaver pelts and other skins.

Then it happened. Colter saw Lisa pulling up to the dock on the Missouri River at the mouth of the Powder River, and off the boat jumped his old friend George Drouillard. The Rockies still tugged on Colter's inner compass. In the next few hours he accepted an assignment for Andrew Henry, who described the overland route he had in mind as well as the help he needed. Henry would later build the first fort west of the Continental Divide, but for now his intention was to have Colter lead his eighty men from Fort Manuel Lisa to Three Forks where they would build a stockade on a narrow tongue of land.

Upon their arrival at the site, construction began. But misfortune struck on April 12, 1810. While some of the trappers worked on the fort, five more headed upriver about ten miles to the Jefferson Fork. Here the Blackfeet struck again, determined to end the infringement on their territory. When the building crew found them, two were dead. The three missing included Colter. Most of their equipment, weapons, and supplies were gone as well.

But fate still favored Colter. Once again he survived and struggled back to Fort Raymond—the exact events lost to history. This time he had no intention of waiting around to change his mind. As he threw his exhausted body through the gate of the fort he said that if God will only forgive him this time and let him off, he would leave the country the day after tomorrow—and be damned if he ever came into it again.

He did just that, arriving back in St. Louis that fall. Later he would learn that Drouillard had ignored his advice to follow quickly, over-confident in his ability to outmaneuver the wily tribe. It was just a few days after Colter's departure that the Blackfeet captured Drouillard and two other trappers. After killing the other two they completely mutilated Drouillard, leaving his decaying body as a warning message for any white man to find.

Back in St. Louis, Colter leaned over William Clark's shoulder as they expanded the map with their knowledge about the West: its rivers, mountains, basins, lakes, and of course the mysterious land of geysers, waterfalls, mud pots and wildlife that would become Yellowstone Park.

Only then did Colter turn to a more peaceful occupation. He accepted the land promised when he first signed on with Lewis and Clark, selecting acreage in Daniel Boone's Missouri neighborhood. He married a young woman named Sally Hiram and had a son, although a recent book, *The Fate of the Corp* indicates there were no children.

In late 1813, with Colter not yet forty, jaundice accomplished what no Blackfeet had been able to. John Colter was dead.

Although considered literate by most historians, Colter left no writing except his signature. Today Colter's measure is that of folk hero—trail blazer for the oncoming mountain man era. Students of Colter's Rocky Mountain era speak in awe of his prowess—two winters in the Big Horn Basin, thousands of miles traveled on foot, his physical stamina matched by a resourceful mind. Lewis and Clark had been wise to select Colter, and were more than repaid for tolerating his early antics. Future inhabitants of Two Dot country and the Big Horn Basin, too, would revere the man who roamed their wilderness when its glories were new to the white man.

CHAPTER TWO
The Final War of the Nez Perce

Cattle spread out across the meadows. (Courtesy Jane Riddle Thompson)

FOR A FEW DAYS IN early September of 1877, the remote lands that would someday be called the Two Dot Ranch became a designated war zone. There Chief Joseph and his band of seven hundred Nez Perce would be squeezed into surrender by a military force much larger and better equipped—at least that was the intention of General Oliver O. Howard and Colonel Samuel Sturgis.

For that one week the nearly uninhabited northwestern region of Wyoming was filled with people. There was an influx of U.S. soldiers come to end Chief Joseph's flight. Small bands of marauding Nez Perce were striking out well in advance of their leaders. The army, too, had its outriders: the glint of a rifle or the shadow of a horse might reveal a spy, a Crow scout, or a messenger between army camps. Then, led by Chief Joseph, came the whole village of Nez Perce, including the elderly, women, and children. The band would slip into the Clarks Fork Valley and, to the frustration of Sturgis and Howard, slide back out again the same day. More than a thousand people were ranging back and forth between Heart Mountain and the Absarokas, between the Clarks Fork River to the north and the Stinking Water (now known as the Shoshone River) near present-day Cody.

Certainly Pat O'Hara, who until that point had been the area's only white settler, must have wondered what was going on. In fact he may have been one of the unnamed prospectors Sturgis referred to as a scout. That might explain why O'Hara would tell John Chapman a year later, as the young Oregonian took over his land, that this country was getting overpopulated and he was eager to get out.

Chief Joseph certainly had no desire to be caught in those circumstances. He had received notice in late spring of 1877 that he and his people had thirty days to gather their belongings and leave their beloved Wallowa in northeastern Oregon, the valley of winding waters.

It made no sense to these Nez Perce. Joseph's father had signed the treaty of 1855, not ratified until four years later. It left the lands to Joseph and his tribe, the hills and valleys they knew as home—where the bones of their ancestors were buried. Old Joseph was insistent they must never abandon those graves.

Then came the miners, the settlers. Pressure developed as whites began gnawing at the edges of the reservation lands. Soon they were greedily devouring more and more.

This led to a revisiting of the treaty in 1863. Under pressure to open more lands, the government proposed to slash the Nez Perce holdings to one sixth, maybe even less, possibly one tenth, of their current size. Tribal leaders protested. Old Joseph left the negotiations. Upon his return to the Wallowa he marked their homelands with poles planted along the borders to designate his own boundaries.

Together Joseph and his father vowed, no matter what, not to leave their home—not to move to any reservation far away.

Young Joseph was born *Hin-ma-taw-ya-laht-qit*, "Thunder Coming Up Over the Land," in 1840. His father, Tuekakas, the leader of the Wallamwatkin band of Lower Nez Perces in the Wallowa Valley, had been renamed Joseph by Reverend Henry H. Spalding at his baptism. The older Joseph was one of the first to take that step after the arrival of the missionaries. His son would be baptized at age five and from then on was referred to as Young Joseph until his father's death.

The Nez Perce were semi-nomadic. They learned farming practices from the missionaries. The nation was also famous for the Appaloosa horses they bred, raised, and trained. At the same time the tribes spent much of their time hunting, fishing, and gathering food.

By the time Young Joseph was twenty-three, his father's health was failing; he was growing blind and feeble. So this son, the eldest of seven children, accompanied him to meetings with soldiers and Indian agents. He sat in on councils of the Nez Perce leaders, listening to his father and the other non-treaty chiefs who had refused to sign the altered compact as they debated their future. Those who had signed the 1863 treaty were known as the treaty Indians. It is interesting to note that the treaty Indians retained their lands while those who refused to sign were losing theirs. The government did not seem to understand that the Nez Perce felt so strongly about their homelands.

The young leader gradually took over more and more of his father's duties as the old chief's health deteriorated. Young Joseph had a charismatic personality, deep intelligence, kindness, and a winning smile acknowledged by whites and fellow tribesman alike. At six feet two and two hundred pounds, he was broad-shouldered with an athletic build. He wore his hair in two long braids over his shoulders.

All these details were noted by a young woman who would sculpt him in later years. She especially noticed his large strong hands when he took her small one—so gently, but with a power she sensed could do great harm if he chose. His eyes, too, were magnetic: as an artist she wanted to capture their riveting brightness.

While Joseph and his brother were often mistaken for each other, Alokut was much better known for his military ability. Sometimes Joseph was credited for his brother's fighting prowess.

But Joseph spent his early adult years honing the ways of diplomacy. While he was usually successful in negotiating with whites in person, those agreements would be voided by higher authorities he never had the chance to confront. That might explain his oft-repeated request to travel to Washington himself.

It must have been difficult for Joseph to understand the ever-vacillating decisions of the white man. For nearly sixty years relations had been favorable amongst the Nez Perce, the mountain men, fur traders, French explorers, and even early white settlers.

John Chapman's family was one of the first to follow the Oregon Trail into the land of the *Nee-Me-Poo*, "The Real People," as they called themselves. He had Nez Perce youngsters as his playmates and close friends.

And Chief Joseph's people were the ones who saved the lives of Captains Lewis and Clark and a contingent from the Corps of Discovery when they arrived at his village starving in 1804. The Nez Perce provided supplies, encouragement, and information. They even kept Lewis and Clark's horses over the winter they were camped on the Pacific, attempting to fulfill the dictates of President Jefferson. Lewis and Clark's journals gave the tribe that credit.

Chief Joseph had not planned to lead his people on a trek that would stretch seventeen hundres miles from their homeland. He did not wish to place them in the path of progress or of an army eager to devour him. On his deathbed in 1871 Old Joseph had told him, remember the treaty that gave us the Wallowa Valley. Never leave our ancestors alone in the land.

The new chief used every diplomatic effort to isolate his people from the whites. But there were too many after the gold, too many settlers claiming the land, too many for General Howard or even President Ulysses Grant to hold back, despite the promise. The struggle finally came to a head early in 1877. A young Nez Perce, not even of Chief Joseph's band, knowing that whites had slain his father, was finally baited into retaliation. He and a comrade broke the tightly held ranks of their own leaders, striking back and killing whites. When he heard this, Chief Joseph realized fate had stepped in. He could no longer remain in the Wallowa Valley. The government finally had the excuse they had been waiting for and the soldiers would now confine them to a reservation.

Pressure from all sides forced the chiefs' council to order the move eastward to the reservations of their friends the River Crow and Mountain Crow in Montana Territory. Chief Looking Glass was especially sure of the Crows' support.

Yet as Joseph gathered his people for the move toward the buffalo grounds and perceived sanctuary, perhaps he visited his father's grave, vowing to bring his people back home when this was over. Sadly, that would never happen.

The summer of 1877 was spent in clashes and skirmishes as the Nez Perce pushed eastward. The battle of White Bird Canyon, Idaho, was only the beginning. There was Fort Fizzle, where the Nez Perce outmaneuvered the soldiers. At one point Chief Joseph's band was close to the Canadian border where Sitting Bull had found sanctuary. There, in a still-unexplained maneuver, they once again turned south. Then there was Tolo Lake, the battle of Big Hole, and another skirmish at Camas Meadows, where the Nez Perce had gathered roots each year for winter food. Here the Indians slipped into Howard's camp in the night to steal horses. Instead it was mules they cut free. The Indians joked with each other about their mistake, but in fact Howard was hobbled by the lack of those pack mules.

By August 25, the Nez Perce were deep within Yellowstone National Park, the world's first area so designated. Conflicts, both civilian and military, took place almost daily. Though it wasn't clear how the Indians would exit the park and the wall of mountains—the Absarokas to the east—there were two routes available: one following the Stinking Water and another, a more challenging one leading through Sunlight Basin and out through the Clarks Fork Canyon.

As General Howard forced his men and animals across the park he left wagons behind, rebuilt a bridge the Indians had attempted to burn, and sent a small force ahead to track the Nez Perce. He had already sent a message to Colonel Sturgis, instructing troops to barricade the passes when Chief Joseph spilled out of the Absarokas, wherever that might be. So sure of victory, Howard sent a message to Fort Ellis, and a telegram to General Irwin McDowell at headquarters in San Francisco, announcing the army's success before it was realized.

But while Sturgis knew Howard was somewhere in Yellowstone, no courier ever reached him. The Nez Perce were one hundred percent successful in silencing the message. Consequently, when he arrived in the area of Heart Mountain the guessing game began.

His Crow scouts assured him that all seven hundred Nez Perce and their two thousand horses—many with the Appaloosa markings made famous by Nez Perce breeders—would come through the Clarks Fork Canyon. Yet one of Sturgis lieutenants had seen Indian boys watering those horses from the Stinking Water to the south. Prospectors and scouts with that lieutenant argued convincingly that if Chief Joseph's people were on the Stinking Water trail, geography would not allow them to cross the rugged terrain north to the Clarks Fork...but they did.

It is believed that the band, now grown to two hundred lodges and stretched out along the trail like a single-file town, suddenly turned on its back right under the army's nose. Like a silent serpent the Indians scaled back up off the trail and crossed the uncrossable, leaving Yellowstone Park behind and disappearing into Sunlight Basin to the northeast.

In the meantime Sturgis, camped about two miles from the

canyon, decided to move south to the Stinking Water. He considered splitting his troops, leaving a contingent at the Clarks Fork. But anticipating up to four hundred Nez Perce warriors, and with no idea where Howard was, he couldn't take a chance on dividing his forces.

He broke camp late that afternoon, loaded the mules and moved out, turning south at the mouth of Blue Bead Creek, the water that still nourishes the land of the Two Dot. He followed it for about fifteen miles, camping that night, historians believe, on Skull Creek.

Just as Sturgis and Howard had scouts and spies roaming the area, the Nez Perce, too, had Indians on the lookout. When they reported the move by Sturgis, Chief Joseph knew it was safe to bring his people out.

By September 9 Chief Joseph was already deep in the Clarks Fork Canyon, the guardian of the camp, the caretaker of the women, children, elderly, and lame; he was moving deliberately and cautiously. There, said a soldier in Howard's army, the Nez Perce "passed through a narrow chasm, which opened into a towering canyon with cliffs scarcely twenty feet apart. This gorge abruptly opened into the Clarks Fork Valley after a course of three or four miles."

• •

Chief Joseph realized his was a "sacred trust," according to biographer L. V. McWhorter. Joseph once described his tribe's creed to an interviewer.

Our fathers gave us many laws, which they had learned from their fathers. These laws were good. They told us to treat all men as they treated us; that we should never be the first to break a bargain; that it was a disgrace to tell a lie; that we should speak only the truth; that it was a shame for one man to take from another his wife, or his property with-

out paying for it. We were taught to believe that the Great Spirit sees and hears everything and that he never forgets; that hereafter he will give every man a spirit-home according to his desserts: if he has been a good man, he will have a good home; if he has been a bad man, he will have a bad home. This I believe, and all my people believe the same.

On this race to freedom Chief Joseph lifted his weapons only in self-defense as the protector of the unarmed. Yet as his people spilled from the canyon like the water of the Clarks Fork itself and he turned them north, he would start making more military decisions.

Chief Looking Glass, who had been so sure of his friends, had just learned that the River Crow had joined with the U.S. Army, probably on the promise of two thousand horses available upon the capture of the band. The Mountain Crow were remaining neutral. Neither would be opening the gates to their reservations. Chief Joseph readjusted his destination plans and set his sights on Canada.

As he made the correction in his mind's map and the tired people started through the Clarks Fork Valley determined now to join Sitting Bull, Chief Joseph may have held out hope that the Sioux would come to their aid if needed, but that wouldn't happen either.

In a strategy to confuse Sturgis, Indians were sent east to stir up dust south of Heart Mountain. Dragging brush behind their speeding horses, the Indians raced back and forth, back and forth. When army scouts saw the cloud rising skyward, they assumed the Nez Perce were still headed for Crow country, and the soldiers raced in that direction to do battle. Unfortunately for them, the dust cleared and the Indians seemed to evaporate. The main Nez Perce village, after skirting the Absarokas, was probably already crossing the Yellowstone by the time Sturgis realized his error. Chief Joseph had not only slipped from the trap on the Clarks Fork, he continued to outwit and outmaneuver Howard and Sturgis.

But the army summoned more manpower as the Indians continued north through Montana. General Miles left Fort Keough—at what is today Miles City, at the confluence of the Tongue and the Yellowstone rivers—marching with well-fed men and rested horses. He would be the one to bring the Nez Perce down in a nearly week-long battle fought in the snowy Bear Paw Mountains, less than fifty miles from the Canadian border.

While some of the chiefs and their forces were able to escape into Canada, Sitting Bull did not come to help. And Chief Joseph would not leave his people. Upon his surrender the Nez Perce leader asked that a message be delivered to the enemy he could ultimately not shake free of.

Tell General Howard I know his heart. What he told me before I have in my heart. I am tired of fighting. Our chiefs are killed. Looking Glass is dead. Tu-hul-hut-sut. (A tiwat/medicine man and chief of the Pikunanmu) is dead. The old men are all dead. It is the young men who say yes or no. He who led on the young men is dead. It is cold and we have no blankets. The little children are freezing to death. My people, some of them, have run away to the hills, and have no blankets, no food; no one knows where they are—perhaps freezing to death. I want to have time to look for my children and see how many of them I can find. Maybe I shall find them among the dead. Hear me, my chiefs. I am tired; my heart is sick and sad. From where the sun now stands I will fight no more forever.

The broken promises only continued. Before making his speech Chief Joseph had accepted the word of Miles, backed by Howard, that he and his band would be returned to the Northwest. They just needed to travel to Fort Keough, Montana, for the winter.

But other generals took over and despite efforts of both Miles and Howard, the Indians were shipped on to Bismarck, North Dakota, then the following spring to Fort Riley, Kansas, then to Leavenworth and on to Indian Territory where they stayed until 1885, many dying of malaria.

In the meantime Chief Joseph remained patient, waiting for change. He was told that generals in the East refused to keep his captors' promise because more bloodshed would surely occur between the Nez Perce and relatives of the whites whose murders had triggered their flight. Even now, Chief Joseph never asked anything to make the situation more comfortable for himself. He only made requests out of concern for the care of his people. He steadfastly believed that someday his people would be returned to their beloved homeland.

When a few of his people, 268 to be precise, were returned to the Northwest in the spring of 1885, the band was broken in two. With about 150 of those left, Joseph went to the Colville reservation at Nespelem, Washington, where he lived out his life. He was only allowed to return to the Wallowa Valley once, on an overnight trip under guard. He indicated he was grateful to stand before his father's grave although he could not fulfill the promise he made on his father's deathbed. He would not be staying.

Before Chief Joseph died in 1904 he would develop friendships with many prominent people, including Buffalo Bill Cody. While his earlier requests to go to Washington had been denied, he was finally allowed to take his concerns to the great white fathers in 1897, when white squatters were encroaching upon open lands within the Colville reservation. His compelling presence ignited a grassroots movement among white leaders and intellectuals including Professor Edward S. Meany, who wrote so well of Chief Joseph's concerns and wishes. The movement grew into a full-blown, but fruitless, campaign to return his people to their home.

●●

A year after the Nez Perce War, John Chapman would locate his ranch headquarters just south of Clarks Fork Canyon. Other settlers, including his Oregon cousin Priestly Riddle, would homestead in Sunlight Basin west of the ranch. While the trail followed in part by Chief Joseph became well-traveled by locals, hunters, and eventually a few tourists including Ernest Hemingway—who learned the meaning of "stuck in the low spots"—it remained a wagon and cattle trail until 1909, when Sunlight Basin residents gathered to upgrade the section over Dead Indian Hill, an 8071-foot high point about twelve miles west of ranch headquarters. It was so named for a Nez Perce Indian wounded and left behind as the tribe spilled into the Clarks Fork Canyon.

By the 1930s the United States Forest Service had carved switchbacks down the mountain's side, making travel a little easier. In the 1940s came discussions about improving the stretch from Cody to Cook City as a more rugged and northerly alternative to the east entrance of Yellowstone National Park. Some initial road work was done.

By the 1960s money was allocated and paving actually began, thanks in part to Cody businessman Bud Webster, who served on the Wyoming Highway Commission at that time. Initially Webster favored paving the route through the canyon itself—Chief Joseph's path. When environmental concerns blocked that route, the old dirt road that peaked atop Dead Indian was designated instead. That road had previously been known as the Sunlight Road, the Dead Indian Pass Road, and Wyoming 296. Another Wyoming highway commissioner, Bob Fagerberg, picked up the reins in the mid-1980s when interest in completing the project was lagging. The commission officially renamed the road at a board meeting on November 23, 1988, dubbing it the Chief Joseph Scenic Highway.

When it was completed in October of 1995, it was not only Wyoming's last state road to be paved, it was also one of its longest-running projects, taking more than three decades, thirty million dollars and including at least a dozen contracts addressing specific sections of its forty-six miles. This included 11.8 miles through Two Dot private property.

The mountainous terrain is steep with jagged peaks. Its deep canyons are traversed with broad-span bridges; tons of boulders had to be removed from every mile. From the top of every windswept rim, the beauty takes one's breath away. The clear water creeks and the surprise of springs bubbling out of the ground add to the splendor.

Exactly 118 years after Chief Joseph brought his people through the Clarks Fork Canyon, on September 12, 1995, Wyoming Governor Jim Geringer cut the ribbon dedicating the completion of a roadway that many have described as the most awe-inspiring view in the world.

CHAPTER THREE
The Bennett Butte Battle

Butte where the battle between Miles and Bannock Indians
took place on September 4, 1878 along the Clarks Fork.
(Photo by author)

A YEAR HAD PASSED since Chief Joseph and the Nez Perce passed through Two Dot country striving for freedom. Now scouts under orders from Colonel Nelson A. Miles spotted a Bannock band at about eleven o'clock the morning of September 3, 1878. The sentinels watched all day as riders in single file dropped down off Bald Ridge, following a narrow, rocky trail into the Clarks Fork Valley below. The tribe's intended campsite for the coming night: an island in the Clarks Fork River.

The Bannocks had suffered a long year. Grasshoppers, fire, and whites, particularly the military, had driven them from southwest Idaho to northeast Oregon and back. Now autumn was once again showing its rich colors, signaling winter preparations. Like Chief Joseph's people, the Bannocks led by Chief Ploqua had been reeling from skirmish to standoff across the mountains from Fort Hall in southeast Idaho through Yellowstone National Park, with the same destination in mind: Canada, where Sitting Bull was established. Instead of going peaceably to the reservation as they were ordered, this desperate band of Bannocks chose war and flight. History would know their year-long resistance as the Bannock Indian War.

There they were—finally, spilling out of the Absarokas, twenty lodges, some eighty tribal members and a couple of hundred horses. Their hearts lightened as safety seemed near. They must have believed they were at last free of the U.S. military, which had seemed only a breath behind them most of the way. The Indians set up camp on the island. Running out of room there, some lodges spilled onto the west shore.

Before entering Yellowstone Park from the west, the band had engaged in some attention-grabbing raids that made them the target of three U.S. government entities. On the evening of August 25, they had fired on a U.S. Geological Survey crew, a division of the Hayden Expedition headed by A.D. Wilson at Henry's Lake. Wilson and his crew footed it sixty miles to the main camp to report that they had been robbed of their equipment, twelve mules, and two horses.

Having heard that report, Captain James Egan managed to catch up with the same group two days later. In a short battle Egan was able to capture fifty-six horses.

On August 29 Lieutenant William Clark attacked the Bannocks at Index Peak with no casualties on either side. He hit the beleaguered band again the next morning, capturing one prisoner. At that time the Indians withdrew in the direction of Clarks Fork Pass. In his rush to catch them, Clark nearly overran thirty Indians, but the warriors scattered out of his grasp like chickens dodging a skunk.

Reaching the Clarks Fork may have convinced Ploqua and his weary people that they were nearly free. Unfortunately for them, Colonel Miles was wise to their probable route. He received word of trouble as he headed toward Fort Custer, at the confluence of the Big Horn and Little Big Horn rivers. Miles was with an exploration party of family and friends bound for Yellowstone, but he immediately interrupted his vacation.

As he studied a map of the area, Miles quickly discerned two potential routes into the Big Horn Basin. He wrote later, "I was obliged to divide my limited force in order to intercept them at either point." Forty men under Lieutenant Hobart K. Bailey struggled over a treacherous trail to Boulder Pass. Miles would march his own men to Clarks Fork Pass, the more likely choice. In the meantime Lieutenant Colonel George P. Buell, post commander at Fort Custer, sent scouts to advise Miles he would join him. Miles didn't wait.

He force-marched his troop of thirty soldiers, gathering seventy-five Crows on the way. While the Crows may not have been eager to join him, the colonel threatened that the Bannocks would overrun the Crow reservation. He added the promise of food, ammunition, and all the horses captured from the well-stocked band. The Crows straggled in a few at a time, probably with no intention of actually fighting.

The Crow contingent included an interpreter named Little Rocky, who had reportedly crossed Yellowstone with the Bannocks. Married to a Bannock, he had lived with the tribe for years, but for some reason had a falling out with them, according to historian Bob Edgar. He arrived at the Crow reservation in time to be picked by Miles's men to provide intelligence on the Indians' whereabouts. (While Miles's memoirs tell a different story they were written many years and many battles later.)

By late afternoon on September 2 Miles's troops, volunteers, and animals were settled in a swale amid the foothills of Heart Mountain. Camouflaged in vegetation, scouts on buttes nearby saw the Indians coming down the Bannock Trail from the northwest about twelve miles away. As the soldiers watched, the Bannocks set up camp. While there is debate about exactly where the Bannocks located their campsite, Kyle V. Walpole in *Bivouac of the Dead* places it at the confluence of Little Sand Coulee and the Clarks Fork River.

Miles estimated a six-mile march to attack. He would wait to move his troops under cover of darkness.

As Miles waited, a fierce rainstorm took over the landscape quickly turning dust to mud. Miles ordered the men to move out anyway, after telling them to wrap "all bits, picket-pins, carbine snaps or other jingling appurtenances." He wanted a silent march. The soldiers knew they were going into battle outnumbered four to one. One soldier commented later, "We knew that if we didn't get the Bannocks, they most assuredly would get us." After crossing the Clarks Fork to the west bank, Miles positioned his troop in the area of three hills closely aligned, later to be named Bennett Butte. From there Miles estimated the camp to be about two miles east.

Miles planned carefully, yet it would all be for naught if the camp could not be located in the driving rainstorm. Scouts searched through the night. Before light Miles ordered his troops to move although the camp had not been pinpointed yet. They marched literally inch by inch toward the river, pressing to be in position before dawn but afraid to stumble on top of the camp unawares.

Suddenly, well toward dawn with the darkest of the night past, they saw a glow of light. A fire was being lit at the camp. There was the target. Miles ordered Captain Andrew Saydam Bennett, a Civil War veteran, to form a skirmish line to lead the charge. They continued to slip through the tall sagebrush toward the bend in the river, keeping their eyes on the campfire.

As Miles ordered the bugler, Snyder, to signal the attack, he reminded him of their plan. Snyder was to run from one end of the line to the other, blowing varying musical signals to make the soldiers' numbers appear much greater. Snyder blew until he fell over a root, then he grabbed a gun and joined the firing.

At first it was easy, with the majority of Bannocks still asleep in their camp on the island and the west shore. One early riser did wound Two Crows as the scout tried to gather his portion of the promised horse herd. As the sky cleared, some Bannock Indians joined the battle, others attempted to escape.

The initial attack lasted about twenty minutes. When Miles thought they had done enough damage he ordered Bennett to charge the camp, then turned to his own troop. Bennett probably didn't take more than a step or two when he went down with a bullet to his chest, dead. But the soldiers knew not to stop and forged forward, guns blazing.

When a sudden silence fell, one of the soldiers checked the time: six o'clock. While an occasional crack of gunfire rang through the battleground during the next few minutes, for all practical purposes it was over. The entire horse herd was now being driven to the Crow reservation, eleven Bannocks were dead and thirty-one were captured, including Chief Ploqua. While the rest escaped, many would be picked up far from the site in the next few weeks.

Besides Two Crows, who would die later that day, a Private McAtee was wounded in the arm. Little Rocky, too, was dead. Then, with shock and sadness, Miles learned of Bennett's death.

Much later, in January 1880, he would write a letter to Mr. Charles W. Bennett, Waukasha, Wisconsin.

Capt. Andrew S. Bennett, fifth U.S. Infantry, has been an officer of my regiment for years. During the great civil war he served his country with distinction, and enduring all the hardships incident to that long and desperate struggle for human rights, and the maintenance of a just and liberal government. After the war, the fortunes of service placed him on the western frontier where his services have been valuable to the government and to the frontier settlements. He has served in most of the western territories east of the Rocky Mountains, maintaining an honorable record for devotion to his profession, and faithfulness in the discharge of every duty; he was engaged in numerous campaigns and several battles.

It seemed appropriate to name a hump rising from the floor of the Clarks Fork Valley Bennett Butte; a creek also bears Bennett's name. A second stream running parallel nearby was named Little Rocky after the translator.

The troops moved their camp to the Clarks Fork that day as they buried the dead and prepared Bennett's body for shipment to his home in Waukesha, Wisconsin, where he had been the first from that area to enlist in the Civil War.

• •

The next day, as John Chapman slowly surveyed his land claim, he ran into Colonel Miles at his camp on the Clarks Fork. He heard the story of the battle from Miles, then a different version from Lieutenant Colonel Buell, who had finally arrived from Fort Custer. Buell blamed Miles for Bennett's death. He believed that the whole Indian camp could have been captured without firing a shot.

When Chapman learned that Miles was heading west to continue his vacation and keep an eye out for escapees from the battle, Chapman joined the entourage through Yellowstone Park. By November he was back in Oregon.

The exact site of the Bennett Butte Battle on the Clarks Fork is unknown. Despite field notes, military reports, Miles's memoirs, Indian stories, an archeological site survey, and the recovery of artifacts and remains, the location of the island is disputed. A river's route can shift. At the Clarks Fork, silt, floods, and the carving of new channels have given us a seemingly unsolvable puzzle. But we can be sure that upon Chapman's return with livestock, the land he claimed and grazed for many years included the site of the Battle of Bennett Butte, mystery though it may be, it was his.

CHAPTER FOUR

Pat O'Hara:
The Elusive Mountain Man

Pat O'Hara shakes hands with Buffalo Bill Cody as he heads out of Cody for the last time.
(Courtesy Buffalo Bill Historical Center)

Pat O'Hara's imagination was in overdrive that warm summer evening in 1873. The wiry mountaineer, a jack-of-many-skills typical of those attracted to the Rocky Mountain region, would face his own demons that night. Eventually he would find safety in the countryside where a mountain and a creek today bear his name.

O'Hara and two comrades, prospecting down the Clarks Fork River, had reached Blue Bead, the creek that spills into the river just below the canyon. The stream was known for the azure clarity of its waters by the many Indian tribes that hunted and fished there.

As the prospectors gathered firewood and set up camp, they heard a rustling noise. All three stopped, reached for their guns, and waited. It was an era when white incursion frequently drove Indian tribes to the warpath. Constant vigilance could age a man, but carelessness could kill him.

Then O'Hara's companions heaved sighs of relief when they saw a few antelope bob over the ridge, disappearing into the darkening horizon beyond. The two laid their guns down—O'Hara did not.

Some combination of fear and near-sightedness had convinced O'Hara he was surrounded by Indian enemies. His companions, E. S. Topping and Nelson Yarnall, were unable to calm him. He saw warriors where they saw wildlife, a small band of game vanishing single file over a distant ridge. They even walked out far enough to show O'Hara the hoofprints, but he still wasn't satisfied. As Topping and Yarnall settled in for the night they watched O'Hara pace, gun in hand, keeping a steady eye on the ridge. Finally he headed for the picket line where the horses were staked. He threw a saddle over one horse and his supplies over the other. The men protested, but O'Hara mounted up. They watched their paranoid comrade disappear toward the back trail to the Clarks Fork Mines.

• •

Topping, who later told this story in *Chronicles of the Yellowstone*, had first heard O'Hara's name three years earlier, in the summer of 1870. A friend told of meeting O'Hara at the Crow Agency when a party of prospectors stumbled into headquarters reporting an Indian attack and the theft of their horses in the mountains where they were mining.

O'Hara had come to the region some years earlier—possibly around 1850, according to some historians. He may have been a trapper for the American Fur Company at the end of the mountain man era. He was a man who found it easy to come and go, always packing light, and the miners' story intrigued him.

Along with four others, O'Hara accompanied the team back to the site of the attack. They learned that the prospectors had found samples of both gold and silver nearby, and they all stayed to try their luck.

As summer stretched into early fall, the men had no more trouble with Indians. They also found an "argentiferous galen" vein (as Topping reported it)—silver. They continued to pan and dig until heavy snows on the ten thousand foot slopes drove them out in

September. By that time they had realized that while their placer mines had little value, the silver ore lodes were of high quality and they staked those out. When they arrived back in Bozeman, the newspaper was glad to share the good news, naming the site Clarks Fork Mines, according to Topping. Investors were more than a little curious.

The original miners returned to the site the following spring. Many others were enticed there, too, as news of the silver strike spread from Bozeman. But late in 1872 the profit-seekers found their dreams caught on a snag. It was discovered the Clarks Fork Mines actually lay on the Crow Indian Reservation. Eager investors backpedaled, spilling their promised financial support into other projects. Capital available for a strike-it-rich opportunity at the Clarks Fork Mines vanished—although that would change a decade later when the Rocky Mountains of the Crow Agency were ceded to the United States. In the meantime O'Hara had faith enough to return to his mining claim as soon as the snow melted in the spring of 1873.

That was when he met Topping and Yarnall. The two partners had mapped out a trip to search the region's waterways, hoping that if there was silver in one place there might be gold in another. In June when they passed by the Clarks Fork Mines, O'Hara eagerly bought into their plan and packed up to join them. The trio panned for gold and silver, following the Clarks Fork down to the Big Horn Basin. It was there that O'Hara got spooked.

• •

Now O'Hara was gone and the night returned to its own voices. Topping and Yarnall questioned the wisdom of O'Hara's flight, yet the code of their culture was to let each man make his own decisions. They stuck to their plan and packed up the next morning, moving on. They would not hear the rest of O'Hara's story until much later.

When they did, they learned that it took the frightened man six days to get back to the miners' cabins, a trip that should have taken less than half that time. Along the way, O'Hara's paranoia must have escalated into something like schizophrenia. Finally he arrived back at the mines, afoot, exhausted, and hungry, reporting a not-so-unreasonable tale of Indian attacks and loss of horses and supplies.

The men listened to O'Hara describe riding away from camp that first night, the shooting he heard behind him, and running headlong into Indians himself before he could return to help; ten miners immediately started packing gear to answer the call.

When they started firing he jumped from his horse and threw himself into a ravine nearby. He figured he could elude their trackers more easily without his shoes so he quickly took them off, hid them in the brush, and traveled barefoot until he found a place to hole up overnight. He felt safe enough to head back late the next afternoon, but he was hungry and sore-footed.

Eventually O'Hara came across an elk, shot it, ate some raw, and used parts of the hide to wrap around his feet. He limped back to camp with his latest tale.

The miners located O'Hara's campsite on Blue Bead Creek, but there was no sign of Indians or any sort of attack. Eventually they found O'Hara's horses and the scattered pack and saddles. At first the men were puzzled as they studied the area: they could only see O'Hara's own prints. Then they suspected that he had been ambushed by a terrified mind. The mountain man eventually came to the same conclusion himself.

O'Hara vowed that he would make no more trips into that mountainous Indian country. According to Topping, probably writing around the turn of the century, it was a "resolution

A relaxed Pat O'Hara in 1913 visiting the Hoffmans on Monument Hill.
From there he disappeared from history.
(Courtesy Buffalo Bill Historical Center)

he has kept to this day."

Topping and his partner had witnessed a true O'Hara "crazy" event. In another oft-repeated O'Hara episode, a band of Indians who captured him found his actions so bizarre that they diagnosed him as filled with the power of the Great Spirit and let him go. After the night he did battle with the crazies, O'Hara lived for five years on the waterway now known as Pat O'Hara Creek. Perhaps as the story of his imaginary encounter spread throughout the region it was described as happening at Pat O'Hara's Creek. Thus the name stuck.

While his first home on the Two Dot was probably a cave, he described a dugout with canvas over the front in later years and may have even built a cabin, all just below what is today the Lower Two Dot Ranch. In his book *Cattle Drive in 1885* Jim Redfera tells of Pat O'Hara, "An old trapper and prospector had lived [on the creek] since the late fifties…" While O'Hara may have called this home, more often he seemed bent on restlessness. With some questions about exactly how the transaction took place, John Chapman's friend and partner John Weaver took possession of that parcel, calling it O'Hara Ranch. It kept that name until Lloyd Taggart bought it from George Heald in 1950.

O'Hara disappeared after his business transaction with Chapman. Perhaps he felt safe enough to go into the mountains at that time, or perhaps he turned his horse in another direction. At any rate he told Chapman that the country was becoming too crowded. But O'Hara would be back.

On Christmas Eve in 1913 the *Cody Enterprise* reported Pat O'Hara's return. He had been hired to help Ranger Sparhawk catch coyotes. The story indicated that O'Hara had spent his life prospecting: "There are few mineral districts in the West that haven't known Pat's pick. Twice he has found what he has sought, until the result that two different fortunes have passed through his generous hands." The writer suggested that O'Hara was now in his eighties, but still spry and frisky.

Noah Riley, a youngster who sold rodeo tickets for Cody's annual Stampede, was introduced to O'Hara by Buffalo Bill himself and told to provide a good seat for him. Riley obliged. But it was the Walter Hoffman family who could claim to be the last people to share a few days with the aging mountaineer.

Since 1907 Walter and Manuelle Hoffman had lived in a cabin on Trail Creek, northwest of the new town of Cody and not far from the neighboring Two Dot. By 1913 the Hoffmans were ready for the homesteading challenge. They filed a claim on Blaine Creek, moving into their new cabin on the road into Sunlight in 1914. One day that year the mountain man rode up to the cabin, leading a pack horse and sparking the lifelong interest of the Hoffmans' three-year-old son, Walter, Jr.

O'Hara stayed overnight, laying his bedroll on the grass, and left the following afternoon, saying he was headed to Oregon.

During his visit, Walter Hoffman, Sr. questioned him about local landmarks. He pointed to a cave in the bank of Pat O'Hara Creek. O'Hara remembered wintering there during his early days, trapping beaver in ponds above it. He stored his pelts there until he had enough to take to Fort C. F. Thompson to trade for traps, shells, knives, clothes, and salt. The cave was protected with six-foot tall sagebrush completely covering the entrance. O'Hara kept a buffalo hide across the opening to keep varmints out.

One day, he told the Hoffmans, warming to the story, he packed up his furs in the cave. He slung a pack over his shoulder and prepared to step out, but as he lifted the buffalo hide it was suddenly pelted with arrows. He backed up, dropping the hide. He waited. For two days and a night he sat at the back of the cave, prepared for an attack. Obviously the Indians either had seen him enter the cave or tracked him there.

Finally he decided they weren't after him, but his furs. The second night, when darkness had enveloped the landscape, he slipped away with his gun in hand. The Indians could help themselves, and he learned later that's just what they did.

In another story O'Hara recalled traveling with two men. As they were dismounting to prepare a noonday meal O'Hara sensed that something was wrong. He could see that the game in the distance seemed spooky but were ignoring the threesome. "I told the other two, don't loosen your cinches," he explained to the family sitting around the dining table.

With O'Hara's own reputation for spooky-headedness, it wasn't too surprising that his companions eased their cinches anyway to let their animals relax, drink, and graze a little. Unfortunately for them, this time O'Hara was interpreting reality pretty clearly.

The Indian attack came suddenly, and it was vicious. One of O'Hara's comrades was killed when his saddle turned as he tried to mount. The second man mounted and got as far as a coulee that dropped away nearby. He was on the verge of escape when his saddle rolled under the horse's belly and he went over the side, easy prey. O'Hara himself took an arrow so deep in his leg that he had to leave it there. Eventually, O'Hara said, he had it surgically removed in St. Louis by a doctor he knew and trusted. In fact, the Hoffmans believed that he was returning from that surgery when he'd arrived back in the Cody area.

Another time, O'Hara said, he and his partner were fleeing from a band of Indians. Adding to the crisis, O'Hara found himself suddenly ill, feeling more ready to be slain by his mortal enemy than to try to go on. He was deathly ill. Unable to travel, he told his partner to go on without him. Understanding the need but unwilling to just leave him, the man killed a deer and laid the carcass next to O'Hara just in case his health might improve and he became hungry. The man mounted his horse, leaving O'Hara to die, be killed by the Indians, or get better. Then he was gone.

O'Hara knew little for the next few days, but gradually his health improved. Finally, although he still wasn't hungry, he felt he needed to eat and he carved off some deer meat spoiling in the hot weather. As he described it to the Hoffmans, the tainted meat acted as a purgative, first sickening him, then saving his life.

Occasionally O'Hara traveled to St. Louis. On one of these trips he ran into William Clark, and they talked about the heart-shaped mountain that John Colter had described so many years earlier. Eventually the Two Dot Ranch would wrap its lands around the west and northern shoulders of this famous landmark, Heart Mountain.

• •

When his storytelling ended, the Hoffmans could see that Pat O'Hara was getting anxious to be on the trail. He told Manuelle that he had a niece in Polson, Montana, and other family in Oregon. He packed his frying pan, coffee pot, blanket, and a slicker. When the Hoffmans offered him supplies he accepted only a few grounds of coffee.

Then he was gone, leaving as quietly as he had come, saying little of his plans or his ultimate destination. What O'Hara thought of the developments at the Two Dot and at his own ranch, then owned by Midwestern transplant George Heald, are left to our imaginations. Without a doubt O'Hara knew he had helped settle good country. Whether he approved of what his successors had done with it is a matter of supposition.

In later years Walter Hoffman and his mother searched in vain for further records of the mountaineer's life. And the quest didn't end there. Walter's son Jim has inherited the interest and remains alert for tales of the elusive Pat O'Hara, first white settler of the Two Dot region.

PART TWO

THE SETTLEMENT YEARS
1878-1918

A Biography of Place

CHAPTER FIVE

John Chapman:
Founder of the Two Dot Ranch

John Chapman leaving on a business trip.
(Courtesy Jane Riddle Thompson)

ONE EARLY SEPTEMBER day in 1878, John Chapman topped the rise sixteen miles north of what would later become the town of Cody, Wyoming. He looked down into a richly meadowed valley. This was what he had been searching for across more than two thousand miles, from Riddle, Oregon to Fort Keough, Montana. This country fit his vision. It would be home.

Here—just south of the Clarks Fork River, whose winding waterway he had been following for days—there he would build the headquarters of the Chapman ranch. As he turned his horse and dropped over the ridge down to Blue Bead Creek, he saw a rough-hewn cabin protected by the creekbank, smoke drifting from the chimney. For a moment he wondered if this land might already be claimed—but only for a moment. Being a confident man, he shook off the feeling, resetting his resolve. He hadn't ridden this far only to be thwarted.

The fur trapper in the cabin was Pat O'Hara, an eccentric individual, already concerned about an overrun of newcomers. He would prove no deterrent to Chapman's plans.

While the call rang across America to "go west, young man," John William Chapman had already done that. As an infant he had traveled from Springfield, Illinois, to southern Oregon's Umpqua Valley in the arms of his mother, a widow who was following her own family, but chasing her dead husband's dream.

Little is known about the family's life in Illinois, but Artenecia Riddle Chapman occasionally reminded her son that his grandparents had befriended Abraham Lincoln in his early years as a lawyer.

Chapman grew up surrounded by the aunts, uncles, and grandparents who had traveled the Oregon Trail with his mother. His playmates included many cousins, fifteen half-siblings born after his mother remarried Oregonian William Merriman, as well as Indian children growing up in the area.

As a young man, his travels as a freighter took Chapman to Virginia City, Nevada, when it was the silver capital of the world and the wildest frontier town ever known. In 1878 he signed on as a drover moving a herd of cattle from his home county to the Powder River Valley in eastern Oregon. He was probably among the first to retrace his mother's steps on the Oregon Trail. According to John K. Rollinson, a cowboy for Chapman and later author of *Wyoming Cattle Trails*, says, "I have often heard him speak of that trip and state that, to his knowledge, it was the first time cattle had ever been moved backward over the old Oregon Trail. His exploration would take Chapman toward a territory slightly south, where roads were still no more than animal tracks and Indian trails, a region unsolicited so far. In any case he was also fulfilling the dream that seemed to infect every member of his mother's family: to move far and explore wide.

As it turned out, the region that really intrigued the young man was the land his family had crossed, the region between his birthplace and where he grew up—a land that whites had virtually ignored so far, except for a few fur traders and mountain men: the Rockies. This vision kept him topping every hill, peering into every draw, through the Bozeman Pass, down the Yellowstone River and on to Fort Keough, now known as Miles City. There rumor had him placing temporary roots, although that has never been proven.

Now he was headed for Blue Bead Creek, so named by the Indians who called that region home. As he rode he planned both his headquarters and his future. When he finally reached the floor of the valley below he probably received a warm but possibly wary welcome from the owner of the cabin.

Mountain man Pat O'Hara, who at one time had probably worked for the American Fur Company, didn't see many white visitors. John Chapman learned quickly that what few humans were entering the area were more than O'Hara wanted to deal with. If reports are accurate, O'Hara was glad to turn the region over to new hands. According to Rollinson, Chapman recalled him saying, "...the country's gittin' altogether too settled up with civilization for such old hands as Jim Bridger, Jack Robinson and me."

Later when Chapman returned with cattle and horses Pat O'Hara was nowhere to be seen. He "had vanished on what he claimed would be a visit to Fort C.F. Smith on the Big Horn River," Chapman later told Rollinson. But the rancher honored the old trapper by renaming Blue Bead Creek and Blue Bead Mountain for him.

• •

Pat O'Hara Creek is the very backbone, the lifeblood of the Two Dot, coming down off Pat O'Hara Mountain, winding through headquarters, nourishing meadows, grazing lands, and fields where crops would grow after the sod was broken up, lands that could support only sagebrush without its sustaining waters. What is left takes a bend turning north and eventually spills into the Clarks Fork River. Pat O'Hara Mountain forms the backdrop with rich summer grazing for both cattle and wildlife. It enticed Chapman then, and has each new owner since.

Born on June 15, 1850, John W. Chapman lost his father nine

months later. The elder Chapman had been plotting a move to Oregon with his young wife and in-laws: they would start as soon as their first child was born. His widow kept to his plan, packing up the baby and climbing aboard a covered wagon on a train headed west over the Oregon Trail, her destination Douglas County, Oregon. There her family, the Riddles, built a town that still carries their name today.

By 1878, John Chapman was grown and had already done some exploring. He had finished school at sixteen and cowboyed for ranches throughout the region. Then he became a freighter, driving a meat wagon, his wife would tell *Billings Gazette* reporter Kathryne Wright in the late 1940s. That job kept him on roads and trails throughout the Northwest Territory.

It was at that time that Chapman hired on to drive cattle eastward.

Chapman then used the drive as a jumping-off place for his search. He took two pack mules and an extra saddle horse, following the Snake River along a trail he would grow to know well. Later he and many other ranchers would pour cattle and horses through this funnel into Montana and Wyoming. The dusty road traversed Monida Pass, led through Virginia City and Bozeman, then dropped into the Yellowstone Valley, following that river east to the Tongue River country and Fort Keough.

Still not finding what he sought, he turned back. At the confluence of the Clarks Fork and the Yellowstone he followed the tributary, which led toward the canyon used by Chief Joseph in his flight the year before. When Chapman reached Blue Bead Creek, he again accepted the invitation of the smaller stream. He climbed to higher ground above the waterway for a clearer view of the whole area. Twelve miles later he found the valley.

A Two Dot rodeo held in 1899.
(Courtesy Buffalo Bill Historical Center)

• •

Having concluded his land transaction, Chapman saddled up on September 5 and turned his horse northwest, heading on home. He met some soldiers of the Fifth Infantry led by Colonel Nelson A. Miles and learned that just the day before, the battalion had fought a band of Bannock Indians about sixteen miles north of O'Hara's cabin. Some say Chapman may have even heard the gunfire.

Later the skirmish would come to be known as the Bennett Butte Battle for the officer killed there; it was the Big Horn Basin's last battle in a year of Indian trouble that history would remember as the Bannock Indian War. Chapman decided to travel with Colonel Miles and his troops along with fifty Crow Indians familiar with the area. They would attempt to catch up with the rest of the Bannocks, now horseless and on the run. The entourage traveled across what today is known as Bald Ridge, grazing land that would become a valuable Two Dot Forest Service lease after Chapman's time. (It continued in the hands of Two Dot owners until Yves Burrus's loss due to the fact that Forest Service lands cannot be leased by foreign owners.) According to Rollinson, from there "...they went down Dead Indian Hill, then across Dead Indian and Sunlight creeks, following the retreating Bannocks . . . they trailed up to the head of Clarks Fork, then past Cooke City, a new mining town, and down Soda Butte Creek to the Lamar River and Baronett's Bridge on the Yellowstone." There Miles hoped to overtake the retreating Indians although they had disappeared completely. When declared safe, Miles had officers bring his family from their retreat in Bozeman.

With war parties on the trail, Chapman appreciated the safety of riding with the soldiers. When he separated from them he went on to Mammoth Hot Springs, then south to Norris Geyser Basin and the Lower Geyser Basin toward the Madison River, still in Yellowstone. After passing Henry's Lake and Mud Lake in Idaho Territory, he was back on the trail to Oregon retracing his own steps.

That same year President Hayes appointed John W. Hoyt governor of Wyoming Territory. Hoyt rode the territory from end to end, then reported to the secretary of the interior, "The present great resource is livestock: The stock business in Wyoming, for security and the magnitude of its profits, is today unequalled by any other of which I have knowledge in this part of the world and in these times."

When Chapman returned to Wyoming Territory in late winter of 1879, he was accompanied by Andrew and Henry Chapman. (They were no relation then, but would later become brothers-in-law. The frequent intermingling and business ties of the two Chapman families has often caused confusion, even among historians.) Another round trip in 1880 found the team bringing in

Affie Chapman after the move to Red Lodge, Montana.
(Courtesy Jane Riddle Thompson)

five thousand head of cattle and a hundred head of horses.

Some other cowboys sharing in the Chapman adventure were Jim and John Weaver, J.A. Bradley, and Charley Morrison. The team picked up Chapman's own cattle in the Powder River Valley and purchased more to make up a drive of twelve hundred cattle and eighty horses. John Chapman's heart must have beat a little faster as he swung into the saddle and headed east again.

When he had the livestock settled in the meadows along Pat O'Hara Creek grazing the first grass of early spring, Chapman and his crew went about erecting temporary shelters and selecting logs for a three-room cabin fit for the bride he intended to bring. These early structures stood on the south side of the creek, opposite where a stone house would be built later. For nearly a quarter of a century Chapman would expand his headquarter buildings on the south bank, but today, only foundation remnants and an occasional hewn log remain.

James Weaver and Chapman, believing in an endless supply of grass, began their twelve-year partnership in the stock business. (In the 1890s, ill health would force Weaver out; he returned to Oregon.) Weaver's brother, John, also frequently played a part in their dealings. Jim Weaver stayed in Wyoming the fall of 1880 to man a skeleton crew while Chapman returned to Oregon to enjoy several months of pre-nuptial celebrations before he married his bride, Alphia "Affie" Chapman, daughter of Addison Chapman and no relation to her betrothed. Just four days after their April 20, 1881 wedding, the couple started for Wyoming Territory.

• •

John Chapman was a thin but powerful man. He towered over his delicately built wife, although few were foolish enough to question her strength—certainly not the hired hands who worked with her. John was extremely modest and soft spoken, a thinker and a doer but not much of a talker. At the time of his death writers lamented that because he was no storyteller or bragger, much of his rich life history had died with him. Although supportive of nieces, nephews, and other relatives, the Chapmans had no children of their own, so that too limited their family lore.

While Rollinson's description of the honeymoon trip places Affie Chapman sidesaddle on her favorite horse, she told a different story in an interview for the *Red Lodge Picket* shortly before her death.

"That was a trip full of a lot of fun," she said, "but a lot of grief, too. There were seven of us in the party—J. W. Chapman, Ed (last name unknown), who was practically a member of the family, Bronc Twister, one of the hands, the cook, another herder and me."

According to Mrs. Chapman, she was driving a rig drawn by a span of white horses, a wedding gift from her bridegroom. An early *Picket* article had mentioned "a pair of young plains horses hitched to a buckboard, the most refined mode of conveyance known in those early days."

"I'd lend a hand to the cook when he needed it," she said. "Cooking was nothing to me. I'd been a 'biscuit shooter' in my mother's hotel in Grant County. Was a darned good one, too. It isn't so much what your job is, it's how you do it," she added.

The trip wasn't all fun; she recalled an accident on a bridge in Idaho. One end of the span went down just as she moved her rig onto it. Immediately water washed over her, nearly throwing her from her seat. "I stuck with the horses," she said. "Mr. Chapman and Ed called to me, 'Stay with 'em, gal.'" Then each of them got a loop on the buckboard and started pulling her back towards the intact end of the bridge. She in turn encouraged the team backwards. Inch by inch they reversed their steps until she and her team were safely on firm ground.

At the Snake River crossing they ran into more trouble. John

Dave Good and John Kirkpatrick were homesteaders, neighbors and frequently cowboys for the Two Dot. Dave Good had come to Two Dot country with his friend Oscar Thompson.
(Courtesy Denver Museum)

Chapman had always crossed it easily earlier in the season, but this time the Snake was running full and the ferryman refused to move until "the hump goes outen her back." They waited ten days.

At Bozeman, the group rested several days, letting the stock graze while they replenished their supplies. Affie's new husband warned her that this would be the last pocket of civilization.

Before they broke camp Mrs. Chapman demonstrated the business acumen and common sense that would stand her in good stead over the years. When a local banker came out to the camp to visit he admitted that he had been quite taken with her team when he saw them in town earlier. "Mr. Chapman had gotten them for me and he said selling them was up to me," she explained. "Well, I thought, why not?" The banker offered her $450 for the horses and $100 for the rig. "I knew if we ever got to where we were going to have a home, I'd be too busy to do nothing but ride around, so I went the rest of the way down to Wyoming in the cook wagon."

They arrived at the ranch in November, seven months and eighteen hundred miles from Oregon.

Upon her introduction to the ranch headquarters Affie was left to her own devices. After the crew turned the stock out, the newlyweds accepted belated congratulations from the men who had kept the operation going; many were old friends. Then Affie explored her new three-room log cabin. Although it was windowless, she was so glad to be "home" that any concerns she might have had with this man-built house were left unstated. Already a few pieces of furniture ordered from St. Louis and shipped via the Missouri River to Fort Benton had been delivered by wagon. Another was quickly dispatched to Bozeman for additional pieces and necessary supplies.

Was she prepared for the future? Affie would spend her first two and a half years there without seeing another white woman. Most of her early visitors were Crow Indians. Her husband made two trips a year to Bozeman for supplies and the mail—her only link to family and home.

• •

At market time in the fall, the cattle were pushed along the Clarks Fork and down the Yellowstone. The shipping site was gradually moving west according to how much railroad track had been laid that year. Coulson, Montana, a town east of present-day Billings, was one of the early shipping sites.

It was during those first years that Chapman became acquainted with Otto Franc, who had come west on an 1877 hunting trip and later returned to start the Pitchfork Ranch. Henry

Lovell was another cohort, establishing his own operation on the east side of the Big Horn Basin along the Big Horn River. Englishman Richard Ainsworth of the Hoodoo just south of the Shoshone River, came a little later. There were W.A. Carter and Captain Henry Belknap, an Englishman who had ranches on the middle South Fork of the Shoshone River as well. Most of these ranchers were bringing in cattle from Oregon. They would become northern Wyoming's cattle barons.

To the north Chapman and his crew worked closely with N.R. Tolman of the Dilworth Land and Cattle Company. While Hank Chapman, Affie's brother, also trailed cattle into Wyoming territory with John, he is better known for bringing sheep into the region. It appears he came to stay in 1881.

The Chapmans had five years' grace: good weather in which to build their cattle and horse herds. Years later Affie recalled her husband's foresight. "Oregon was known for their good stock and we brought some of the best to our ranch," she said. "Early on we focused on breeding our mares to imported Percheron stallions." The colts were trained and marketed nationwide for fire departments, livery stables, freighters, and dray companies. Recognizing that the Homestead Act of 1862 was bringing the free-range era to an end, Chapman bred strong saddle horses that could also do a farmer's work. New homesteaders would need to break sod and pull irrigation ditches if they hoped to grow the crops they had grown in the Midwest.

By the mid-1880s the demand for such horses was ebbing and the cattle business was at its height. Chapman's early importation of Durham cattle out of Oregon would ensure his survival in the coming years.

While the Chapmans were getting established, wildlife was still plentiful. Buffalo hunters were shipping hides east—forty-five hundred reported in 1880 alone—but in December 1884 Vic

Arland, a trader on Meeteetse Creek, wrote to a friend back east that "the buffalo have entirely disappeared from the surrounding areas."

The Chapmans fell into the free-range schedule of twice-a-year roundups, with neighboring ranchers joining forces to collect all their cattle, from mountaintops to sagebrush plains, into a single herd. Then they sorted them out by brands. In the spring the cattlemen branded the newborn calves; in the fall they selected stock for market.

During one of these early roundups when her husband was gone, Affie Chapman met her first grizzly.

She was returning the milking equipment to the barn that evening: in Oregon Affie had developed quite a reputation as a cheesemaker, a practice she continued in this wild country (her earliest customers were mostly Indians, who "just loved it"). She did the milking herself in the beginning, until her husband concluded he could spare one of the cowboys for the job. But Affie herself cleaned the pails and other equipment to her strict specifications, returning them to the barn in time for the next session.

That particular evening as she carried her buckets, Affie had an eerie sense of trouble but ignored it. The feeling continued despite her best efforts to shake it loose. As she entered the barn she let the big double doors swing open, letting in the late afternoon light as she put everything in its place. Starting back to the house, her sense of unpleasant company overcame her again and as she spun around, there it was—a mother grizzly and her three cubs nosing around the side of the barn. At the sight of the woman, the mother grizzly rose snorting on her hind legs to her full height, her three furry babies dangling around her feet.

Affie looked to the house: too far away, and besides, she had no intention of running. "I wasn't going to let those critters have free rein of the place. We'd already been missing too much meat from the smokehouse, and here was the outfit responsible for it," she later told an interviewer. No time to reach the doors and pull them shut. The grizzly seemed frozen. Affie didn't dare do the same. Then she remembered a rifle her husband kept on the barn wall. She ran for it, pulling it down. She tried to raise it and aim, but it was too heavy. She looked out to the fence that could provide a prop, but that would put her in line with the grizzly. Could she get set up and fire before the animal reached her? It was her only chance.

The mother bear seemed puzzled by this woman running toward her, instead of away. The animal paused long enough for Affie to position the gun on the log and squeeze the trigger. As the rifle roared in the young woman's ears she watched the grizzly racing toward her, and imagined the attack. She saw the luxurious rippling coat of fur, the blazing red eyes, the open-jawed mouth with the razor sharp teeth; she heard a growl, a snort. She even sensed that flash of death that comes in perilous circumstances. Then suddenly, nearly at her feet, the mother grizzly fell dead. Affie's aim had been accurate.

The shot brought the milking hand out of the bunkhouse at a run. When he found her at the corral, she calmly handed him the gun. He finished off the cubs and together they dragged the bears closer to the house where the animals could be skinned for the hides and meat. Affie headed for the kitchen, taking pride with every step that she had been so calm.

It would be hours before she realized the toll this incident had taken. Late that night her husband slipped home from the roundup to surprise her. That he did. As he came through the kitchen door in his dark brown coonskin coat, she took one glance and fainted.

● ●

As more and more cattlemen settled in the region the twice-a-year roundups provided a system that seemed to work throughout the four-state area of Wyoming, Montana, Colorado, and Idaho. This system allowed the big ranchers to claim a percentage of

The men in this picture, ready for their annual pack trip, include Pres Riddle in middle, and Glen Brough, Dick Hinkle and Hardy Schull around 1902. The others are unkown.
(Courtesy Jane Riddle Thompson)

the mavericks—unbranded calves—according to the sizes of their respective operations. Although practical, the process encouraged stealing by smaller operators and homesteaders throughout the West trying to "grow" their cow herds.

While the Montana-oriented John Chapman never joined the Wyoming Stock Growers Association, he did abide by their roundup rules. He also worked closely with Montana ranchers and gladly accepted the maverick law.

The Wyoming Maverick Law of 1884 countered the assumption that unbranded animals on the open range were fair game for anyone with a branding iron. It gave roundup authorities permission to sell mavericks—but only in large lots. Small operators claimed this was unfair. They didn't have the money to buy large lots, especially when their own missing stock was part of the deal. Then some ranchers started paying their cowboys for every maverick they brought in. From there it was an easy step for the cowboys, who were laying out their own homesteads, to gather from this unbranded pool for their first herds, placing their own brands on calves missed during the gathering. Some homesteaders, seeing how this practice worked, took advantage of it as well.

For Chapman the traffic in mavericks, and his own vision of where the western country was headed, led to some of the first barbed-wire fences in the northern Big Horn Basin. He also started fencing valley meadows, more to keep other cattle from grazing what he considered "his lands" than to keep his own in.

In 1886 the Wyoming Legislature declared it unlawful for any person at any time to brand any maverick, except on the official roundup under the supervision of the roundup foreman. Members of the Wyoming Stock Growers Association found it most effective simply to blacklist any cowboys suspected of stealing stock so there would be no jobs available for them anywhere.

The next two years rang out suffering for the cattle industry. Blizzards, floods, drought—all were thrown at producers and investors alike. The devastating winter of 1886–1887 was slightly less so for ranches whose grass was knee high and dried to a highly nutritious content, and whose livestock had serious survival instincts. Cattle out of Oregon did considerably better than newer shipments from Iowa. While the Big Horn Basin appeared to fare better than elsewhere, no one was left without injury before the first blades of green returned in the spring. That year beef steers brought only twenty to twenty-five percent of the 1883 selling price on the Chicago market. Stock cattle fared even worse, with cows bringing scarcely five dollars a head, down from a high of thirty-five dollars.

With prices so low, the count became even more vital to ranchers' economic futures. Their losses made them develop better tracking systems for their animals. Ranchers strung barbed wire and filed on claims that had simply been land grabs.

The plight of homesteaders trying to build their herds became even more desperate. Cattle rustling took on deadly ramifications; serious money could be made in that profession even as it was being lost by the cattlemen. At the same time, as author Byron Price points out in *Cowboys*, "Many cattle raisers encouraged their hands to file homestead claims on desirable acreage in order to preempt other settlers from buying it." Chapman's later purchases suggest that at least some of that was going on.

Records indicate that even during those tough years, the Chapmans never missed any opportunity—they kept building their land base. Frequently the patents carried Alphia's name: she had her own brand, her own money, and managed much of her own operation. Almost every year their names were added to courthouse records for land purchases as well as sales. Many of their real-estate transactions read like exchanges more than outright purchases. Like many ranchers, the Chapmans encouraged not only hired hands but also relatives to file on homesteads in the area. Soon some of that land was in Riddle hands. In 1899 Chapman purchased a South Fork property from his cousin Priestly Riddle for one dollar, and another in Sunlight Basin at about the same time. For years Chapman held the land on the Riddles' behalf while they moved back and forth from Oregon, trying to decide where they wanted to settle. Eventually Wyoming would win.

Priestly Riddle first came from Oregon to work on the Chapman ranch when he was barely seventeen. He had tried out his entrepreneurial skills near Hardin, Montana, where he ran cattle on the Crow reservation with Senator John B. Kendrick. According to *The Historical Encyclopedia of Wyoming*, he was a good friend of Counsellor Bob Yellowtail, for whom the Yellowtail Dam is named. Both Kendrick and Yellowtail are credited with a tenacious vision for the development of the dam on the Big Horn River, which winds into Montana at the northeast corner of the Big Horn Basin, becoming a one word river inthat state, the Bighorn.

By 1917, when he married Mary Nichols, a close friend of his younger sister, Riddle was already well established in Sunlight Basin and would earn an outstanding reputation for his Hereford cattle and Quarter Horses. He and John Chapman would bring the first Silver Horn registered Herefords into the ranch from Oregon. Meanwhile, after the pivotal year of 1886, with grasses grazed to a nubbin, some cattlemen looked to other opportunities. "Needing less food and water than cattle, sheep are more suited to grazing on the arid winter range of Wyoming," author B. Byron Price points out in *Cowboys*. In 1887 Chapman staked A. C. Newton, owner of the neighboring Trail Creek Ranch, to a band of sheep; he also brought several bands in for himself. Fremont County tax records show that Chapman was assessed for 2,250 sheep valued at $2,812. It was the first sheep herd officially recorded in the Basin. More would follow, according to David Wasden in the "*Annals of Wyoming*, Fall, 1977 #2 Vol. 49."

• •

During this period, many Wyoming ranchers along the border of Montana Territory and the Crow reservation struck agreements to graze their cattle on Crow lands. At the peak of his cattle numbers, Chapman, like Otto Franc, did the same. Agency heads wanted more permits sold to increase their budgets. As for the Indians themselves, they just knew they were hungry.

By September of 1887, relations between whites and Indians were becoming more and more strained. Complaints about horse stealing were added to reports of slaughtered cattle. The Cheyenne-based Wyoming Stock Growers Association once more alleged that ranchers as far away as the southern tip of the Big Horns were reporting cattle slaughtered by the Crow. One rancher who saw a horse with his brand in Crow hands protested that he had no recourse. It didn't help that Indian agents were keeping the Crows hungry to force compliance with U.S. government rules.

For the Indians, three years of tension exploded at the agency on September 30, when twenty-one young Indians held what some termed a parade, a celebration. Actually they rebelled. Led by twenty-five-year-old Sword Bearer, a medicine man who had spent much of his youth with dissident tribal chiefs, they raced into the agency headquarters, guns blazing. After threatening an interpreter, the Indian agent, and his wife, they left—still shooting, mostly in the air and at buildings.

When eight soldiers from Fort Custer arrived at nightfall to provide protection, a mass of young Crows surrounded them and pressed them back until the outnumbered soldiers feared for their lives. It took older and wiser headmen to force the younger bucks away so the soldiers could set up their station. But the Indians continued their harassment. Shots were heard throughout the night. In the morning Sword Bearer once again presented his challenge to the troops, but they held their weapons silent.

Although the medicine man had traveled the reservation from end to end trying to incite an uprising, even soliciting Sioux and Cheyenne leaders, none took place. As soldiers waited out the Indian storm, Sword Bearer disappeared.

Having amiable relations with the Crows from the beginning, the Chapmans were not particularly worried, but they did keep up with the news coming out of the Billings area. John Chapman still joined his cowboys each morning, heading north before dawn to work cattle. Then, late one morning as Affie went about her chores, she saw Indians descending the ridge above the ranch house.

"I never even thought a thing about the raids," she said years later. "They just rode up. Got off their horses and came in. I fed 'em what I had, just like I always did, and they sat around enjoying it." Was Sword Bearer among those dinner guests? Affie's friends were concerned when she told them about the visit. She, in turn, explained that her story was meant to show there was nothing to worry about.

By November 1, troops from across the region were in place

at the order of the secretary of war, who told General Alfred Terry to "take such action at once as may be considered necessary to prevent an outbreak." Brigadier General Thomas Ruger, the Civil War veteran in charge of the region, fully intended to prevent this potential uprising. He did not understand that few Crows were willing to join the prophet, as Sword Bearer was frequently referred to. Pretty Eagle, one of the leaders, acknowledged the young Indian's charisma and power. "He is a great man," he said. "All things bend before him and the very ground is shaking before he does his great deeds." At the same time Pretty Eagle admitted that armed resistance was futile.

Despite Sword Bearer's efforts to wreak havoc on the reservation and end agency rule, ten Indian leaders who met with Ruger on November 5 assured him that while the young Indian had impressive powers, none of them planned to follow him. Finally, after a white fatality from Indian gunfire, they agreed with the brigadier general that something must be done to prevent further bloodshed.

The U.S. attack was ordered. Sword Bearer raced through the Indian camps promising to use his medicine to prevent any harm to the Crows, but the majority of warriors were not impressed.

Wounded during the ensuing battle, Sword Bearer attempted to escape alone. He raced his pony across the prairie toward the Little Bighorn River. He must have been surprised, after fording the river and coming up onto the far bank, to find the Crow policeman Fire Bear waiting for him. While Fire Bear admitted later that the fleeing man had demonstrated no resistance, the officer shot him in the head. Sword Bearer died instantly.

While the Crow would not follow Sword Bearer, they recognized a powerful shaman, a medicine man, among them. As he lay in state for the rest of the day, the whole tribe came to pay its respects. More than a century later descendants of those mourners continue to tell the story of his death.

One day many years later when the Chapmans were settled in Red Lodge, Affie found herself at Yegen Brothers' Store in Billings. One of the brothers, a frequent hunting partner of Buffalo Bill Cody, helped with her purchases. Then he pointed to an Indian peering from a corner. He suggested that the Indian must have a reason for watching her so closely and warned her to be careful. Then, Affie recalled later, the old Indian came right over to her, looked her up and down, put his hands on her shoulders and grunted his approval: she was a good woman. In a mixture of Crow and English he reminded her how often he had eaten at her ranch. It was then she recognized Little Face, one of the Indians who had come to the ranch that day along with Child-in-Mouth and Harry Moccasin. As for the others, she never did know the names of the many she fed or if Sword Bearer had truly been among them.

• •

Gradually cattle rustling waned, but by 1887 more and more Montana Territory horse thefts were being dealt with by the vigilante method: simply string up the suspects without advantage of the court system. The outlaw problem seemed to leak south out of that state as vigilante organizations dedicated themselves to solving the crime by killing the criminals.

While this did not end the stealing it did drive it underground and professionalize the system, making it more portable. By 1889 a horse-trafficking network spread over at least a seven-state area; so did the owners' outrage, surpassing even their anger over cattle thievery. John Chapman, with his reputation for Percheron crossbred and straight line stock, found himself in an explosive situation.

There were rumors that well-known robbers Butch Cassidy and Al Hainer had been camped at the far reaches of Alkali Creek northeast of the ranch. Chapman counted horses—two hundred missing. Cassidy had worked at the Pitchfork as late as 1881. Otto Franc reported to Chapman that he had already signed a complaint against the two men. Two horses from the Grey Bull cattle outfit just north of the Pitchfork had disappeared with the men.

Chapman saddled up in front of the ranch house that autumn day in 1891. As he adjusted his saddle for the long ride he studied the posse gathered around him. Expenses for the men were to be paid by the ranchers who remained at home. They turned their horses south where, rumor had it, the team was holed up on the edge of the Owl Creek Mountains.

While much has been made of Robert Leroy "Bob" Parker's name change, Butch Cassidy's reputation grew over time: bank robbery after train robbery after horse theft. Cassidy was often described as the folk hero of the poor and oppressed, championed by small homesteaders struggling for their very existences in a raw frontier dominated by cattle barons and railroad magnates.

Chapman and most of the area ranchers from Montana to South Dakota and back to Idaho put little stock in the growing legend. They just knew they had trouble keeping up with Cassidy's travels—and so did the chroniclers throughout the last century who tried to track his movements during that nineteen-year period of lawlessness.

Chapman stopped to tell Franc he was on his way, then rode west expecting to find them at what was called the Mail Camp Road Ranch on the south slope of the Owl Creeks. James Thomas, who knew Cassidy, suggested to Chapman that the partners were traveling southwest toward Evanston. With a little encouragement Thomas remembered seeing Cassidy shoeing the same three horses Chapman described while talking about the trip to Uinta County. At Chapman's next stop, Fort Washakie, the clerk of the Shoshone Tribal Agency, a man named Rorick, told him that Cassidy and Hainer had left just a few days before.

At Evanston, Uinta County Sheriff John Ward provided Chapman with the talents of his best deputy, Bob Calverly, a Texan. They checked ranches in the area, always with an eye to the sky. Winter was rolling in.

While the posse may have actually located their horses in the Teton Basin of Jackson Hole before they were driven out by blizzards, they chose to come on home to wait until spring to arrest the outlaws, probably guessing that Cassidy felt safe and would be limited in his travels from the snow-locked area.

According to Otto Franc's diary, Chapman was back in home country by December 26, 1891. What may have seemed an unsuccessful hunt to some was a ride that helped Chapman sleep better that winter. He knew where his man was and he would surely find him. As winter wore on he became even more determined to get Cassidy. By spring all-out war was declared on horse thieves across the West but Chapman stayed focused on two men.

The first of April, 1892, found Chapman and a number of eager volunteers back in their saddles. They headed their horses toward Evanston. The posse may have included Dave Stewart, a Pitchfork hand who, according to the Franc diary entry of March 1, 1892, had been sent to join Chapman's party at the Dilworth Ranch, where plans were laid for the general campaign to rid the West of rustlers. The capture of Cassidy and Hainer would be just one step in a far-reaching plan. There may also have been an unnamed law officer from Montana and, at some point, Charles Davis, later the sheriff of Park County. In addition, local authorities would become involved because Calverly, once again riding side by side with Chapman, was actually out of his jurisdiction. They needed to be legal. Cassidy had been slippery before and they needed the charges to stick.

Coming out of Evanston, the posse picked up speed as it

headed north toward Afton, a town just eight miles from Auburn. The men had a tip that Cassidy and Hainer were now using a young ranch neighbor, Kate Davis—Charles's sister—to run errands and pick up their mail in Afton. Chapman and his team wanted to catch up with the girl before she returned to Auburn and the sawmill-ranch where the two men were reported to be staying. At some locale, perhaps the Afton post office, they were able to intercept her and either follow or get her help in reaching the Cassidy-Hainer hideout.

Upon their arrival there that early April day, they moved quietly through the trees, locating Hainer at the sawmill. They were able to surprise and capture him with little effort and no noise. Once he was gagged and tied to a tree, Calverly nodded toward the cabin and the men moved forward. With a little encouragement, Hainer had admitted that Cassidy was sleeping on a bunk just inside the door. At the entrance, Calverly called out to the outlaw. "Cassidy, I've got a warrant for your arrest."

Before he could say anything else Cassidy reportedly hollered back, "Well, get to shooting." With that the team hit the door, Calverly first. Aiming at Cassidy's stomach the deputy fired, again, then again, but the bullets went wild. The outlaw fired himself but was bumped in the process by one of the posse, possibly Chapman, and that bullet, too, strayed far from its intended target.

Although the shootout lasted only seconds, it seemed longer to Calverly. He finally got off a fourth shot which plowed a furrow across the left side of Cassidy's forehead, rendering him temporarily unconscious.

Once Cassidy came to, Chapman showed his compassion in cleaning and wrapping Cassidy's wound as they prepared for the trip to Evanston. Not unlike many others, Chapman probably found Cassidy likeable but dangerous. In fact the two men actually had at least two things in common. They both admired good horseflesh as well as loving the challenge of becoming top horsemen early in life.

Affie and John Chapman at the back door of the Stone House.
(Courtesy Jane Riddle Thompson)

As soon as the thieves were locked away in Evanston awaiting Sheriff Charlie Stough, who would return them to Lander for trial, the posse saddled up again. By now an expanded band, they headed north, their destination the Cunningham Ranch in Teton Basin, where Chapman believed they would find the missing horses.

By April 15, they were mixing it up in a gun battle with rustlers there. Two outlaws, George Spencer and Mike Burnett, were killed. Unfortunately, the majority of the horses had already entered the stolen-horse pipeline in an ever-widening circle of states, either trafficked with altered brands or sold to packers at a penny a pound. Chapman came home with only fifty-three horses of mixed ownership—a token return.

Finally settled in the Fremont County jail at Lander, Cassidy got word to a lawyer from Rock Springs, one he had befriended at an earlier date. Preston would eventually serve as attorney general of the state of Wyoming. Those who questioned Cassidy's ability to hire such a high-powered lawyer were puzzled. They didn't know that Preston had gotten into his cups—as they once described the use of an excess of alcohol—and Cassidy had saved him from a severe beating.

According to the District Court's "Information," #144 dated July 16th, 1892, the two men "unlawfully, knowingly, and feloniously did steal, take and carry away, lead away, drive away and ride away...one horse of the value of forty dollars of the goods, chattels and personal property of The Grey Bull Cattle Company, a corporation duly organized and existing under, and, by virtue of the laws of the State of New Jersey, and doing business within the said County of Fremont, State of Wyoming."

John Chapman and Otto Franc were just two of the prosecuting witnesses who also included David Stewart, James Thomas, and Joseph "Billy" Nutcher, the young rustler who had actually sold the horses to Cassidy, if rumor was correct.

Friends of the men made their bail and both were released on their own recognizance for a period that would turn out to be a year when the District Court next convened. William Simpson, of the well-known political Simpson family, sat at the prosecutor's table the first day but he quickly turned the case over to a special prosecutor, M.C. Brown. Simpson's reasons are unrecorded although his friendliness to Cassidy over the years may have been a factor.

The trial moved quickly. The prosecution presented its witnesses and evidence, then turned to the defense, which did not make a case at all. The jury was sequestered and a bare two hours later returned with "not guilty" verdicts for both men. Still, it was far

Few get a chance to rebuild a house. Affie Chapman took pen and ruler to her stone house, expanding it in Red Lodge with much more decoration. Seen with family, Affie is second from left and John Chapman is far right.
(Courtesy Jane Riddle Thompson)

too early for the outlaws to celebrate.

Otto Franc had already signed a second complaint concerning a horse of a different color than the one originally cited, and the name in this warrant was changed from that of the Grey Bull Cattle Company to that of its owner, Richard Ashworth.

A date was set for the next court term scheduled for November. The two men were again freed on bond. In November the trial was postponed once more. Cassidy bounced from town to town just as he had before the first trial, but just as dependably as ever he was back in town ready to await his fate in late June of 1894. By that time it looked like a problem had developed between Hainer and Cassidy. Simpson was prosecuting the case himself and the witness list was altered somewhat. Ashworth, the horse owner, was present; Nutcher, the rustler who had supposedly sold the horses to Cassidy was not.

While Simpson's case was systematic and his witnesses well prepared, Preston's case, developed around the "Bill of Sale," crumbled.

This time the results were different, starting with a long deliberation. The jury returned with their verdict late on Saturday, so Judge Knight, who had presided, sealed the results until Monday, July 4.

After a testy weekend of street fights and near riots, Judge Knight ordered all strangers removed from the courtroom. While the courtroom was still filled, many were there as volunteers to protect those involved in the case. The verdict, which was signed by jury foreman George S. Russel, was read. "We the jury find the above named defendant George Cassidy guilty of horse stealing, as charged in the information, and we find the value of the property stolen to be $5.00. And we find the above named defendant Al Hainer not guilty. And the jury recommend the said Cassidy to the mercy of the court."

For the first and only time, Butch Cassidy was transported to the Wyoming Territorial Prison across the Big Laramie River from the town, arriving at the "Big Stone House" on July 15, 1894.

He would leave prison on January 19, 1896, with a full pardon from Governor William A. Richards, much earlier than his sentence called for and with new intentions. No more petty thievery of horses and cattle. He would become a major outlaw known on two continents. He would partner with Harry Longabaug and together they would build new lives for themselves as "Butch Cassidy and the Sundance Kid."

• •

Eighteen ninety-two was also the year the Crow reservation was thrown open to settlers, displacing the ranchers already grazing it.

On June 24 of that year a writer for the *Stinking Water Prospector* described the Chapman ranch: "...it contains thirteen hundred acres of deeded land, principally in meadow.... Last season's hay crop footed up about eighteen hundred head of fine graded Hereford cattle and several hundred head of inferior grade. He also owns one thousand head of fine horses, among them being an imported stallion costing one thousand dollars."

For John Chapman the gates of the American frontier swung both ways. The grass looked at least as green in the business world as in the livestock industry. By the mid-1880s he was already developing a reputation as a man with an extra dollar or two in his pocket and a willingness to lend it—at a monthly interest rate that has been debated locally. Stories vary with the teller: some were grateful, others might have lost everything despite the help. Some remember him as "old two-percent Chapman." Later, in a September 19, 1901 piece the editor called Chapman "the constant friend of those requiring assistance...these beneficiaries have nothing but words of praise for his liberality of treatment."

Banking would become his profession. In his first joint venture, with Paul Breteche, French owner-manager of the Trail Creek Ranch to the south, Chapman invested in butcher shops in the new town of Red Lodge, and in Billings. Then in 1895, the year Montana's Carbon County was formed, Chapman and Breteche were instrumental in creating a financial institution in Red Lodge with partner W. F. Meyer, a man who would eventually find politics to his liking. After Breteche sold Trail Creek and returned to France, the bank was renamed the Banking House of Meyer and Chapman with Meyer as president. In 1912, it was reorganized as the Meyer & Chapman State Bank. Chapman—already president of branch operations at the Bank of Belfry and the Big Horn County Bank at Hardin, as well as director of the Yellowstone Bank at Laurel and the Park City Bank—took over as head of the Red Lodge facility upon Meyer's death.

But Chapman's livestock and land interests were so vast that it took him eight years of divestment around the turn of the last century before he made a permanent move to Red Lodge.

For a time, the Chapman ranch continued to grow despite the change in focus. In 1896 the couple started building a three-story house which still stands today. A 1901 article in the *Cody Enterprise* states that the Chapman "home and fireside has always been open for travelers without price or charge, and his prosperity is gratifying to the entire community."

When the house was finished in March of 1900 the Chapmans organized a housewarming party of major proportions. Affie cooked for days; she decorated and polished. Her final walk-through in late afternoon filled her being with pride, she later told Mac Taggart. Never one to shirk her duties, she still had to feed the hired lambing crew at the Pat O'Hara place, which they had purchased from Jim Weaver in 1890. It was lambing time and the workers' meals came first.

Unfortunately, by the time she finished cleaning up there and made her way back to her new house, the party had already started. With early arrivals, a missing hostess, and no food, John Chapman had thrown the liquor cabinets open wide and the celebration was beyond full swing when she came through the doors in her chore clothes.

• •

By this time Martin and John Jobe were firmly settled on the ranch as a management team focused on the operation while John Chapman targeted his other business interests. Highly respected, the Jobes would stay twenty years, successfully managing operations for two more partnerships.

The Chapmans had started selling down in 1897 when a Nebraskan by the name of Valentine bought a thousand head of Chapman cattle. By 1901 they had signed away several sections of land. Yet John Chapman continued to be a hands-on rancher to the end, as a December 16, 1902 *Cody Enterprise* story demonstrated. The autumn had been mild and Chapman allowed a herd of his cattle to continue grazing at his summer camp on Crandall (Crannel) Creek deep in the mountains. It was one of the few times that Chapman was found to use poor judgment: After a blizzard struck, his cattle were literally penned in, with no way out and the snow much too deep to find feed underneath.

Fortunately Chapman had sixty horses running on the same range. He forced the horses into a band and headed them in the general direction of home, allowing them to pick their own way. Then he started the cattle out on the trail packed by the horses.

According to the paper, "He came very near being too late in the season...but he succeeded by hard work in getting two hundred cattle down to his ranch on South Fork with a loss of only two head." The fact that he moved the animals to his South Fork place is the first indication that he actually utilized the ranch that he had purchased from his relatives, the Riddles, for one dollar.

Starting in 1901 and completing the transaction by 1903, the wealthy partnership of E. M. Bent and J. P. Allison purchased the ranch headquarters. While area newspapers lamented every step, the transition, with the Jobe brothers managing the operation, was so smooth that it hardly formed a ripple on the home front. Still, the Chapmans retained much of their property on both sides of the Wyoming-Montana border.

While John and Alphia Chapman focused on their new life in Red Lodge, they continued their livestock and ranching operations from Bozeman, Montana, to Worland, Wyoming. One article written at the time of the Chapmans' move to Red Lodge listed a Bozeman ranch, half interest in the bank, as well as mining property in the Wood River district. One bank grew to four. Known for entrepreneurship, both John Chapman and his brother-in-law Henry were quoted in the *Cody Enterprise* in 1922 as "talking up a telephone line from Red Lodge to Cody [already] in 1897."

Singlehandedly, Affie tackled the design of a more luxurious version of the Stone House, which they built on Hauser Street in Red Lodge. It became known for the exquisite gardens and is still a striking residence yet today.

John died in 1933 at the age of eighty-three and Alphia took over his seat at the bank until her own death in 1949.

While the Chapmans are gone, the nieces and nephews they supported and the generations that followed thrive, their ranch lives on, their bank is now a part of Wells Fargo, and the rock solid marriage and commitment they demonstrated to each other lives on in the thousands around the world who have experienced this land.

CHAPTER SIX
The Stone House

A Biography of Place

The Stone House, Christmas 1995.
(Courtesy Keith Voyles)

No ONE KNOWS when Affie Chapman first dreamed of building a new house—maybe when travelers overran her three-room cabin for the hundredth time, spilling into the bunkhouse and maybe even the barn. At any rate we know she kept her eye out for the perfect location, settling on a spot across Pat O'Hara Creek from the cabin her husband and friends had built for her. Here a rise would protect the home from prevailing winds. She would turn the house so that large front windows would look out over the irrigated meadows stretching out below.

The three-story Stone House was built within the protection of a shallow ridge. The buildings of Two Dot headquarters have sprung up around the house to meet the needs of the ranch, and cottonwood trees surround it. It was Affie Chapman's dream. Its design was her vision; a scale model was still in the hands of its later owners, the Taggarts, in the 1990s.

The fourteen-room home with its wide veranda and covered porch looks out over valley meadows, standing as a century-old monument to her talent. Its two bathrooms, one on each floor, made it unique for its time. The immigrant artisans who labored in the construction brought their own European enhancements to the design and interior finishes. A large dining room with its long plank table could seat more than a dozen comfortably. A large fireplace and oak trim throughout enhanced the beauty.

Envisioning the house, clearly Affie had at least three criteria in mind as she worked on the plans within the lamplight's glow. Surely she longed for plenty of space, after fifteen years in the log home begun by her husband and completed by his friend Jim Weaver. There would be room for company, too: she could host their many friends and family, who came often and for long stays. Other travelers could be provided overnight accommodations as well.

And it would be a home commensurate with their financial place. By this time—the 1890s—the Chapmans were doing very well. John was already lending money to those in need and eyeing the prospect of founding a bank in Red Lodge. They had a great deal of land together and Affie had many acres in her own right, so they could afford such a home whatever the price. Newspaper estimates of that cost ranged from $6,000 to $50,000. The lower end was more likely; when the Chapmans later built their Red Lodge home, which expanded on the original Stone House floorplan, headlines in the *Red Lodge Picket* said they had spent $6,500 for that one.

The Stone House was a convenient overnight layover for travelers, but not a stage stop, as some have suggested. More and more homesteaders were staking their claims in Sunlight Basin and along the Clarks Fork, a two-day trip from Red Lodge. Others traveled the Red Lodge Freight Road, a spur of the Red Lodge–Meeteetse Trail that went on to Lander. Affie often found herself arranging wall-to-wall beds for those in need of one. Some observers point out that the numbers above each of the second-and third-floor bedrooms indicate a commercial establishment. Others argue that Affie and later owners were merely saving themselves the stair climb to direct the guest traffic. In any case, Affie's open-door-

A seldom seen view of the back of the Stone House in 1943.
(Courtesy Jane Riddle Thompson)

policy, started in the days when her only guests were Indians, was upheld by residents of the Stone House well into the 1960s. With the construction of the Cody-Billings highway travelers could make the trip in a day, thus putting to an end most overnight stays of the past.

Construction began in 1896, with stones quarried from a nearby bluff. The Chapmans did not look far for skilled laborers. Their ranch was surrounded by talented craftsmen-homesteaders, one of the best of whom was stonemason Samuel S. Carteen, the first homesteader on Paint Creek. An exotic rumor had it that Italian stonemasons carved the blocks, but actually it was homesteader teaching homesteader and cowboy. There were seven who worked with Carteen over the four years of construction.

Martin Jobe, the Chapmans' ranch manager, also worked on the structure along with Hardy Shull, another Oregon native. Shull eventually homesteaded on North Fork. The two men developed an easy friendship, though one which would eventually prove detrimental to Jobe: Shull apparently taught him the fine art of moonshine making.

Charles Marston, an Oregon friend of Chapman's, also worked on the house, as did O. C. Bevelhymer, who arrived in Cody on June 22, 1899, from Baker City, Oregon, and became a rider for Chapman. Bevelhymer and Carteen worked well together and ended up neighboring. Bevelhymer also takes credit for planting the cottonwoods that grew up to surround the house.

Some of the basic lumber, too, came from the ranch. Mrs. Chapman told new owner Mac Taggart years later that much of the lumber for the carved interior woodwork, the golden oak stairways that dominated the front hall in those early years, and some of the furnishings were hauled by team and wagon from Livingston, Montana, through Red Lodge.

In some early photographs the veranda that now spans the façade does not appear. Apparently it was either torn off at some point and replaced, or simply added by later residents.

Just a year after the house had been warmed and celebrated, Carteen was murdered at his Paint Creek homestead, where he had been living in a tent. That morning he was across the creek, using a shovel on some unexplained groundwork.

An unknown individual arrived. By the looks of the ground in that area, they had a terrible fight. Then, according to Bevelhymer, "Whoever it was knocked Carteen's brains out with the same shovel that he was working with. Then he took the dead body of Carteen and drug it with a rope and saddle horse about four hundred yards and cached it in a washout. There the body remained for several days on account of there being nobody living in that country at that time."

Carteen's body was finally buried on a little hill on the east bank of Paint Creek. There was much speculation about Carteen's death: Did he owe somebody money? Did it have something to do with the Chapman construction?

One folk tale still repeated today has Carteen knocking on the Stone House door, asking for his money, and being killed on the spot. In fact the murder, while never solved, happened on his own property.

• •

Affie took great pride in the house and repeated the layout in Red Lodge a few years later, though its décor was more ostentatious. Mac Taggart said, "You could certainly tell that Mrs. Chapman was responsible for both houses."

In the late 1940s Mac and his wife Janet enjoyed showing Affie the Stone House again, from end to end and basement to attic. "Even though she was almost blind and must have been nearly ninety by then, she was madder than hell about any changes," Mac said. "We did seem able to defend our alterations to her satisfaction, though."

By the time Mac Taggart had taken over the management in 1946 heating and cooking were done with coal and electric power from a Koehler plant—a gas or diesel-operated generator that charged six volt lead acid batteries in glass cases to provide energy. "Ten years later the government established Rural Electric Association power, with lines installed across the country and propane gas became popular," notes a local history book. Eventually natural gas was piped in from a well developed on the ranch.

Frances Curtis remembers preparing meals in the cooking kitchen in the 1960s. Like the midwestern "summer kitchen," this was an addition at the back of the house where meals were cooked for the cowboys, hay crew, and irrigators.

The Stone House, home to dozens who either owned or worked for the ranch, provided overnight lodging for hundreds passing by. It was also home to an arguably unusual visitor—a ghost.

While early owners scoff at the idea of a spirit being, Teddie

A Biography of Place

Ryan St. Clair, longtime manager of the Two Dot,
and his wife Teddie.

St. Clair, who came to the ranch with her husband Ryan in the late 1970s, accepted its presence. So did her boys; Keith and Kyle remember visiting with him as they played in the third-floor attic, little concerned with the male spirit's presence. Ryan St. Clair was heard to say that he didn't believe in such things, he just made sure he never went to the third floor.

Teddie St. Clair told of an overnight guest who awoke from a deep sleep to feel her covers being pulled away from her face, then dropped aside. As she held her breath, footsteps crossed to the door, and the presence was gone. She fell back to sleep chuckling, thinking that Keith had come home late, found himself in the wrong room and went elsewhere to sleep. There certainly were plenty of rooms, so she slept soundly.

The next morning at breakfast, the guest couldn't wait to give Keith a bad time—but Keith hadn't come home at all, nor had any other visitors arrived.

While she never spoke to the ghost, Teddie continued to be aware of his presence on an almost weekly basis: a sense of breeze, heavy footfalls, and other unexplainable sounds. Teddie, like her sons, was never fearful despite the sense of someone watching her.

After Teddie and Ryan moved, Yves Burrus decided to restore the Stone House as closely as possible to its original state. Jackie and George Keesler were hired to restore the oak trim, floors, and staircases throughout the house, among other projects. They were joined by Jackie's twin sister, Jo Holmes.

The twins had recognized that from early childhood, they had been open-minded receptors for spirit beings, the first sign being a tingle in the back of the neck. Jo was the more sensitive to such spirits and had been able to converse with an occasional ghost over the years. Jackie could not.

During the five or six months of work the twins could feel the ghost's presence most of the time, especially on the second and third floors. "We had a sense that he wasn't a dangerous spirit, more lonely and lost," Jackie explained. "On occasion I remember getting a tingly feeling and realized he was following me down the stairs. We were all so fascinated with the restoration project, peeling away the wallpaper layer by layer, stripping the paint that camouflaged history. The European style woodworkings and the overall workmanship were unbelievable, so we weren't especially bothered by his presence."

Yet the ghost never gave up. He seemed especially interested in Jo and was quicker to make his presence known to her. Jackie was aware and watchful but it was her sister who eventually struck up a conversation with the tormented spirit.

"His name was Charles W. Green," Jo explained. "He arrived at the Two Dot Stone House by stage where his fiancée, Amanda, was to meet him the next day." As he explained it to Jo, the couple was preparing to buy a ranch or farm and he had a great deal of money with him. He put it in the resident safe overnight and after a pleasant evening went to bed.

Shortly after midnight he was awakened to loud noises in the hall outside his door, he told Jo. He rushed to open the door and was shot dead as he stepped into the line of fire. It had been a setup.

When Amanda showed up the next day, no one had ever heard of Charles W. Green. They told her they were certainly sorry for her plight, but the man simply had never arrived. The ghost was tormented by the fact that the woman he loved believed that he had run off with their money, and he had no way to prove to her otherwise.

The wonder for him was that right here, standing in front of him, working around the house, was his Amanda. It had to be. She looked just as he remembered her. He just had to find a way to tell her his story. Sure that Jo was Amanda, he shared the tale with her.

As the twins debated how to send the ghost away, they came up with a plan calling for some serious acting on both their parts. Jackie said to Jo, "Amanda, you realize that Charles didn't desert you, don't you?" Jo turned to the space she sensed Charles W. Green occupied and said, "I know that something happened to Charles, he would never have left me alone without explanation or without money." Then Jo added, "Charles, it's time for you to go now."

The spirit disappeared as the twins stood there in silence. While their work kept them busy in the months to come, no ghost took part in their restoration efforts from then on.

When the rest of the story was told to Teddie St. Clair, it made perfect sense to her. To others it remains ridiculous. Without records and a burial plot no proof is possible—but Jo and Jackie don't need proof.

When the McCartys took over the ranch management for Yves Burrus in 1996 and Mark McCarty moved into the newly restored Stone House, there was no sign of a noisy-footed spirit.

For sure if Affie Chapman were to return as a ghost in her own right, she would find nothing to complain about except the addition of a third bathroom on the second floor—a concession to modern master bedroom-and-bath convenience. Or perhaps she would approve, after all. She would certainly be proud to see the Stone House hosting international visitors as well as neighborhood gatherings.

CHAPTER SEVEN

John Allison
and the
Elusive E. M. Bent

A Biography of Place

Horses graze in corrals across the creek where little remains
of the headquarters built by Chapman on that side.
(Courtesy Keith Voyles)

By THE TURN OF the century wealthy Midwesterners were joining Europeans and Easterners in investing in the development on America's western lands—men like John Allison of Sioux City, Iowa, sinking money into lands west of their own borders, land, water, and livestock.

Allison appeared on the Rocky Mountain scene in 1885, invested a little in Bozeman, Montana, a little in the Miles City area where another local was settling, then finally was able to purchase the Chapman ranch from its owners.

An area publication described the ranch at this time. "The model mountain home of this section is that at the Allison-Bent ranch," wrote the editor of the *Wyoming Stockgrower and Farmer* in 1905, two years after Chapman sold the property.

The location is ideal and remarkably romantic. On the east towers the somber head of old Hart mountain, a grand and lonely monument on the level plain, and on the west rise the pine-clad peaks of the Shoshone range, dark, somber and grand, while the musical creek bustles past the ranch buildings and spreads out over the fertile acres making

John P. Allison, Sioux City entrepreneur who started investing in the Two Dot
area in 1885 and bought the Two Dot from John Chapman.
(Courtesy Sioux City Public Museum)

glad and green and beautiful the entire surroundings.

The buildings consist of a palatial cut sand stone mansion, a number of bunk and mess houses, large, roomy stone barns, a laundry, etc. Ample corrals, substantial fences, stock scales, etc. make the place a model cattle ranch, surrounded by the finest range. Within the spacious residence everything is homelike, and the visitor breathes the air of a rare hospitality and is entertained in the most gracious manner by the accomplished hostess.

The article also noted that "in returning by Mr. Bent's ranch, one passes the Kimball Sheep company holdings on Pat O'Hara Creek. The Kimball brothers have by diligence and good management, built up a fine business and acquired a most desirable ranch property." The Kimball Ranch is still part of the Two Dot today.

The *Cody Enterprise* of September 19, 1901 reported that John W. Chapman sold his ranch to John P. Allison for a total of $70,000: $30,000 for eighteen hundred deeded and leased acres, a thousand head of cattle at $38 a head, plus miscellaneous charges. Still, the Chapmans didn't actually move until 1903.

Allison himself never lived at the ranch full time, but he spent summers in the area and visited the ranch periodically, overseeing his business investments. It appears that E. M. Bent was a partner only briefly, from about 1903 to 1906, apparently living in the Stone House. The Bent-Allison partnership raises many questions. Why did Allison, who had investments in Red Lodge, turn his attention to the ranch south of town? How did he and Bent meet? What were Bent's origins, and where did he disappear to so quickly, four years before Allison's death and the eventual resale of the ranch? Those questions remain.

During the first decade of the 1900s many called it the Allison Ranch, but topographic maps of the period show it as the Bent

Ranch. Community notes published in the newspapers refer to many social events at the "Bent Ranch" between 1903 and 1906. In fact if it weren't for the maps and the newspapers there'd be little evidence of the Bent family's involvement at all.

The "Over in Wyoming" column of the Bridger, Montana *Free Press* referred to Bent several times on March 25, 1904: "The two Card boys, Bert and Ed, are busy every day feeding cattle for E. M. Bent...John Ruff, one of Mr. Bent's riders, suffered a broken leg some three weeks ago by the fall of his horse. He is now able to get around on crutches." The next mention had deeper implications. O. C. Bevelymer, Chapman's Oregon friend who had helped complete the Stone House, had "commenced working on E. M. Bent's ranch, where he and his brother, Jake, will break up about 150 acres of land. The boys expect the work will last all summer." This was the first indication that the ranch owners were turning to farming, adding hay and grain crops to the grazing of natural grasses.

Further references continue to vary the ranch's name. In 1905 Ed Brown went to work at "Bent's ranch" in the capacity of chef— yes, chef—according to "Paint Creek Points" in the *Wyoming Stockgrower and Farmer.* (Early homesteaders in the area recalled the number of servants on staff at the Stone House during this period.) A month later it reported that S. D. Thomas "commenced work at the Allison & Bent ranch last Monday," without indicating his exact job. In May of that year "Miss Esther Brown will spend the summer at the Bent ranch;" in June she and "Uncle Sam Thomas of the Bent & Allison ranch visited in the Creek country Sunday."

Those community notes also indicate that Bent was an innovator. On August 9, 1905 the *Stockgrower and Farmer* reported, "E. M. Bent is preparing to put a track and car into his coal mine on Pat O'Hara, to get out fuel for use on his ranch." Coal mines had also opened on the west slope of Heart Mountain, and coal was dug there to supply the ranch's winter needs. Eventually water problems at the

John P. Allison, a man who like John Chapman understood banking,
stands with his partner George Weare in front of their Sioux City establishment.
(Courtesy Sioux City Public Museum)

Heart Mountain mine forced its closing.

The last published reference to the Bents came on May 17, 1906 in the *Stockgrower and Farmer* under the headline "A Pleasant Wedding."

> *On last Friday, Rev. and Mrs Cates drove out to the beautiful ranch home of Mr. E. M. Bent to unite in holy wedlock Mr. Edward M. Card, the foreman of the ranch, and Miss Gerda R. Carlson, Mrs. Bent's greatly esteemed housekeeper. The wedding was performed at high noon and immediately Mrs. Bent served a sumptuous luncheon.*
>
> *Mr. and Mrs. Bent displayed their true greatness by arranging for all the servants to be seated at the table, while they themselves attended to the serving. Mr. and Mrs. Bent are among the most beloved people in Big Horn County and it is needless to say that they never have to worry over the servant girl problem.*

Significantly, the publication's next reference to the operation, in September 1906, used a new name: "The ladies of the Allison ranch gave a big dance last Saturday night. Nearly all Paint Creek turned out." Late that year it also referred to the "Jobe Allison ranch," suggesting that while the Jobes were therethroughout, the name had now taken on an elevated status, possibly replacing the Bent management/partnership. Clearly some shift had been made; perhaps Allison had forged new alliances, or revived old ones.

• •

John Perry Allison is best known as one of the twin fathers of Sioux City, Iowa. He was born in New Hampshire and became a lawyer after attending Harvard. He moved to Sioux City in the spring of 1857, joining other New Hampshire residents in the new town.

One of them was George Weare, who had opened a bank in an attic of one of the early buildings there. The business consisted of a three-drawer chest containing the funds Weare had brought with him in a box. While Allison was involved in a number of other partnerships he eventually joined Weare.

The partners influenced the growth of the Missouri River town—the site of the only death during the Lewis and Clark Expedition nearly one hundred years before. There John Colter had helped bury the fallen Sergeant Charles Floyd.

Eventually Allison built a mansion in what is Sioux City's downtown today. Later he sold it to be used as the Hawkeye Club headquarters, a gentlemen's club for businessmen and capitalists.

Early sources indicate Allison only became interested in western pursuits after his retirement. His interests in the West may have been influenced by his daughter Fannie's marriage in 1885 to E. M. Ferris of Bozeman. With John Chapman's many investments in that area, perhaps the two could have met there. Chapman may have then steered Allison toward the Wyoming border. In fact Allison was involved in land purchases and water development there for fifteen years before purchasing the ranch. He applied for water rights several times: on May 1, 1885, for ninety-three acres on West Pat O'Hara Creek and 208 acres on East Pat O'Hara; thirteen months later for sixty-nine acres from Big Springs; in May of 1900 for Roberts Creek off Pat O'Hara; and a week later for Blaine Creek No. 2. The 1885 transactions were adjudicated by district court on April 16, 1907, perhaps implying that those lands were incorporated into the ranch he had purchased in 1901 from Chapman.

A *Sioux City Tribune* item on December 24, 1909 reveals two notable facts: first, Allison apparently served as a judge, and second, he was running sheep at his ranch—perhaps in addition to cattle, or perhaps exclusively. "Judge J. P. Allison has arrived from Cody, Wyoming to spend Christmas with his family. Mr. Allison owns a ranch eighteen miles northwest of Cody. He said things were in a prosperous condition there. The weather has not been as severe as it has here, and on that account the sheep are in excellent condition."

After Allison's sudden death July 19, 1910 in Iowa, his estate was filed for probate in district court at Basin, the county seat, on October 2. Appraisers S.C. Parks, Jr., Martin A. Jobe, and A.J. Martin found that the ranch now encompassed 3510.79 acres valued at $46,000.

While the mystery of the Bent family has never been solved, some evidence regarding their prior location may come to light with the obituary of S.C. Parks, Jr., in the March 16, 1949, *Cody Enterprise*. Parks was the one who, along with E. Amoretti, launched the first privately owned bank in Cody, one that would eventually become the Shoshone National Bank. Its first stockholders included Parks, Bent, Allison, and an S.S. Newton.

Amoretti and Parks both came from Lander, Wyoming, where a number of Bents had registered land claims in those early times—perhaps indicating that E.M. Bent was a member of this family. Regardless, Bent's residency at the ranch was short-lived and his disappearance permanent.

CHAPTER EIGHT

Ganguet and Barth:
A Young Immigrant's Opportunity

Joseph Ganguet meets the airplane from Canada that provided his favorite French brandy during prohibition. The year is 1922 according to granddaughter Jacqueline Benning.
(Courtesy Jacqueline Benning)

IN THE FRENCH Alps above Grenoble, a young sheepherder sat high atop a boulder in his father's pastures at Villard, St. Pierre, watching over the family flock. Born in 1872, Joseph Ganguet had steadily increased his knowledge of the animals, first by working with his father and later on his own. He had learned to recognize their changing bleats: their seemingly quiet conversations among themselves as they grazed, their louder drone as they went on the move, and the fearful sound that called for help.

At the same time Joseph was dreaming—mostly about seeking his fortune in America. The dream always ended with himself as an adult, standing once again at his father's door, a rich and successful man.

Others may have scoffed at his vision, then again he may have kept it to himself, but in 1888, at the age of sixteen, he stood at the desk of an immigration agent filling out the papers. Joseph was going to America and he already knew just how he would become rich.

He also couldn't help noticing the pretty twelve year old girl standing shyly behind her father there in the office. Her smile was wonderful and Joseph was fascinated. In the next few weeks while he awaited approval of his application he shared his dreams with the

1

Le présent Livret, contenant quarante pages, appartient à

Nom
écrit en bâtarde.   *Ganguet*

Prénoms : *Jean, Joseph, Léoneus*

Surnoms :

Né le *3 Octobre 1872*

à *Poligny*

canton de *St Bonnet*

département des *Hautes-Alpes*

résidant à *aurrouze*

canton d

département d

Profession d

Fils de *Joseph*

et de *Camille Escalle*

domiciliés à *Ste Eusebe*

canton de *St Bonnet*

département des *Hautes-Alpes*

Marié le

à

alors domiciliée à

département d

autorisation d

Jeune soldat (1) *Appelé*

de la classe de 18*92* de la subdivision de *Gap*

n° *6C* de tirage dans le canton de *St Bonnet*

Signalement.

Cheveux

Sourcils

Yeux

Front

Nez

Bouche

Menton

Visage

Taille : 1 mètre _____ cent.

Marques particulières :

ou Engagé _____ an _____, le _____ 18 ___

a _____, département d _____

A été compris sur la liste de recrutement de la classe de 18___, de la subdivision

d _____, n°_____ de tirage dans le

canton de _____

Numéro au registre matricule du recrutement :	Partie de la liste du recrutement cantonal.	Numéro de la liste matricule.
562	*1e*	

(1) Appelé ou classé dans les services auxiliaires.

Joseph Ganguet (pronounced Gangay) birth certificate.
He was born in the town of Poligny, County St. Bonnet
in the region of Hautes-Alpes
(Courtesy Jacqueline Benning)

young girl, Lea Escalle. Before he boarded the ship to America he promised Lea that he would send for her as soon as he was successful. Successful, of course, meant rich—but rich would come slowly.

Arriving in Bakersfield, California, the boy hired on with a French sheepman as herder for one of his bands running in northern California. It was a five-year contract and Joseph requested that the sheepman hold his wages until the end of the term.

As the sixteen year old headed his sheep out toward the high mountain meadows of the strange land, he surely must have felt good about this plan. What could possibly go wrong as long as he was diligent? Certainly in those lonely years when he had time to imagine his future, always including the pretty Lea, he saw no obstacles that could stop him.

Five years later Joseph returned to his countryman, his hand out for the wages he was owed. There he learned no money had been set aside for him. He had worked five years for nothing. While he was not the first man—for Joseph was certainly a man by this time—to fail this way, he mourned the dream lying at his feet, a broken mirror shattered, the shards of bad luck all around him.

He shook off the depression and loneliness, vowed to make his own luck this time, and started over. This time he would be in charge of the money. He would find his own sheep to run.

Joseph went to Walla Walla, Washington. There he found ways to partner with the sheep owners, taking a certain number of animals for himself. Then he learned of the Big Timber, Montana, grass country. Heading east, he probably followed in John Chapman's footsteps.

Big Timber saw its first sheep in 1865, a band trailed in from California. Within twenty years the town, which was part of what would become Sweetgrass County, was the world's largest sheep-producing region. By 1900 that record had moved on down the road to Billings, where each year the rail center shipped more

Wedding photo of Joseph and Lea Ganguet in 1903.
(Courtesy Jacqueline Benning)

pounds of wool to Boston than any other community in the country.

Upon his move to Big Timber Ganguet met August A. Barth, known as Gus, a Billings blacksmith and sheepman. A member of the Montana Wool Growers Association since 1872, Barth was always looking for a good investment in people and in land. He found both possibilities in Joseph Ganguet. They formed a partnership there.

In 1903, at the age of 31, Joseph was ready to invite Lea to come to America. As dreams go, though, Lea's arrival by train at Fromberg, Montana, was disappointing.

Joseph did not meet her at the depot. Furthermore he didn't arrive at all that day. Lea spoke no English, but finally a man who had watched her pace in front of the depot communicated to her she could wait just as satisfactorily at a local boarding house owned by a Canadian woman. Joseph would be able to find her in the small community easily enough, and he did—three weeks later!

The bridegroom had come down with typhoid fever, which prevented him from meeting Lea's train, but he quickly made up for it by introducing her to every aspect of his American life. They were married in Red Lodge. Two years later their first daughter, Lea, was born at Fromberg. Maybe it was the birth of his daughter, or maybe Joseph had reached some inner measure of success, but gradually he began to long for France. His wife's loneliness must have influenced him, too.

Joseph told Barth of his plans to return to his homeland. He moved the family to France in 1907, investing the money from his American ventures in several businesses there, including a hotel.

Although he had vowed there would be no coming back, Joseph's fascination with American opportunity outweighed his desire to stay put. Seven years later, when Barth called on him to manage the ranch he had just purchased for their partnership—a large operation in Park County—Joseph couldn't help himself. He returned in 1914.

More cautious now, he left his wife and three daughters in France until 1916. That was well after his one-quarter ownership to Barth's three-quarters partnership had been settled.

The March 29, 1916 *Cody Enterprise* made a puzzling announcement concerning Gus Barth's purchase. Had the Two Dot property briefly changed hands again—back to its original owner? The article states that Barth and associates purchased the Heart Mountain ranch on Pat O'Hara Creek near Cody from John Chapman of Red Lodge and his associates.

The deal is said to have involved a sum ranging from $150,000 to $200,000. Mr. Chapman purchased the ranch from the Allisons of Sioux City, Iowa several years ago. It is said to be one of the best ranch properties in northern Wyoming, commanding a good range and

*Ganguet's daughter Lea sits astride the hood of the car with her dad,
Joseph Ganguet on the right, Victoria next to him and Mary Louise on the end.
Jacqueline Benning is unable to identify the rest.*
(Courtesy Jacqueline Benning)

From left, Victoria and Mary Louise Ganguet in 1919 on the ranch.
(Courtesy Jacqueline Benning)

The schoolhouse in the meadow just down the two-track road from the stone house.
(Courtesy Jacqueline Benning)

possessing a large acreage for hay and capable of supporting a vast amount of stock. It consists of 4,000 acres of deeded lands and about 7,000 acres of leased and script lands. The sale also included some 11,000 head of sheep. Mr. Barth, Mr. Chapman and Martin Jobe, who was interested with him in the ranch, are now invoicing it.

Throughout the Two Dot's sale history, it is often difficult to see exactly which of its scattered properties were being purchased, and sometimes from whom.

Ganguet and Barth had already changed the name of the ranch to one that would remain to this day. Until then its name had always followed that of the family most directly involved. While some historians have speculated about a link with the town of Two Dot in Montana or a ranch of that name near there, it actually refers to Ganguet's own sheep brand of two dots.

*Sheep barns and other headquarter barns
with the stone house in the far distant right across Pat O'Hara Creek.*
(Courtesy Jacqueline Benning)

Sheep branding irons resemble those used on cattle but they are smaller and instead of being heated, they are dipped in paint and stamped on the animal. According to Charlie Blackstone, a cowboy for the Two Dot in the 1950s, it really started with a drunken cowboy dipping his beer bottle in paint and branding twice with the bottom of the bottle. Plausible, perhaps, but it proved more story than fact.

• •

Of all the earliest families involved in the Two Dot, the most has been written about the Ganguets. Children and grandchildren of their neighbors continue to have stories to tell. Clytie Williams tells of pen-pal correspondences she and her sisters enjoyed with the girls. They must have been interesting, well-liked people because the tales abound.

*Joseph Ganguet and his wife Lea on the porch of the stone house
with Mary Louise, Lea and Victoria with two unidentified men.*
(Courtesy Jacqueline Benning)

In a paper prepared for a historical Two Dot tour, writer Dave
Wasden described Ganguet as a large man, close to 230 pounds. His
wife, too, was large, with a reputation for being stronger than most
men. According to a neighborhood story the only thing she feared
was the family goat, an animal that vented hostility on anything that
moved across his path. Mrs. Ganguet tried to avoid being that object,
but one day she inadvertently became the target of his attack and was
forced to take to a tree. There she waited, not so patiently, on her
perch with the goat stomping down below, until finally a ranch hand
came to the rescue.

The three girls, Lea, ten; Vicki, seven; and Marie, six, remember their arrival in Billings. According to Vicki and Marie, this time their father sent a driver and a Huppmobile to drive them to the ranch some eighty miles to the south.

While the Ganguet girls did not speak any English, they were quick to learn. John and Martin Jobe continued to work for this new partnership and John's wife, Rena, frequently rode horseback with the girls, all three using it as a bilingual opportunity. The girls also credited the ranch's own school, which included the children of resident employees as well as neighbors' children, for helping them with this new language.

The first schoolhouse was a roughly hewn shelter. Later Ganguet would make an improved school out of the homestead cabin John Jobe built in the meadow next to the headquarters. Still later, with more students, Ganguet built a larger one, which by 1918 was also used as a community polling place during elections. By 1922, although the Ganguets were no longer residing at the headquarters, the census showed ten children between the ages of six and eighteen attending school there. Today the building rests in the first meadow in front of headquarters as if waiting for its next students.

Vicki Ganguet remembered life on the Two Dot in an article June 28, 1977, "Looking at Agriculture," in a *Powell Tribune* publication. She said that Ganguet ran twenty-six thousand sheep and had no involvement with cattle; Vicki and her sisters tied wool fleeces for their father's employees as each sheep was sheared. In those days, no one operated a ranch of that size without a large crew.

"We lived in the large Stone House," she said, recalling that the cookhouse, which included a dining room and kitchen, was used for family and employees' meals. A few animals may have also lived under that roof; other people have described a combination house and livestock shelter at that time—a heat-conserving arrangement common to Europeans, with animals housed below or beside the living quarters. Perhaps the Ganguets kept a milk cow, goat, chickens, or pigs in such a facility attached to the cookhouse.

• •

When Barth and Ganguet bought out the Allison heirs, their sheep numbers were already running as high as twenty thousand and they were eager to expand. In fact that number could double by the hour as Ganguet speculated about the country.

Ganguet was in the habit of buying bands of sheep anywhere in the region if he felt the price was right. Known as a sharp trader, he would then start the sheep toward the home range, whether government lease or deeded property, wherever that might happen to be at the time. His philosophy was that everything was for sale so any offers he received for his new flock along the way, if they met his price, were transacted on the spot.

Consequently, although his family might know of his intention to bring a large flock home, he could just as easily arrive with nothing or only a few stragglers. If that was the case, hired hands waiting at the gate could bet there was money in his pocket.

Despite Ganguet's marketing approach that made him more a seller than a buyer, the ranch generally ran around twenty-six thousand sheep at any one time. The animals grazed on three large government permits and on deeded land. They wintered on Chapman Bench, a relatively flat region on the northern reaches of the ranch where animals could find protection from winter storms in the sagebrush. This also kept them close to headquarters during lambing season. The rest of the year they ranged from ranch pastures to forest grazing permits. In summer sheepherders headed them up into the Bald Ridge region, one of those federally owned areas that would become important to the ranch as lease property over the years.

By 1918 Barth's health was failing and Ganguet was becoming eager to retire once more to his homeland. On January 3, 1919, they signed the papers selling the ranch to Frank L. Hudson of Lander.

But the Ganguets stayed in the area for a time, moving closer to Cody so the children could attend school there. Joseph downsized his sheep operation considerably, although in 1924 he couldn't resist buying some prize ewes, as noted in the *Park County Enterprise*.

Ganguet enjoyed many benefits to success in the sheep business—pleasures unimagined when he had herded sheep in the Alps and the Sierras. Determined to always have a bottle of his favorite cognac in his liquor cabinet, Ganguet had his spirits flown in from Canada during Prohibition. He also enjoyed annual trips to New York City to attend the opera and plays. Vicki and Marie noted, however, that their mother never joined him on those trips.

Gus Barth died at Rochester, Minnesota on March 25, 1920. His obituary in the *Billings Gazette* called him "one of Billings' sturdiest characters and one whose life irrevocably refutes the allegation that America is no longer a land of opportunities." It went on, "Mr. Barth soon after learning his trade as a blacksmith, came to Montana and established a shop in Billings, where in due time, he obtained the nucleus of his fortune, the upbuilding of which was based largely on land and livestock investments."

It was Gus Barth's intention to honor Billings by building a magnificent hotel at Second Avenue and Twenty-ninth Street, to be without peer in the state. Whether the hotel came to fruition after his death is questionable. Certainly Barth's appreciation of his good fortune in the area was valid.

Ganguet was granted ancillary letters of administration in regard to the estate. According to Vicki, they ranched a number of smaller acreages east of Cody. The next year, when Frank Hudson defaulted on his agreement to purchase the Two Dot, it was Ganguet who once again stepped in, not only handling the legal issues but seeking another buyer as well. That buyer would be James N. McKnight of Texas, who carried on with a sheep operation, albeit briefly.

It was at that time that Ganguet was able to sell off his other two ranches and the rest of his property, gather up his family, and return to France to finish out the remaining steps of his dream. Unfortunately that plan was cut short when he died of complications from pneumonia only five months after returning to his homeland.

Still, Ganguet had come full circle, and had prospered at the ranch now named for his own brand. He had sustained the Two Dot during some difficult times—just as he had his own dreams.

CHAPTER NINE
Their Own Kind of Partnership: The Jobe Brothers

*John and Rena Jobe on their honeymoon, pulling up in front of the cabin John built
on land he had homesteaded nearby in John Chapman's front yard.
John and Rena in front seat, Martin Jobe and his wife, Nellie Conlin Jobe,
who were themselves married in Missouri February 24, 1897, accompany the newlyweds.*
(Courtesy Beth Jobe Spears)

WHILE OWNERS CAME and went and partnerships were built often to dissolve, the one constant at the Two Dot Ranch from 1896 to nearly 1920 was the management team of Martin and John Jobe.

Both capable and independent individuals, the brothers joined forces for twenty years during which the Two Dot prospered through their efforts as well as those of the owners. The Jobes were seen as master managers and, during their brief tenure as owners, the name "Jobe Ranch" even hung over the arched entrance. Clearly their relationships with partners were complicated and individualistic but the brothers did lay claim to the title of Two Dot owners at the turn of the century according to their children.

After first teaming up at A.A. Anderson's Palette Ranch at Meeteetse, the brothers hired on with John and Affie Chapman sometime after 1896. Martin helped build the Stone House and provided the leadership on the ranch as the Chapmans dealt more and more with their business interests in Red Lodge.

John took over much of the bookkeeping. According to John Jr., his dad talked Chapman into letting him build a cabin in a beautiful meadow adjacent to headquarters. He needed privacy; it was proving difficult to pore over ledgers and receipts in the evenings at the bunkhouse with cowboys "jawing" all around him, he explained.

Several years later Chapman learned that in fact he had neglected to claim that little parcel of land himself, and John Jobe had filed a patent on it. John Chapman had to face his mistake every morning he was on the ranch, as his large living-room window provided the perfect frame for the Jobe cabin. Eventually he would buy the land back.

The Jobes' first contract with Chapman granted them the opportunity to buy into the livestock operation, adding their own stock almost from the beginning. The brothers also started buying and leasing land wherever it was available.

Ownership of the ranch's scattered properties was often in a fluid state. In one major transaction in 1901 or 1903 (it appears parts

Jobes running sheep through the docking chutes on the Two Dot in 1915.
(Courtesy Beth Jobe Spears)

John Jobe docking sheep at the Two Dot in 1915.
(Courtesy Beth Jobe Spears)

Rena Long well before she met John Jobe on her first trip west,
camping with a group of school teachers.
Rena is second from left in the white dress eating watermelon.
(Courtesy Beth Jobe Spears)

of the property were sold at different times), "Chapman and a partner, Martin A. Jobe, sold the ranch to Allison. The sale included eighteen hundred acres deeded and leased and a thousand head of cattle at $38 for a total of $70,000." Old-timers referred back to the "Jobe-Allison Ranch" in the five years before 1910. Later Martin Jobe is reported again as selling a parcel of land to Chapman. Just as always, land was easily shifted back and forth. It wasn't easy to distinguish what was Jobe's or the owner's. Probably only John knew for sure as he pored over the books.

*A 1920 photo of Irenia (Rena) Long Jobe with her son John,
taken in Newcastle where she had homesteaded years before.*
(Courtesy Beth Jobe Spears)

Rena and John Jobe headed out on a pack trip up into the far reaches of Yellowstone
and the Thoroughfare from Bear Creek on the South Fork southwest of Cody.
(Courtesy Beth Jobe Spears)

There was certainly a period when Martin and his wife lived in the Stone House—probably after 1906, when the Bent-Allison partnership dissolved quietly, so quietly that outsiders hardly noticed.

The Jobe brothers ran cattle and sheep in Sand Coulee, Elk Basin, Badger Basin, and on leased railroad land, especially the sections with water on them. They continued to manage much of the Two Dot operation after the Ganguets' arrival. Records indicate a form of partnership with Joseph Ganguet, probably separate from Barth. The Jobes probably ran sheep with Ganguet on both of their properties.

In 1916 Martin sold land to Chapman for $25,000, then went to California where his ability to put a ranch together stood him in good stead, according to Glen Jobe, his nephew. "Uncle Mart was a heck of a businessman but he had a bad habit when he made a sale, and had big bucks in his pocket—he always had to take two to three months off to do some drinking," Glen said. "Then he had to start all over."

John Jobe married Rena Long, a Missouri schoolteacher and talented artist, in 1917. She joined him in the homestead cabin, and later told her boys of horseback riding with the Ganguet girls, trading French and English lessons along the way.

But a year later John and Rena sold out all their interests to the Two Dot Ranch Corporation and went into partnership in a large cattle operation with Gordon Kneisely, another of the many homesteaders, whose business lives partnered with those of the Two Dot. When that dissolved, they spent time in the Newcastle, Wyoming area where Rena had investments of her own, as well as family. Then John hired on as foreman for the Hoodoo Ranch north of Meeteetse. Eventually the couple purchased the Nuckols Ranch east of Cody, where the boys, John Jr. and Glen, grew up. There they lived for thirty-eight years until retiring and selling to Harold Davidson, who had recently sold the Paint Creek Ranch.

But the Jobes' Two Dot story wasn't over yet. At some point Martin returned to the Cody area from California and went back into business with Hardy Shull making moonshine. They had become friends when Shull first came to the Two Dot from Oregon to work on the stone house while Jobe was managing the operation for Chapman. But one night in 1928, Martin's luck ran out.

When raiders struck that North Fork still at two in the morning, they found two hundred gallons of whiskey in kegs lined up along the trail, and "barrels and barrels of mash." They found Martin Jobe asleep, arrested him, and dragged him to jail under guard. Although it was clearly Shull's still, the owner was nowhere around, and the evidence against him was inconclusive. Jobe pled guilty April 1, 1929, and was sentenced to two to three years in the state penitentiary. Many understood Jobe's loyalty to his friend; Jobe had no children and Shull was responsible for a large family.

Glen and John Jobe know that after his release from the penitentiary, Uncle Mart left again for California, never to return, as far as they knew. Like the Chapmans the Martin Jobes had no children to pass their story on to. Martin was probably too ashamed to contact his brother or return again to the place where he'd had so much success—and then sullied that sterling reputation.

A Biography of Place

PART THREE

THE HOMESTEADING ERA
1918-1933

CHAPTER TEN

Evolution of a Homestead:
The Heald Operation

Lower Two Dot Ranch.
(Courtesy The Park County Historical Archives)

HARRY HEALD DIDN'T see himself as the family pied piper as he bicycled west from Grinnell, Iowa, selling horse-drawn buggies along the way. He'd never heard of the Two Dot, the Pat O'Hara Ranch, or any other. But when he arrived in Cody and realized the potential for his family, it took only a little encouragement for his brother George to join him in 1910. His brother Ed followed shortly after that.

The Heald brothers' arrival would launch an era of expansion north of Cody. First they worked diligently to accumulate the funds to buy ranch properties in that area. Harry settled on the Clarks Fork; George bought the Pat O'Hara Ranch—becoming Ganguet's northern neighbor. Ed was able to get the Trail Creek south of the Two Dot and just north of town. Another brother, Walter, came later, settling on a ranch on the Clarks Fork River north of Belfry, Montana.

George and Ed took unity one step further when they became attracted to the Painter sisters, daughters of a pioneer Sunlight Basin family. Courtship required dedication to dangerous travel. It wasn't so hard to reach the Dead Indian Mountain trail by crossing Bald Ridge or following Blaine Creek. But descending that steep trail to the basin

Gathering at Lower Two Dot Ranch ca. 1920.
Martin Zinn, Orin Kepford and George Heald, Jr. are in the photo.
(Courtesy The Park County Historical Archives)

was truly perilous. Although George Heald later claimed that they drove their wagons "acourtin'," they likely rode horseback most of the time.

Wagon travel on that trail was perilous. Travelers often dragged logs behind their rigs to keep them from overrunning the horses. Paul Phillips, who later married Ed Heald's daughter Marguerite, recalled that "a lighter load might need only a tree dragging behind to slow down the momentum. With heavier loads the wheels were rough-locked by tying light poles across the wheels and through the spokes to keep them from turning. This made like a sled which slowed down the descent," he explained. His mother-in-law, Marguerite Painter, could drive a four horse team and wagon into Cody for supplies, then navigate the Dead Indian trail by herself. Some of those logs were still stowed at the base of Dead Indian in the 1970s.

It was that Margeurite who caught Ed's eye. When the two men had their ranches established, Ed married her and George was wed to her sister Mary in separate ceremonies, both in 1917. Mary had their first child, George, Jr. in 1919, but died in childbirth a few years later, leaving George to raise his son alone. Grandmother Painter helped out in the early years and later housekeepers kept an eye on the adventuresome boy.

George Jr. often spent the winters with his Uncle Ed attending the Trail Creek Ranch school. Later all the ranch kids were bused into the Cody school. Marguerite Phillips described the treacherous roads often so slick with mud that it was amazing that the bus driver kept the vehicle upright. Still, she remembered with pride, they never missed a day of school due to bad weather.

The Pat O'Hara Ranch thrived and grew under the excellent management of George Heald, as he invested in homesteads when they became available and took advantage of government leases, as well. The original property apparently was developed by James Weaver, John Chapman's Oregon friend. It is uncertain whether Weaver purchased it directly from him, or from Pat O'Hara, as Alphia Chapman claimed in an interview in the late 1930s. No written record of the sale exists—but then, the long trip required to record a land purchase was prohibitive in those days.

Weaver then partnered with Chapman for twelve years before admitting to health problems in 1890 and selling the Pat O'Hara to Affie Chapman's brothers, Henry and Andrew. They, too, had been enticed to the Big Horn Basin by their adventuresome sister and brother-in-law.

When George Heald purchased the operation it included the Little Sand Coulee, Heart Mountain, and Chapman Bench. Heald

*The Lower Two Dot about 1933 when Frank L. Clark and George M. Heald
held the lease on the Two Dot Ranch.*
(Courtesy The Park County Historical Archives)

ran three bands of sheep of a thousand each, and some hundred head of cattle. More than likely the sheep were grazed during lambing time on Chapman Bench. After shearing, the bands were gradually moved on up the trail to summer range in the Beartooth Mountains. The winter range was on Chapman Bench, Little Sand Coulee, and the lower north slope of Heart Mountain.

Lambing was by far the busiest time of year, when herders and camp tenders brought their bands to headquarters sometime in April. Then shearing companies arrived for a week or so around the first of June. Wool was then packed for shipment to Billings, where it was sold and sent east. In the annual cycle for the sheepherders, they were soon driving their flocks back to summer pasture in the mountains.

Lower Two Dot Ranch.
(Courtesy The Park County Historical Archives)

By the time the sheep had left the corrals, the irrigators were already hard at work, having been hired shortly after the spring thaw. Water permits had been obtained earlier for Pat O'Hara and Blaine Creeks. The irrigators stopped only long enough for the hay crew to get started, then were immediately back at it trying to keep the alfalfa growing for a second crop, always aiming to beat the first frost. Both the Trail Creek and Pat O'Hara ranches produced tons of alfalfa and native grass hay, as well as hundreds of bushels of grain for the livestock.

The hay crew, a group of twenty-five or so, spent the summer at work with buck rakes and overshot stackers. Haystacks dotted the meadows and more hay filled the barns at headquarters.

The original log house, probably built by Weaver and used by Chapman's hired help, was turned into a bunkhouse after George Heald built his new bride a big ranch house before 1920. After Mary died, George remained a widower until 1939 when he married Beatrice Wanner, someone he had known during his youth who had by that time lost her husband.

In 1933 when Jim McKnight lost the Two Dot Ranch, Heald

was leasing the Two Dot hay fields bordering his ranch—an arrangement that survived the eventual transition to the Taggarts. Paul Phillips' dad had leased the cultivated land between the hayfields and the Dead Indian road, and Frank Clark, a banker from Belfry, leased the Two Dot itself. Paul worked for Clark on the hay crew that summer.

Betty Heald, who had married George Jr. shortly before the ranch was sold, called the Healds "the quiet ones." George had worked hard and by 1942 thought it was time to retire. He sold Pat O'Hara to Lloyd Taggart and over time the Pat O'Hara name was replaced with a more apt term for modern purposes—the Lower Two Dot. Today, though, it is still often referred to as the Heald place.

When the Curtis-Skoglund partnership purchased the Two Dot from the Taggarts in 1963, one of the brothers, Dick Curtis, settled at the Lower Two Dot. He was in charge of the Quarter Horse breeding operation, building a new facility specifically for those needs. Over the next ten years, the Curtis family developed an outstanding reputation for their Quarter Horse genetics.

Today the Lower Two Dot is a vital part of the operation, serving since the 1990s as calving headquarters. As one of the four main ranches that form the Two Dot, the old Pat O'Hara Ranch is still a vital asset in its success—due in part to the hard work, business acumen, and vision of George Heald.

CHAPTER ELEVEN

Frank Hudson: Great Sheepman
Right Place, Wrong Time

A Biography of Place

Ellen Hudson, center, with playmates in front of the schoolhouse,
including Tommy Barlett and others.
(Courtesy Hudson grandson Bruce Finley)

FRANK HUDSON grew up in the Lander area during an era when cattle were king but sheep were making men rich. He started with bum lambs and built that first bunch of orphans into an outstanding sheep operation by the turn of the century. He could have been called a sheep baron, one of the richest in Wyoming, and he lived the life of prosperity.

By the time he purchased the Two Dot from Joseph Ganguet and Gus Barth, along with the Heart Ranch on Heart Mountain, Frank Hudson's success as a sheepman was well established. His quick climb to wealth in a risky business generated much talk—talk that frequently turned to his idiosyncrasies. He owned a small fleet of white pickup trucks, driving one everywhere in those early years when others were still cowboying it or hiking. He enjoyed wintering in warmer climates such as California. And he had a passion for stocking high mountain streams with a variety of trout, the legality of which was questionable.

But Hudson's success was such that it wasn't too surprising that he turned his eye northward toward the Two Dot, one of the larger sheep operations in the region, when Ganguet and Barth placed it on the market.

Frank Hudson, foreground, with his brother Dan in the high country.
The woman is possibly a dude as the Hudsons stocked creeks with trout for guests.
(Courtesy Bruce Finley)

Born in Salt Lake City in 1878, Frank moved with his family to the Lyons Valley near Lander in 1885. His parents had chosen a small farm with poor soil, but the whole family reached deep to pull itself up by the bootstraps. Hudson finished eighth grade and started building his first flock. He eventually married Harriet, a young woman he met at local dances, and continued his expansion in an industry he loved so well, building a home in 1912.

At the same time part of his family was developing the town of Hudson, between Riverton and Lander. His brother Dan had a ranch in the Sweetwater country and served the government as a U.S. marshal and state commissioner for the Game and Fish Department.

Frank Hudson purchased the Two Dot in April of 1918 and formed the Two Dot Sheep Company. He signed the contract with Barth on January 3, 1919. Of the principal sum of $83,000, he paid $11,000 on signing the agreement, and issued a note promising to pay the balance by January 3, 1922, at eight percent interest.

The sale included 4,481 acres of deeded land, interest in a large number of land leases, "all farm machinery, ranch horses, swine and farm implements, cattle, wagons, harness and household furniture now on said ranch." The buildings were to be insured for $10,000 for the duration of the loan.

No mention of sheep was made. With other lands owned and leased, Ganguet and Barth had left with their flocks and Hudson brought in his own. One can only imagine the movement of masses of sheep across the mountains and up the valleys of the Big Horn Basin, across the lip of that bowl, and pouring down into the meadows John W. Chapman had discovered forty years before.

According to the family, Hudson also bought land called the Heart Ranch at the same time. Part of that would become a Japanese internment camp during World War II.

According to Ellen Finley, Hudson's oldest daughter, the family continued to live in Lander, retaining a hay farm there as well

Two Dot sheep camp 1914.
(Courtesy Beth Jobe Spears)

as a ranch in the canyon north of town. The Hudsons spent summers at the Two Dot Ranch headquarters, but Frank Barrett actually ran the ranch. They hired Mexican sheepherders, who migrated through looking for work, as well as Arapaho and Shoshone men to help during branding and shearing. Ellen remembers the two dots of paint about an inch in diameter that the men placed on each sheep. Hudson and Barrett also hired Glen Billings, a Kansas cowboy fresh out of the Navy at the time. He was one of the few locals who worked for them throughout Hudson's tenure.

Ellen also remembers the one-room schoolhouse in the middle of the meadow, where the six children she played with all summer went to school. She remembers their favorite game was hide and seek: "such wonderful places to sneak away to until you raced into base safe—or not—depending on who was 'it.'" While she was probably glad to return to Lander and her friends there, she surely must have longed to stay on the Two Dot and go to school with Timmy Barrett and the other children.

Hudson was one of the first to buy into the new mechanical generation. He drove his signature white trucks everywhere he went, even into the mountains delivering supplies to the sheep camps. Ellen also remembers him driving his wife in one of those trucks out onto frozen Bull Lake near their home at Lander, scaring poor Harriet until she begged him to return to shore.

While planning their move to the Two Dot, the Hudsons also ran a dude ranch in the mountains north of Lander, according to Ellen. It may have been there, leading dudes on fishing trips, that Frank Hudson came to understand the value of stocking the lakes and streams with trout. His grandson Bruce Finley recalled Hudson had special metal panniers made to carry fish to the high lakes. "He planted Loch Levin [lake] trout and native rainbows," he explained. "I still have some sheetmetal panniers that my grandfather used to haul Mackinaw trout up into the lakes of the Wind River Mountains to plant. Probably not a good idea in retrospect, but I did manage to catch one of them a few years ago at Lake Christina."

In the winter of 1917, Hudson, who loved traveling as much as fishing, spent three months with his family at Ocean Park, California. While there he had an opportunity to buy Signal Hill, some very pricey real estate by today's standards, for very little money. He declined, one of the first of many errors in business he would make in the next few years—errors that family members still shake their heads over.

It was Bennie Itorroran, a Spanish Basque sheep foreman and friend to Hudson, who finally told him, "Frank, you're a helluva sheep man but you don't know nothing about business." That fact, combined with the skidding sheep and wool market, brought Hudson's reputation as the wealthiest sheepman in the state to a close. By the end of 1921 he was in trouble.

After Barth's death on March 25, 1920, Joseph Ganguet became executor of his estate and on December 15, 1921, submitted that Hudson had contacted him saying he would fail to meet the deadline on his loan for the Two Dot Ranch.

Hudson went back to Lander, the place where life had been so good to him. After Ganguet took the ranch back, cowboy Glen Billings headed up South Fork, where he worked for ranches in the area for much of the rest of his life. His wife's family had been among the earliest settlers in the upper reaches of that tributary of the Shoshone River, when Red Lodge was still the only place to shop.

What the ranch manager, Frank Barrett, did next is uncertain. While many saw him as a partner to Hudson, no contracts seemed to carry his signature.

Back in Lander, Hudson's youngest son Fred was born in 1921. Even as a little boy, Fred drove his father out to tend the flocks. "Dad taught me to drive by the time I was nine years old," he said. He learned much from his dad about herding sheep as well.

He also remembers the day—January 17, 1935—when he went to find his dad down by the creek with his flock. The teenaged Fred discovered him there among the sheep, just lying so still. Realizing his dad was in trouble, he raced for help but it was too late. Although his father was only fifty-three years of age, and had lost much of his worldly property, he died where he had always wanted to live—with staff in hand, taking care of his sheep.

CHAPTER TWELVE
The McKnights' "Big" Ranch

*No matter the owners, the Lower Two Dot seemed the ideal location
for working sheep, whether lambing, docking or shearing.*
(Courtesy Jane Riddle Thompson)

FROM THE TIME Frank Hudson turned the Two Dot back to the previous owners, Joseph Ganguet had been searching for a buyer. It was during that time—the early twenties—that the W. F. Marlin family moved to the Clark area north of the Two Dot from their Texas home.

Clytie Williams, a pioneer of that area and young lady at the time, remembers Mrs. Marlin because she was so beautiful, was always dressed up and wore hats even to the store. It was Mrs. Marlin, sister of Mrs. James N. McKnight, who encouraged their exploration of economic opportunities in the area. Being a sheep producer himself, the Two Dot would have seemed tailor-made for his investment.

James McKnight, born in 1889, came from a well-known Throckmorton, Texas, ranching family and knew sheep as well as cattle. He had married Alice Elizabeth Davis, also from an influential Throckmorton family. The little Texas town still calls itself the "Capital of the Cow Country," and members of the McKnight family still ranch there today.

The couple was immediately enthused with the beauty of the mountains and the financial opportunities. When McKnight learned that Ganguet was looking for a buyer for the Two Dot so he could return to France, he made an offer and purchased the ranch from Joseph Ganguet and Annie Barth in 1924.

McKnight was welcomed into the business community. As a visitor to Cody one day in May of 1924, he was introduced at the Cody Club luncheon. According to the newspaper report, "He is a stockman of many years experience and plans to develop his new holdings to the utmost."

Probably because of the Marlins, the McKnights quickly became part of the communities from the ranch headquarters to Clark. They appeared in both the "Pat O'Hara" and "Paint Creek" newspaper columns throughout the 1920s and "Beyond Bald Ridge" into the 1930s, visiting neighbors, entertaining at the Stone House and participating in neighborhood activities.

Interestingly, the ranch quickly picked up the nickname of the "Big" ranch, a term used interchangeably with the Two Dot throughout the period of their ownership.

Through the 1920s homesteaders and small ranchers alike were dependent upon extra jobs to keep their outfits afloat. Many worked occasionally or full time for the Two Dot.

• •

Others hired on as stage drivers. In 1924 Jody Brown drove a regular run from Clark to Belfry while living on Bennett Creek. F. L Brough, a homesteader, took on the stage for the Sunlight line running from the Two Dot to the basin. He never realized that one of his first trips early in an April snowstorm would require six hours to drive three miles, then camping under "the lee side of a friendly pine," according to the *Northern Wyoming Herald*. Others like Henry Purvis became mailmen for the Paint Creek and Pat O'Hara sections.

The McKnights stepped quickly into the cycle of livestock management adopted earlier by their neighbors. Sheep were brought up from Sand Coulee the last of March, just as they had been under Ganguet's management. They would be fed at the Big ranch until after lambing there.

It was noted in the same paper that lambs were going for ten cents a pound that spring with one million lambs on feed in the state of Wyoming, according to J. B. Williams, secretary of the Wyoming Wool Growers.

Although ranchers in the area counted on a mild early spring, 1924 was plagued by one blizzard after another. Ranchers in the area were forced to feed more hay than usual. In the middle of the worst of it, McKnight needed to return to Texas, which he would do with great regularity throughout his tenure at the ranch. He pointed out that the bad weather wasn't just in northern Wyoming, it extended from Montana to Texas.

By May 7, 1924, lambing was in full season. Then there was more. An article in the May 29, 1924, edition of the *Northern Wyoming Herald* indicated that Joseph Ganguet hadn't stepped aside completely from his interest in the Two Dot.

FIVE THOUSAND BLOODED EWES FOR TWO DOT

Joe Ganguet closed a deal last week for the purchase of five thousand choice yearling ewes for the Two Dot ranch, the sheep to be delivered the first of June. The two bands of 5,000 each are blooded Merino and Corriedales and were purchased from Henry Doores of the Gooseberry country who runs some of the best stock in the southern part of the state. The price paid is said to be between eleven and twelve dollars.

The sheep will go to stock up the Two Dot ranch, which was recently purchased by J. N. McKnight, and according to Mr. Ganguet is one of the finest bunches of sheep in the country. The Two Dot ranch, one of the finest in the northern part of the state, represents an area of 28,000 acres of deeded and leased lands, and adjoins the Shoshone Forest, which furnishes summer range for the sheep and cattle of this outfit.

One thing McKnight would learn, as did others later, is that summer can be short-lived. Winter can come early as it did that year, when an October first snowstorm caught the McKnight sheep up in the mountains.

Any moisture created havoc with mud roads, although the locals tried hard to keep them graded and improved. While cars were becoming more prevalent, they became useless in bad weather. McKnight found himself trying to pull cars that had slipped from the grade above him back onto the roadbed or providing them with an overnight stay as they gathered horses to go on, frequently abandoning their vehicles until drier days.

Community events in that era were usually held at the schoolhouses. Rev. McCorkle came through once a month to lead the "Sunday Sing" and old time meeting at the Paint Creek school, and provided a resounding sermon as well.

Halloween parties and box socials with entertainment were also part of the neighborhood events well attended.

October also triggered the annual Sunlight roundup of cattle and sheep. Those not involved were off on hunting trips. This was when McKnight would bring in his spring lambs and get them ready for shipment. During that period cattle were no longer being shipped to Chicago, as in Chapman's time, but to Omaha.

Elections brought everyone out to the various schoolhouses to vote. Pat O'Hara school was within view of the Stone House and the *Paint Creek Reporter* indicated that Mr. and Mrs. McKnight served dinner to the election board there.

By the end of November it was time to move the sheep to

winter camp in Sand Coulee. After trailing the bands to that area, McKnight stayed with the sheepherders for a week or so and helped to get them settled in. He indicated in 1924 that the sheep were in fair shape, and he'd had no losses despite the snowstorms.

The winter of 1924-1925 proved to be a tough one. Ranch hands were kept busy baling hay on the stationary baler to be hauled to the sheep in Sand Coulee. George Heald moved a band of his sheep to Line Creek, taking the animals to hay he'd purchased, rather than hauling the hay to them. Grain was high and hay already in short supply.

With deep cold for long stretches, McKnight chose to develop the coal mine that Bent had started nearly twenty years before. He reported that the miners were bringing out some good coal.

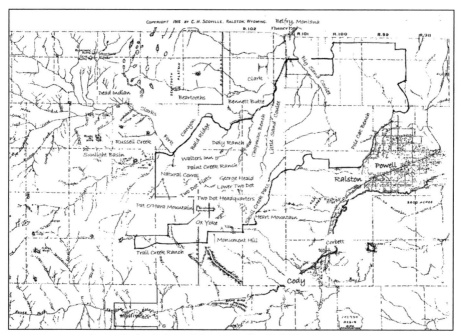

A rough depiction of the area of today's Two Dot Ranch

By summer of 1925, the McKnights had refined the annual cycle taking sheep to the Forest Reserve mid-July following George Heald, who drove his to the Beartooths the first part of the month.

By fall of 1925 McKnight had decided to hire his thrashing done, bringing in an outfit from Montana who finished on the Two Dot first, then went on to Paint Creek.

As McKnight moved into 1927, he and his wife decided to send son Jimmy to military school in Fairbault, Minnesota. He came home for summers and holiday breaks. Mary Nielsen, who grew up on Monument Hill, can still picture him driving what she remembers as a big fancy car, one like the locals had never seen before.

The 1929 school census of District No. 29 includes Jimmy, Jr., aged seventeen, and Jack McKnight, seven.

Despite rumblings in the stock market and heavy loans, McKnight made plans in April of 1930 to put in a crop on what was known as the Luce place. Homesteaders had settled there at the base of Bald Ridge and farmed for a number of years. Then it was left fallow for a long time before McKnight decided he wasn't going to have a shortage of grain or hay again. Today the area has a lake by the same name, which provides good fishing for anglers and the range is used strictly for grazing.

Those stock market rumblings became a giant thunder on October 29, 1929, the day that would become known as Black Tuesday, when "thousands of investors tried to sell off their stocks, ending the prosperity of the Roaring Twenties," according to a Houghton Mifflin definition. Investors lost billions in a matter of hours. Banks and businesses, heavily invested in the stock market, went under. "Although the crash did not 'cause' the Great Depression to come, it was the opening event of that era."

At the Big ranch in late May of 1930, life was going on normally, at least on the surface. Crews were once again preparing for shearing.

Bad luck seemed to be creeping into the McKnights' charmed lives. In August of 1932 fire took their big barn, moved on to the sheep sheds, and destroyed everything. McKnights' trips back to Texas seemed to increase.

Mrs. McKnight's shoulder was badly burned by a lamp tipped over at a local dance.

While McKnight's hold on the ranch was slipping, nationally the Great Depression, which would last from 1929 to 1940 when World War II started, was growing. More and more people were losing their jobs which caused them to withdraw their life savings from the local banks. Banks failed because they did not have enough cash on hand to meet the unexpected demands. This caused depositors to lose all their money and other banks to panic. President Franklin D. Roosevelt put a stop to the cycle on March 5, 1933, declaring a Bank Holiday. The president then called Congress into a special session where they passed the Banking Act of 1933. This set up banking regulations, and after examination most banks were back in business by April 1, 1933.

In the case of Cody, Powell and Meeteetse banks, they reopened more quickly—March 15, following a nine-day holiday. While there was deep concern, one of the banks reported that depositors showed their confidence by depositing $2,500 the very first day. According to a *Cody Enterprise* report, "There seems to be an attitude to do business other than by the banking and checking method," was out of the question.

But that did not help the McKnights. A front page article September 6, 1933 told the story.

HEALD AND CLARK BUY TWO DOT RANCH

A deal was closed recently whereby George Heald and Frank Clark became the owners of the Two Dot ranch and all the leases and range which this ranch has controlled. The deal, it is understood, was made by taking over the large federal loan which had been acquired by J.N. McKnight on his ranch property.

Both Heald and Clark are among the older and successful stockmen of the Clarks Fork and Pat O'Hara sections, several years ago having been partners in the sheep business. Mr. Heald has a large ranch on Pat O'Hara Creek, just below the Two Dot, and Mr. Clark has extensive holdings of range on Heart mountain and a big ranch in the Clarks Fork valley.

The change in ownership of the Two Dot marks a real estate deal of considerable note, as it is a large ranch, and controls an enormous area of range land.

Although this transaction would be short-lived and the newspaper may have actually gotten it wrong, that it was a lease agreement rather than a sale, it erased any hopes McKnight had of restoring his "Big" ranch rights.

On January 10, 1934 an article titled "Cattle at Two Dot Sold At Auction," followed by a sale of personal property two weeks later, seemed to bring to an end the tenure of James N. McKnight.

At an auction sale held on Thursday of last week, the cattle and sheep and a number of horses were sold to the highest bidders at the Two Dot, J. N McKnight ranch.

The sheep brought a very good price, six-year old ewes going for $4 per head and a band of lambs sold for $4.50. Mr. Hime, Belfry banker, purchased the woolies. Henry Sayles bought a bunch of the cattle at varying prices, the largest bunch of cows and calves going for $10.50 per head.

Horses sold at very moderate prices with the exception of one *heavy work team, which brought $310.00. The hay on the ranch sold at $5.00 per ton and a quantity of oats at $.75 per bushel. The sale was ordered by the Regional Credit Corporation, the business being handled by Attorney Paul H. Greever of Cody, assisted by E.S. Hoopes as auctioneer.*

In another twist, it was announced August 7, 1935, *TAGGART BROTHERS BUY TWO DOT RANCH.*

The article states that Charles and Lloyd Taggart bought the property, a ranch "last operated by J.N McKnight and considered one of the finest ranches in the country. Comprising several hundred acres of irrigated land, several thousand acres of range land, together with vast state and railroad leases which make it an ideal stock growing property. The property was foreclosed about a year ago and since that time had been under lease to Frank Clark, a Clarks Fork sheep man. The Taggarts receive possession in May, 1936."

• •

McKnight was in Cody for several weeks at that time closing out the deal. Then again on August 12, 1936, *Cody Enterprise* mentions J.N. McKnight for the last time when he returned to Cody to attend to business matters while "he has been making his home in Texas for several years."

Thus, the rough and rocky twenties came to a close deep into the thirties. From there the Two Dot would grow and prosper through more fortunate times and management.

CHAPTER THIRTEEN

The Walters Inn:
Travelers' Rest

"The Dry Fork was one of our favorites to ride in," explained Teddie St. Clair.
(Courtesy Wilderness Images by Carla Zerkie Wawak)

LIKE THE CHAPMAN house at the Two Dot a few decades earlier, the Walters cabin on Bald Ridge often had more overnight visitors than it had space for. But Fred Walters and his sister Mary Say never turned anyone away.

Alfred M. Walters had laid claim to his dry homestead in 1916 or 1917, according to local historian Mary Nielsen, who grew up on Monument Hill nearby. Walters finally filed the patent on April 29, 1919. Several miles from Two Dot headquarters, the Walters place lay along the two-track wagon trail over Bald Ridge to Sunlight Basin, Cooke City, and Red Lodge, Montana.

When Fred Walters realized his two-room cabin was a natural first-night stopover for homesteaders and ranchers freighting supplies in that direction, he decided to expand.

He built a two-story log building against the wall of a ravine on the Dry Fork of Pat O'Hara Creek, just below the cabin. Mary Nielsen, who visited the inn a number of times in the next forty years, was amazed at the height of the flat-roofed structure. Its construction must have been quite a feat, she said. Because it was built into the side of the ravine, it stood a full three stories high at the front. Once the inn was completed, Walters set a sink with a hand pump outside the kitchen door on a rock patio where travelers could wash up, according to Nielsen. "A small spring in the ravine was developed and a tall ice house was constructed where meat and other perishables were stored...there may have been a pump house at the base of the ravine as well.

"Because there were no stairways connecting the floors either inside or outside, paths along the side of the hill led to upper and lower levels. Meals were provided and if several people stopped they often shared bedrooms," Nielsen explained.

The Walters Inn was still standing in the late 1950s or early 1960s when Mary and Senius Nielsen, then working at Trail Creek, went exploring on a Sunday afternoon and Mary caught this shot of the three-story inn, which served so many years as a way station for travelers.
(Park County Historical Archives)

On the hill south of the inn they built a log barn large enough for at least a dozen teams. In addition their corrals clearly indicated they served their guests' need for a place to pen larger herds of horses and cattle being trailed in or out of Sunlight. Walters charged two dollars a head. In the later twenties he purchased his first car and added a slab-covered garage.

Elaine Rhoads, a former Miss Rodeo Wyoming and long-time North Fork resident, remembered spending a March night at Walters Inn around 1930, on a weeklong trip to Crandall Creek on the Clarks Fork. She too recalled that it seemed "perched" on the side of the ravine. Inside, its whitewashed log walls were decorated with elk hides and other native skins. "I also remember some fascinating pictures and many post-card pictures," she wrote in 1985.

Mary Say started a weekly column in the *Cody Enterprise* in 1923, trying out various titles and finally deciding on "Off Bald Ridge." She often recounted events at Walters Inn in a bold, humorous tone.

In a column, September 4, 1923, she wrote, "A. M. Walters is back home again. He's been helping the Two Dot with their hay. His sister, Mary A. Say, was running the Inn while he was gone." Many of her comments regarded road conditions—always a concern for the community—and brought a much better understanding of the euphoria that arrived in the community with newly built roads to Billings and Powell. On October 24, 1923 Says titled her notes, "They're Bogged Down on Bald Ridge. Mr. and Mrs. Henry H. Sirrine, Miss Sheila Sherman and Mr. W. Grove and Mr. Orton Sirrine stopped over night at Walters (Inn) going back to Crandall. They were at Red Lodge for a week getting their winter supplies. Mr. Orton Sirrine helped them over Dead Indian with extra teams. The roads are so bad they had to hitch six horses to a wagon." Then a few notes later, "Grover Willock came back after his wagon and a new cookstove which he had to leave at Walters till roads dried so he could make the trip with same."

Another sister of Fred and Mary's, Lydia (Mrs. John) Nielsen, lived just over the hill to the east on the JN Ranch. When Lydia died of cancer in 1933, it ended the whole family's enthusiasm for the area. The Walters family sold their property to the Taggart family on December 31, 1933, shortly after Lloyd and Charles Taggart had purchased the heart of the Two Dot. That concluded their years in the area. In any case, the horse-drawn vehicle era was ending and, with motorized travel, the inn was in less demand for overnight stays.

The inn stood empty for years. Eventually, Two Dot management decided in the early 1970s to burn the buildings to prevent cows from getting trapped inside, a common practice during that period. Therefore nothing is left of the Walters Inn— no reminders of its benefits to the many settlers traveling over Bald Ridge.

CHAPTER FOURTEEN

Bootlegging and Moonshine: The Prohibition Era

A Biography of Place

*Heart Mountain at Sunset. The mountain can be seen from almost every stop
on the Two Dot and from miles away anywhere in the Big Horn Basin.*
(Courtesy Ranee Gonsalez)

IF A SATELLITE SCANNING device circling the earth today could be programmed to detect the remnants and scraps of old moonshine stills scattered across the Two Dot Ranch and Heart Mountain, dozens would be located. Evidence of the Prohibition era still exists at the Natural Corral, all along Pat O'Hara Creek, and on Bootlegger and Paint Creeks as well.

Long before stills were big business, pioneer families concocted wines and cordials from the bounty of their fields and forests, although the law allowed them to make only enough for their own use. The problem arose when Appalachian mountain people, who were ordinary in daily life but exceptional in their moonshining talent, became secret professionals, manufacturing liquor in varying degrees of quality during a period when the law said no.

Some of those professionals started coming down off Stone Mountain in North Carolina, one family after another, in 1903. The Woodruffs, the Royals, and the Spicers were the first who headed for Wyoming and the Two Dot Ranch, their move inspired by Buffalo Bill's Wild West Show, which Billy Woodruff first saw as a young boy. These families adapted to the Absaroka Range of the Rockies as surely as they had called the Blue Ridge Mountains of both North

Carolina and Tennessee home for generations.

They had much in common. They were related by blood or marriage, sometimes both. They were sheepherders by trade and moonshiners, a seemingly genetic artistry carefully practiced and passed on from generation to generation. And they were all drawn to the Two Dot Ranch, the perfect site with its remote location and spiderweb of streams.

They hired on as sheepherders and soon established stills along Pat O'Hara Creek. Then they secretly hired others to help them make the liquor and guard the stills during the winter—often the very men who worked on the ranch's summer hay crew. As sheepherders they could run a flock over the area, scrambling tracks that led to still sites. Even in this rough country the law searched for the whiskey-making machines, but without success. More often they were stumbled on, then reported.

Individual family members quickly became known as the best in the West, developing solid reputations as whiskey makers a decade before Prohibition was enacted in 1919. As Carl Royal explained it, "It was the one thing they all knew how to do."

Billy Woodruff's moonshining history seemed unlikely to many who knew him and his son Bob: He was a hard worker, a likeable guy, and an upstanding member of the community. As Woodruff told it in *Park County History*, when he arrived in Billings in April 1903 with his brother Johnnie, a cousin, Ernest Spicer, and a friend, Avery Wood, they were quickly recognized as experts in the care of sheep.

First Billy took a job with John Tolman, a sheep rancher on the Clarks Fork who also ran the Dilworth Ranch. In 1909 he signed on as foreman for John Chapman's Heart Mountain Livestock Company, which ran thirty thousand sheep at the time.

As wool and mutton prices rose, Billy formed a partnership with Paul Richter of Cody and they took advantage of the range left

By the time Prohibition was coming to an end Jack Spicer boldly walked the streets of Cody in broad daylight, delivering his wares and defying anyone to stop him.
(Courtesy Carl Royal)

on Pat O'Hara, eventually expanding to fifteen thousand acres. By the mid-1920s when his relatives were deep into moonshine making, Woodruff had created a sheep business envied by many.

Elaine Moncur, who runs the E&B Landmark Ranch (which was Bischoff Cattle Company at one time), recalls that according to Bob Woodruff, Billy and Johnnie once walked their sheep from the ranch to Miles City, where they were sold. Eventually Billy grazed his sheep from Heart Mountain to the Beartooths.

Jack Spicer, whose sister married Johnnie Woodruff, arrived in 1907 at age eighteen, possibly with brothers Arlie and Luther, all three cousins to the Woodruffs. Jack would become the leader, mentor, and director of moonshining and bootlegging operations over the next twenty-five years. Ironically, within a few weeks of the end of Prohibition, Spicer's life would end in a shootout more personal than professional.

Long before enactment of the Eighteenth Amendment to the U.S. Constitution, which outlawed the manufacture and sale of any liquor containing more than one-half of one percent of alcohol by volume, an expanding segment of the American population feared the growing misuse of liquor. They wanted it stopped.

Saloonkeepers were their first target, but soon they started addressing the drinkers themselves. Their clever efforts escalated as America came closer to entry into World War I. The temperance advocates claimed that the tons of sugar required to make alcohol should be turned to feeding the troops.

Jack Spicer was already on his way, though, trailing a pack train of relatives west from the Tennessee hills. He arrived on the Two Dot with experience as a sheepherder as well as an underground reputation. He pretty much ignored the efforts of the anti-drink radicals. After all, there were multitudes eager to stick another buck in their pockets while following the Spicer recipe for making moonshine and big money. From 1912 to 1933 he would slip through legal loopholes with the help of thirsty customers and obedient relatives.

Carl Royal, one of those family members who never learned the trade, still owns the miniature *New Webster Dictionary* that Spicer carried. Inside the front cover the mountain boy documented his travels, listing his arrival in Clark, Wyoming, north of the Two Dot, on March 25, 1907, and in Cody on the Fourth of July, 1908. He went to work on the Two Dot for Martin Jobe soon after.

By 1912 Spicer had carved his name in the aspen tree that Jud Richmond would find in the late 1940s, probably to mark an early still as he learned to navigate the rough terrain of this new land.

According to *A History of the North Fork of the Shoshone River*, Jack Spicer built his first still, with its six-horsepower steam engine, in a natural cave on Pat O'Hara Creek, four miles below what was then the Allison Ranch.

The next year he married his snuff-chewing sweetheart, another Stone Mountain native, on the day she turned twenty-one. Etta, better known as Jake, would prove an able partner in their most important endeavor but may have contributed to his downfall and death in the end.

Ray Prante, who often hauled supplies for Spicer, told how his sister, Jessie Lowe, came across one of Jack's stills during her homesteading days on upper Pat O'Hara. She admired how cleverly it had been hidden under a cliff shelf above the creek.

Gradually Spicer's market spread. Bootlegging took him to Billings, Miles City, and Cody. Eventually he established a connection in nearby Powell, where Billings buyers met him to transfer product.

The Lever Food and Fuel Control Act of August 1, 1917, forbade the use of foodstuffs intended for the war effort. The wrath against drink culminated in the Eighteenth Amendment, made into law December 22, 1918 and ratified January 1, 1919. It gave the federal government control over the manufacture, sale, and transportation of intoxicating liquors. The Volstead Act set a first offense punishment of six months in jail or a fine of $1,000. The Jones Five and Ten law upped the ante to five years in jail or $10,000.

But few were convicted. Even if found guilty, a bootlegger might spend thirty to ninety days in jail, or pay only a few hundred dollars. Law enforcement moved slowly and carefully, made sure cases were rock-solid, and even then, oftentimes stepped back. After all, many of the professional whiskey makers carried guns, and one was nicknamed Snake. That was Jack Spicer.

While many in the area disagreed with Prohibition, some were eager to find and report the moonshine factories. Such was the case of that 1914 still Spicer had so carefully tucked away. It was a man named Finley Goodman—related to Buffalo Bill Cody—who turned in Arlie and Luther Spicer, who were working for Martin Jobe at the Allison Ranch as well as for their brother Jack. They provided budget information: the equipment was purchased in Miles City for forty dollars. The boys claimed to have invested another $250 in the plant, which produced seven gallons a day. When the officers found forty gallons of hidden liquor, they followed standard procedure: first tasted it for themselves to be sure what it was, of course, then poured the rest down the creek.

Jack Richard, a well-known photographer and entrepreneur, described Spicer in an undated article. "He made quite an impression on me," Richard said of his childhood encounter with Spicer in a barbershop. While young Richard waited his turn he picked up a magazine. "I kind of watched him over the top of the page when he thought I was tending to my business. He wore flat-heeled lace boots up to his knees—which was different from a lot of men—heavy canvas pants and a wool shirt like most of the others. He had kind of a sparse black beard, but the thing that got me was his eyes. I have never seen on any individual, before or since I'm sure, a pair of icy

Jack "Snake" Spicer and his wife Jake in front of their cabin on North Fork.
(Courtesy Carl Royal)

pale blue eyes like those. They'd really penetrate and he just was a spooky man for a kid to look at." While Richard referred to the man as Jack Smith, readers of the time knew exactly who he was talking about.

Accomplice Ray Prante said, "Jack Spicer was a man who didn't waste words." He would meet Prante on the street and say something like "tonight" or "Thursday." That was Prante's cue to pick up a load of sugar at the Cody Trading Company and bring it to a predetermined location, together with other supplies, at the designated time. He would wait for the bootlegger to take the supplies from the truck, then leave. According to an interview in 1984, Prante was then paid in cash along with a pint of whiskey.

By 1921 Jack Spicer's reputation was attracting the attention of law enforcement. According to *A History of the North Fork of the Shoshone River*, he was arrested December 1, 1921 for manufacturing, possession, and sale of intoxicating liquors. The arrest became case number 354, which dragged on until March 8, 1924, when it was dismissed along with case number 357.

In March of 1922 Spicer grew suspicious of Joe Hill, a partner, and accused him of stealing from their liquor stash in the Monument Hill country south of the Two Dot. Spicer pulled Hill's .32-caliber Savage pistol. When Hill tried to get away Spicer fired four shots, three of which struck the intended target. One shot hit the horse, one went through the cantle of the saddle, and one hit Hill in his side.

Hardy Shull's daughter Frances recalled Spicer: "Most people didn't want to tangle with him. He did tend to foster his villainous, steely-eyed appearance, seldom traveling unarmed. Always had two guns and a knife, no matter where he went. My dad was the only one who dared to cross him."

According to Ester Johannsen Murray in her book on the North Fork, "Those who didn't like him gave him the nickname

'Snake,' but were always careful where they used the term," according to Ray Prante. Morris Simpers remembers Jack as "a tall, muscular man, clean shaven with piercing blue eyes, and not given to frivolity, but he did entertain occasionally with a clog dance at Wapiti schoolhouse dances," he said

Jack and Etta Spicer disappeared from law enforcement records, and also from the Two Dot area, for some years after the Hill incident, mixing their mash on North Fork. There Jack

Norman Dodd and his wife celebrating their 50th anniversary.
Well-known and loved throughout the community, the Dodds
were actually Sunlight residents on Russell Creek,
who worked well with their Two Dot and northern neighbors.
(Courtesy Harold Davidson)

multiplied his stills, becoming part of the fabric of the community and even more arrogant in his sale of moonshine, delivering in person in broad daylight.

Murray quotes Clark Lawrence, who worked at Mike Clark's filling station in Cody: "Jack would come walking right down Main Street with a gunny sack over his shoulder with two gallon jugs in it and leave Doc Kinne one and come on down to Mike Clark's and leave him one." Murray also notes that "Spicer at times sold ' wholesale' to the Green Drug Store in Cody. Here the 120 proof was cut to 100 proof and after being bottled, Canadian labels and tax stamps were glued on and then it could be sold as prescription medicine, legally. Spicer sold it for twenty dollars a gallon wholesale and it retailed for five dollars a pint at the drugstore."

Even the respectable could be brought low by bootlegging. Martin Jobe was arrested at Hardy Shull's still in 1928, found guilty, and became the only area citizen ever sent to the state penitentiary for the making and sale of moonshine.

By this time the pressure was driving many moonshiners to move their stills. The cutoff from North Fork to Pat O'Hara was well traveled as they shifted their operations according to the heat and focus of Sheriff Blackburn and his men.

Norman Dodd, an early homesteader on Russell Creek in Sunlight Basin, told Harold Davidson about the day he cut across Pat O'Hara and over Rattlesnake into Cody. Knowing it was a bootleggers' route and might be dangerous, he kept his nose pointed straight ahead as he rode along the two-track that crossed trails leading to various stills. Suddenly there was the explosion of a .44 or maybe a .45. Still Dodd kept going, not allowing his horse to step nervously to one side or the other. Later Dodd would learn that someone had been killed in that area on the same day, and he knew that he had heard it happen.

It was not unusual for the sheriff to raid a Spicer still only to find a note that read, "Just a little too damn late," but one time the prediction was wrong.

When Spicer returned to the Two Dot in 1929, he left Howard Royal in charge of their biggest still on North Fork. According to his son Carl, Howard also worked for Lonnie Royal, another producer. "Dad had stayed up on North Fork nearly six months. Lonnie brought all his supplies but Dad was finally caught at Spicer's still located up under Table Mountain on Whit Creek." Raiders seized the still, ten gallons of finished product, and nine barrels of mash. Howard said that although Spicer had built the still, it belonged to sometime Two Dot employee Charlie Krause, known to have produced some fine whiskey of his own. In fact Krause claimed that he didn't own the still, and was at work on the Two Dot at the time.

Carl went on, "Jack Spicer and some of his men broke Dad and several others out of jail. The escapees hid out in Sunlight Basin in the Clocktower Creek area where Spicer had another still." There they watched the sheriff and posse scouring the countryside below for them. Finally one of the escapees announced that he had had enough of that life and they broke up.

Howard hid out at the Crow reservation, then took a train back to North Carolina. But bad luck followed him. When he was arrested once again for making mash, law enforcement officers discovered that Wyoming had an outstanding warrant for his arrest. He was extradited to Cheyenne. But there all charges were dropped but one, and Howard spent ten days in jail simply for locating his still on Forest Service land.

Howard Royal, like so many before him, took the fall for others. But unlike many, he learned his lesson. "Dad loved this country but he went back home to North Carolina and became a Baptist minister," said Carl. "He spent the rest of his life preaching the wages of sin in bootlegging and moonshine."

••

In the late 1990s, Two Dot manager Mark McCarty and then-owner Yves Burrus rode into the Oxbow valley. There Mark showed Yves a cave where evidence indicated that whiskey had been made and moonshiners hid. There was further indication that poachers had also used the hideout in later years. The two men imagined that when Hemingway summered in the area his own cache of spirits may have been stored there.

Even today, wagon tracks and pack train trails can be seen from the base of Dead Indian through Whiskey Gulch to Paint Creek, tracing the whiskey barrels' route from still to buyer. Some men in the liquor trade had names as colorful as Red Gulch Pete, who homesteaded the land where Paint Creek flows from the Natural Corral, and Snake River Bill, a homesteader at the head of Alkali Creek—Elaine Moncur has noted remains of his cabin at the site. Others were Black Pete, Pontoon Johnny, Peg Leg Williams, and plenty more with regular names; all had their own stories to tell. Many had learned their part of the craft from Jack Spicer himself.

Early in 1933 the Eighteenth Amendment was repealed by the Twenty-first. With alcohol legal once again, most moonshiners would disappear. Yet no one thought a quality producer like Jack Spicer would go away. Customers would continue to line up for his "fine" whiskey.

In fact it was Jack and Jake Spicer who called for a celebration, hosting a Saturday night dance at the Wapiti schoolhouse in March of that Prohibition-ending year. At some point very late in the festivities one woman reported hearing Artis Royal and Jack arguing, but she couldn't tell over what.

Shortly after that Artis and Lonnie left the party, and although they both lived with the Spicers, they drove to town for the night. The next morning Artis came back to the Spicers', supposedly to pick up his clothes. As Artis pulled up, Jack met him with a gun. Racing to the bunkhouse under a barrage of fire, Artis, too, grabbed a gun and started shooting back.

When the gunfight was over, Spicer was dead from a bullet to his heart. Artis was seriously wounded with three bullet holes in his torso, one through each lung and one high in the chest. Less accurate in his aim, Artis had only struck Spicer with two out of five shots, the second one low in his body. Spicer had fired three times.

Artis was taken to the Cody hospital where he spent six weeks dying, according to the newspapers, but miraculously recovered in the end. As soon as he was able to travel he left for California to join other Royals.

Spicer was given a proper funeral, reportedly well attended. While he may not have been the very first bootlegger on the Two Dot nor the last, his name quickly became the most legendary.

No one knows how many others learned the skill of moonshine making from Spicer; few would spend much time talking about it. Yet the evidence continues to surface with wind, rain and flood. Today those remnants of the Prohibition era remind the cowboy who finds them of that aspect of Two Dot history.

A Biography of Place

PART FOUR

THE ERA OF EXPANSION
1933-1975

A Biography of Place

CHAPTER FIFTEEN

The Golden Age of Expansion:
The Taggart Years

Lower Two Dot Ranch taken in 1950 or 1951 by Louis Huseman,
a young summer employee from Indiana.

"The whole decade of the thirties was dry and dirty—the condition of the animals, the grass, drier than hell," recalled Mac Taggart. By 1933, when the Taggarts stepped in, the Two Dot had been reduced to its smallest common denominator since Ganguet and Barth. The Great Depression and the Dust Bowl had riddled it with economic and climatic bullets that cut Frank Hudson off at the knees early and brought James N. McKnight to near bankruptcy.

But now, under the Taggart brothers, the ranch would flourish and grow as never before. Its seven thousand sheep-grazed acres would evolve into a sixty thousand-acre cow-calf operation. Cowboy Reesa Clute later recalled, "I believe the ranch was at least forty miles long and seven to eight miles wide. The winter range was huge. As soon as we weaned in the fall, we started the thousand head of Hereford mother cows east toward that winter country." It was a golden age of expansion for the Two Dot.

The Taggarts came to ranching somewhat circuitously. In the 1930s, while agriculture was failing, road construction was thriving. The ambitious Charles Taggart had started the Taggart Construction Company in 1905 in Cowley. While Lloyd had done some general contracting work for the company, it wasn't until 1924 that he

A Biography of Place

The Two Dot feedlot at Ralston had once served as a sheep headquarters.
(Courtesy Buffalo Bill Historical Center, Jack Richard Collection)

became a partner. They finally relocated the operation to Cody in 1932 when Lloyd moved his wife, Louise, and their nine children to Cody from their Cowley farm.

Lloyd and Louise both brought powerful family histories to their union. Louise was the daughter of Charles A. Welch, secretary of the Big Horn Basin Colonization Company that led a wagon train to the area in 1900. The expedition was caught in a four-day blizzard on South Pass, which made a strong impression on eight-year-old Louise.

Lloyd's parents had moved their sixteen children to Cowley in 1901. His father was a fine cabinetmaker, in charge of carpentry and construction for settlers east of Cody. His mother had traveled with a handcart community from Council Bluffs, Iowa, to Salt Lake when she, too, was only eight.

After both Louise and Lloyd graduated from college, Lloyd worked a few years for Charles in Montana, then partnered with his father and another brother in a farming operation. Lloyd ran both sheep and cattle, purchasing sheep from a South Fork rancher named Kepford in 1916. He joined the Wyoming Stock Growers Association in those early years, an alliance that would lead to his presidency in 1951.

In 1924 the farming partnership was expanded to include Lloyd's work with the construction business. By the early thirties Taggart Construction was so busy that Lloyd gave up the farm and joined Charles in building roads throughout the region, specifically in Yellowstone National Park.

In 1933 the brothers decided to buy the Two Dot Ranch through an intermediate purchaser, Ernest Goppert, but waited a year for the expiration of a lease held by Frank Clark, Paul Phillips, and George Heald. Lloyd's son Jesse McNiven Taggart, known as Mac, was thirteen at the time. "The conditions in ranching were the very worst during that period which was why we could buy the ranch," he recalled. "Ranchers sure didn't have any money."

Lloyd managed the ranch for the Taggarts, often bringing in construction employees for projects such as blowing up beaver dams. Some stayed on for calving and feeding. For summer employment, young Mac now switched from Taggart Construction errand boy to Two Dot cowboy, which he liked much better.

The Taggarts kept the ranch in sheep during their first decade, lambing and shearing at pens on Ralston Flat. They ran three bands of sheep until World War II, when help was terribly hard to find. Finally the sheep were sold to the Manning Ranch at Douglas.

This was a turning point. Ralston Flat became feedlots for the Hereford foundation cattle the Taggarts bought from the May Ranch above Meeteetse. There was land enough for a farming operation, and growing feed crops to support winter feeding of the animals.

• •

The ranch employed several dozen people, some year-round and many more seasonal: irrigators, farm workers, and haying help. They all needed to be fed, and several Two Dot women told of cooking nonstop. Jane Thompson, who worked at the Two Dot with her husband Oscar in the 1940s, remembers cooking an early breakfast for the branding crew, then fixing them a take-along lunch while she made another breakfast for the haying crew. Then of course she went on to prepare a noon dinner and an evening supper.

The Taggarts hired a Mexican haying crew supervised by George Frame, who also served as interpreter. In 1945 Jack Higham, then owner of the Paint Creek place, bought a baler and Lloyd Taggart put a Two Dot crew on the new-fangled machine. It took four or five men: one to feed the wire, another to pull it through the windrows with a tractor, and the others to help.

The Two Dot's continuous land mass was an even greater

Jane Thompson, niece of John Chapman, and her husband Oscar,
who grew up on the edge of the Two Dot, were vital sources in this historical search.
(Photo by author)

advantage during the Taggart era than it is today. Oscar Thompson explained, "In those days we didn't have horse trailers so you got on your horse and rode to wherever you were going."

Oscar was born about a mile and a half up Pat O'Hara from the Two Dot. He remembered the McKnights, who had lost the ranch to the "dirty thirties," and the early years when fences were rare and neighbors ran their cattle together.

Jane, Priestly Riddle's daughter and John Chapman's grandniece, was raised in Sunlight. There, too, homesteaders threw their cattle into a common herd that circled the valley from early spring to late fall, then wintered in the basins close to home.

The Taggarts leased many homestead lands through those

Oscar Thompson leaving Pat O'Hara Cow Camp headed upcountry
with his pack horse and mule.
(Courtesy Jane Riddle Thompson)

years and as those deeded properties came up for sale, they were quick to purchase them. Their land base would eventually reach sixty thousand acres.

Evelyn Braten was one of those homesteaders. She grew up on the Clarks Fork just below the canyon with a clear view of the Absarokas—the "Shining Mountains," as she called them. Later her family would move to Russell Creek in Sunlight. Even in her youth, Evelyn could tackle anything; she served as a fire lookout, cooked, babysat her younger siblings, carried mail, worked for neighbors. After high school this young woman with true grit took up her own homestead on Blaine Creek where she ran her father's sheep. "Her brothers and her Brough relatives often came and stayed while they cut and hauled wood. While she was 'proving up' her claim, she helped her neighbor, Lulu Brown, with haying and driving cattle to water as there was no stock water on the Browns' range." She liked being alone but eventually sold to the Taggarts, one of the early ones to do so.

Jane Thompson remembers that in five years on the ranch, "We packed ourselves up fifteen times to go a few miles down the road and unpack. Even at that we were at the Stone House from 1943 to 1945." Jane first knew the Stone House as one of those overnighters coming through for supplies in Cody or Red Lodge.

The ranch was still running sheep when Montana cowboy Reesa Clute, known as Slim, started at the Two Dot. His summer camp was close to the three bands grazing on Bald Ridge. "The camp tender, Lester Reed, would drive up to my camp, then he would pack up the horses and head off to deliver supplies to each of the herders. The sheep were run on leased land and the cattle all remained on deeded land."

Oscar Thompson pointed out that in earlier times, ranchers ran sheep on the fringes of the cattle herd. Sheep graze pasture grass shorter than cows do, and that stubble can act as a buffer to keep the

Pat Cremer, who provided this picture, called Reesa Clute
"the gold standard for handling cattle and horses."

cattle bunched together. The sheep were also sent up early on Bald Ridge to clear out the larkspur, a plant poisonous to cattle in spring. When the plant matures, usually by late June, it is no longer palatable to the cattle.

The whole crew celebrated with the Taggarts when they purchased the Heald operation, still called the Pat O'Hara Ranch, in 1942. "It gave them control of the whole creek, and that was great," Clute said. Benny Taggart ran that ranch and Reesa called him "one of the good guys."

Clute lived in the house trailer for cowboys whose hours didn't match the regular mealtimes of six in the morning, twelve noon, and six in the evening. "That way we could fix something whenever we got back," he explained. "We were often in the saddle shortly after three in the morning during the summer." This schedule has been the rule rather than the exception for Two Dot cowboys, even today.

It was Reesa's job to tend the Polecat Bench cow camp twenty-five miles from headquarters through the winter. "I had another cowboy with me and we had to break the ice and keep the holes open for the cattle to drink out of the many reservoirs on that range." Charlie Blackstone, who cowboyed for the outfit in the fifties, also remembers chopping ice and clearing snow from Pat O'Hara and Paint Creeks.

Ordinarily the cattle started for home by March, calving time. After calving the cowboys watched the new moms closely. A Hereford calf sometimes needed a few days to catch up with the mother's milk production. "When I could see that the cow's bag was too full and swollen, I had to catch and milk her out," Reesa explained. "Sometimes I was able to rope the cows by their horns and get them tied up to a tree to milk. Other times I was able to catch them out there in the brush. I had one great horse that, once I had the cow roped by the back legs, would hold the cow stretched out and still

Benny Taggart throwing hay to horses.
(Courtesy Jane Riddle Thompson)

until I got her milked out."

That gelding was a favorite. "He was just a black horse, not very big, but filled with intelligence and what a worker! He just had one problem, you couldn't tie him up. When I grained him in a stall in the barn I just tied a rope across behind him. I figured if he was going to work so well for me I could adjust to meet that little idiosyncrasy.

"Later I heard, after I left the ranch, that his next rider wasn't so patient. I guess he told the other cowboys that he would break the nag of that stuff in a hurry. After putting a chain around his neck, the horse fought until he broke his neck...I don't know who the guy was and that's probably good because I would have gone after him for sure."

Reesa remembers missing a whole week of branding one year. "I kept getting sicker and sicker. Finally Jack Snell just loaded me up

Elie Well and Oscar Thompson moving cattle.
(Courtesy Jane Riddle Thompson)

and hauled me to Cody. They diagnosed me with Rocky Mountain spotted fever, sometimes called tick fever. Then they told me that two guys had already died from it."

While Reesa did not admit easily to serving as ranch foreman as Oscar Thompson had remembered, he did say that when Jack Snell had to leave, "He put me in charge for awhile."

When last interviewed at ninety-six, Reesa still had a special place in his heart for his boss, Lloyd Taggart. "Lloyd was a great guy. He always came out from town prepared with coats, shovels and other equipment in his truck. This was after his brother Charles died in 1944, and he proved to be an excellent manager," Reesa said.

He just had one failing. "Oh, my gawd, the man couldn't make coffee. Whenever we knew he was bringing lunch out to us we knew that we'd be drinking water, just couldn't handle the pale brown rue he claimed was the real stuff," he laughed. "Of course he didn't drink coffee so he didn't even know just how bad it was.

"Whenever Lloyd came out he visited and talked right along with us. He seemed like he liked our kind of people and we sure liked him and his whole family for that matter."

• •

On Sunday, December 7, 1941 Pearl Harbor, Hawaii, was attacked, triggering a declaration of war against the Japanese—all Japanese, whether in the home country or those who had immigrated to the United States, of which there were thousands. American common sense and reason were cast aside in total hysteria.

The Japanese movement to America had begun after the Russo-Japanese War of 1904–1905. They were welcomed on the West Coast as an answer to the need for cheap hardworking labor. While they were reminded that they were "in" America, they were not to think of themselves as "of" America. Yet their numbers grew. In 1924 the Oriental Exclusion Act was put in place to stem the flow of immigration from Asia. By 1941 a large contingent of first and second generation American-born Japanese, called Nesei, were well established throughout the West. Most of them were as shocked as other Americans when the Japanese attacked Pearl Harbor. Unfortunately the fears of the citizenry swelled and these immigrants were an easy target.

To ease the pressure, President Franklin Delano Roosevelt moved to restrict the movement of Japanese Americans with Executive Order 9066 signed on February 19, 1942. A few days later the head of the Western Defense Command designated the western half of Washington and Oregon, all of California, and a portion of Arizona a Military Defense Zone. The order stated that anyone of Japanese extraction had to leave the area—but of course there was no place to go.

Mac Taggart and Jud Richmond, taken by a photographer from Colliers Magazine.

Like a flood washing over the country, the evacuation from the West Coast began two weeks later, and a War Relocation Authority agency was established to handle it. Sixty-four temporary reception centers were established along with ten permanent sites. One of the selected permanent sites was near the Two Dot on the Heart Mountain Irrigation Division of the Shoshone Irrigation Project lands between Cody and Powell. Camp construction began immediately a few miles from the Ralston Flat part of the Taggart operation. Locals were called out in droves to work round the clock in twelve-hour shifts. They were aiming to house eleven thousand people within sixty days.

Jud Richmond, longtime cow foreman for the Two Dot.

The design was simple, and in fifty-eight minutes an assembly line could erect a building, from foundation to roof, large enough for thirty evacuees. The buildings eventually formed thirty blocks.

By August 10, 1942, Wyoming's third largest city was ready for occupancy. Two days later, the first 292 inhabitants arrived by railcar. Eventually the final total would be 10,767, thirty-seven percent of whom were Issei, Japanese born, and sixty-seven percent American born. One thousand students attended the school within the compound. Quickly nine hundred of the adult males entered the U.S. Army, twenty of whom were killed in action.

It may have been the shortest-lived city in the nation's history. By January 2, 1945, the West Coast Exclusion Act was lifted. More than half the residents were gone by September 1, 1945 and the last 205 American citizens left November 10. The Bureau of Reclamation opened the Heart Mountain Irrigation Project to army veterans. Many of the homesteaders lived in the residential quarters while building their own headquarters.

The 20 by 120 foot barracks were hauled off to become homes for the newcomers. By 1956 little was left but a tall smokestack and a few foundation and lumber remnants.

• •

Mac Taggart worked on the ranch both before and after his four years of service in World War II. He married Janet Blackburn, the daughter of Sheriff Frank Blackburn, in January of 1943.

Frank Blackburn had traveled from England to Manitoba, Canada, where he worked three years for his uncle, a wheat farmer. Punching cows seemed a more interesting line of work and eventually he followed a friend back to Wyoming's Big Horn Basin. There on the Greybull River, Blackburn would gain one of the first Forest Service permits for grazing sheep. A man of many talents, he would

*Charlie Blackstone demonstrating the gentleness of Two Dot cows—
or the foolishness of one cowboy.*
(Courtesy Charlie Blackstone)

be elected county sheriff on the Republican ticket in 1926.

Janet had already had several careers after attending the universities of Oklahoma and Wyoming. Her job at the *Cody Enterprise* included serving associety editor; she was secretary for U.S. Senator E.V. Robertson at his Cody office, then became a cashier at the First National Bank of Cody, then at the American Trust Company of San Francisco. Then she said yes to Mac.

They moved first to Ralston Flat where the sheep pens were being converted to feedyards, then later to the Stone House, where "much of the old furniture, original wallpaper and carpeting were still there," said Mac. They also found, as the Chapmans had, that storms could force travelers to seek shelter, and they welcomed the company.

Mac and Janet's children, Leslie, Jessie, Frank, and James, were envied by many of their Cody classmates as they shared tales of their life on the Two Dot. When Jud and Verle Richmond moved to the ranch in November of 1946, the two families became close friends. The Richmond children and other Two Dot kids went to a country school on Paint Creek, then to Cody schools later.

Replacing Benny Taggart, Jud Richmond joined a long and talented list of Two Dot cattle foremen. Already on that list were Jack Snell from Lovell, Clute, who called his tenure "accidental," Monroe Wogamon, Sid Nelson from Meeteetse, and Johnny Griffith.

Jud and Verle started out at the Lower Two Dot, the Heald place on Blaine Creek. "Our house had been part of the Japanese internment camp residences which were sold to many area residents when the internees were freed. The Taggarts had moved several to the ranch, then remodeled them into comfortable living quarters," Verle explained.

Jud had grown up in Thermopolis; his dad, R.M. Richmond, was a stockholder in the LU Sheep Company. "The only cows they had were used to clean up the grasses the sheep didn't want," Jud quipped. Later he worked at the Arapaho Ranch on the Wind River

*Far right, Benny Taggart, Jose driving tractor, and the rest of the haying crew
the first year a traveling baler was used.*
(Courtesy Jane Riddle Thompson)

Indian Reservation at Riverton, Wyoming, an operation so large it still spans sixteen U.S. Geologic Survey topographical maps.

When Richmond arrived at the Two Dot, he learned that it was now strictly a cow/calf operation. As cow foreman he was in charge of more than a thousand Herefords whose yearling calves ran on Bald Ridge.

Richmond liked his cows well marked with not too much white: "I'm not as much a Hereford fan but the Taggarts were sold on them." In late summer, buyers bid on the yearlings and they went wherever the Taggarts could get the best price.

While Jud managed the cattle, Verle fed the crew that first year. "There were eighteen of us to sit down for meals," she said. "We never put the dishes back in the cupboards all summer, just washed them and put them back on the table."

Verle made jams and jellies from wild fruit: plums and

Percy Large in a rare seated moment.

Pat O'Hara Basin Cow Camp with assorted chaps hanging on the wall.
(Courtesy Jane Riddle Thompson)

buffalo berries; currants, gooseberries and chokecherries from Blaine and Pat O'Hara creeks. When sugar was rationed during World War II, she recalled, "The stamps were your permission to buy sugar, just as gas stamps allowed for the purchase of car gas."

While many winters were mild, some were tough. Just days into the job, Jud almost quit when an early storm stranded more than a thousand head of cattle on Pat O'Hara. In the early 1950s, cowboys froze toes and cheeks trying to move cattle out of Badger Basin after a blizzard left thirty-eight inches of snow on the level. When the storm finally cleared out, Verle recalled, "It was so quiet that the one noise we could hear came through quite loud, although we were puzzled at first." The sound was a distant engine: Everett Wallace, the mailman, coming cross-country on a Skidoo

Oscar Thompson moving cattle across the bridge on Pat O'Hara Creek
toward corrals on the stone house side at Two Dot headquarters.
(Courtesy Jane Riddle Thompson)

snowmobile. Fences were no obstacle for the hardy mailman. He just drove right over them.

Keeping track of the cattle on winter feed grounds was tough through that period. "That Pole Cat Bench is a cold place," Richmond said. "We calved right out in Sand Coulee and they didn't get hay," Jud explained. The fact that these animals could survive so many seasons on little or no hay was a phenomenon each new owner and fellow cattleman would marvel at. Today, in the search for better bottom lines, many ranchers throughout the West are now trying to emulate those early practices.

George Frame leaning against the flatbed truck used to haul hay.
(Courtesy Jane Riddle Thompson)

• •

For seventeen years, whenever he rode to the far end of Pat O'Hara Mountain, Jud Richmond passed a young aspen with "Jack Spicer, 1912" carved in the bark. While the tree grew and the signage stretched, the words never faded. Eventually he would learn that the sheepherder so named had also been a notorious bootlegger.

Jud Richmond was a businessman with an uncanny sense of the doings of Mother Nature. He knew how to keep grass growing from mountaintop to river basin and turn cattle into profits for his bosses. There was always enough summer range so that the Taggarts could expand, homestead purchase by homestead purchase. Eventually a herd of a thousand grew to 1,350 with plenty of winter range.

He was willing to experiment, too. After studying the subject in the mid-fifties, Richmond encouraged the Taggarts to spray sagebrush on Skull Creek and the Two Dot Bench, killing enough to thin it out and improving the range environment. They had good results.

While Richmond took the scientific approach to running cattle, when he topped a horse he was pure cowboy. Martin Nielsen, a young summer employee, found a hero in Richmond: "He was one of the best cowboys any of us ever knew."

Jud did appreciate a good horse—although even now he can only remember about ten that met his standards. His philosophy was, "Never get married to a horse."

Richmond liked competing in calf and team roping events when he had time, which wasn't often. It was a credit to his innate ability that he could rope and tie a calf or steer in record time when the opportunity arose, even without practice.

His last award-winning time came at a rodeo in Meeteetse in 1962. "I got first in calf roping there and second in the cow milking. That day I was using a horse that was really good but you never knew when he was going to buck you off."

Calves weren't his only roping target. The day some cowboys discovered a bull moose, Jud just couldn't resist. He had to rope him so the boys could take a closer look.

Jud's favorite days were spent losing himself deep in Two Dot territory, although "Mac was always trying to get me to go to stockgrower meetings or other events in town." Even jawing with the neighbors for too long, much as he might like them, left Jud turning restlessly toward the mountains or eyeing his horse.

Charlie Taggart, the youngest brother, understood Jud's bent to be in the mountains. He spent every spare minute on the ranch, every summer and weekend. One weekend he was joined by his classmate Earl Curtis—future owner of the Two Dot. Admittedly the cowboys had a lot of fun at Charlie's expense, but the boy seemed to enjoy it as much as they did.

Visiting cow camp one day, Jud admired a copper nugget from a New Mexico mine, owned by the guy in charge that summer. It was beautiful, Jud said. "It looked just like pure gold."

The guy gave it to Jud. Later, as he rode past the bunkhouse, Charlie ran out to greet him. Jud just threw the piece of rock down on the ground and went on.

Well, Charlie couldn't get that rock to Lloyd fast enough. Since Lloyd was headed to Helena for a meeting, he showed it to an assayer there who said a full report would take a while but he could see that it was high grade. Lloyd must have driven home thinking they'd all be rich as soon as he found out where that rock came from. Eventually the story came out and Lloyd was fit to be tied.

Everybody loved Charlie; he was enthusiastic, curious, and loved cowboy mischief. One day he found a stick of dynamite in an

Mexican haying crew with George Frame, father of Georgia Close,
who interpreted for the Spanish speaking crew.
(Courtesy Jane Riddle Thompson)

old shed. At some point he broke it in half and, curious, took the longer half and stuck it in the campfire. He stirred it around for a bit. The next thing Charlie knew he was standing in a cloud of black smoke, his right hand gone. When the Taggarts got him to the hospital Charlie held up his arm. "Guess I'll never be a famous baseball pitcher, huh," he said, not looking for an answer. In Jud's words, "He had a lot of guts, that kid did."

• •

After years of committee work for the Wyoming Stock Growers Association, Lloyd Taggart said yes to their highest office in 1951, a two-year term. He took over the presidency of arguably the most powerful organization in the state, making some lasting changes.

Seeing the WSGA needed an office in Cheyenne to boost its influence at the state capitol, Lloyd ramrodded the construction of the building still used today. He also aimed to make *Cow Country* the voice of Wyoming agriculture. At the end of his term the magazine was a money-making proposition and recognized as one of the state's elite publications. Still head of the Taggart Construction Company, Lloyd also used his WSGA presidency as a bully pulpit to rail against the labor unions trying to move into Wyoming.

What Lloyd's presidency meant back home was a shift in responsibilities. Mac took over the management of the operation as well as running the farm. Jud had full authority over the cattle. Yet the cowboys, who by this time referred to their boss as Uncle Lloyd, were never too surprised to see Lloyd racing in his vehicle from one hotbed of concern on the ranch to another.

Jud, too, appreciated Lloyd Taggart. "He was a straight talking, hands-on owner. He gave you an answer when you asked him something and he didn't beat around the bush," he said.

In an era when every ounce of new techonology was celebrated, George Frame stands with a Farmall tractor and the latest grader. The Taggart crew was lucky to have access to road construction equipment when needed. They might have used the grader to even out humps in fields to ease irrigation.
(Courtesy Jane Riddle Thompson)

"He did do a lot of funny things, though," Charlie Blackstone added, recalling a day on the range when he was a newcomer. "Here it was out in the wilderness—the middle of Chapman Bench there where it was wide open with no fences thirteen miles across. I expected only hoof prints and here were tire tracks, a big circle of tracks, spinning wheel kind of marks." He was really puzzled. When he told the crew about it at suppertime, they just laughed. "That's just Uncle Lloyd checking cattle in his two-wheel drive Chevy car," one said.

On another memorable day, Blackstone brought in a big crew from the construction company and started burning ditches. A terrible west wind came up, driving the fire ever wider right toward a fifty-ton stack of baled hay. The stack burned.

"There wasn't a cowboy on the place who didn't say his prayers that he wasn't the one having to tell Uncle Lloyd that night," Blackstone laughed. "That west wind can blow hard out in that country," he added.

"He's one of the good guys," not a phrase cowboys use lightly, but Reesa Clute used it to describe Benny Taggart. Charlie Blackstone used it to describe Lloyd.

Lloyd had a ready wit, Blackstone remembered. One year the Taggarts trailed a big bunch of steers from the ranch to the railhead, loading them onto boxcars. After the last steer entered the train, Lloyd leaped to the bridge to slide the door shut and fell head over heels off the side.

As the crew waited, Blackstone swears, even the horses didn't breathe. All of a sudden Lloyd got up, dusted himself off and said, "I can't decide whether to sue the railroad or can the cowboys who caused this." Everyone grinned in relief.

Elaine Moncur, whose grandmother was a Taggart, remembers a similar story told to her by Bob Woodruff, who by then had a sheep operation out of Powell with his father, Billy, while still running sheep on Pat O'Hara and helping on the Two Dot whenever he could.

Lloyd was helping sort cattle in knee-deep mud, standing in the middle of the corral. "Suddenly there was a bunch coming at him and because of the mud and him in his overshoes, they just sucked down and he couldn't move out of the way. When it was all over the cattle had pretty well buried Lloyd well over his Stetson before hitting the far corral fence in a muddle. He surfaced with a fist in the air yelling, 'I'll sue, I'll sue!'"

Another time Blackstone found Lloyd with his car hung over the edge of a big hole on Pat O'Hara Creek. He had been checking the water, got distracted by a grandson traveling with him, and ended up stuck. Blackstone tied his horse to the bumper and pulled Lloyd out. Once unhooked, Lloyd peeled out, leaving his rescuer in the dust.

Blackstone laughs over these stories but turns serious when he adds, "He did build up a tremendous set of Herefords, he sure did."

• •

With so many characters on board at the Two Dot, it was some kind of place for a teenager to work. Martin Nielsen, whose parents had worked on ranches throughout the area, found his own cowboy heaven at the Two Dot on the summer farming crew. Martin recalled Percy Large, an Indian who turned many heads across Wyoming and Montana. Percy had a twenty foot long bullwhip and could rope calves right or left handed. One day Martin listened as the cowboys discussed their plan to drive Glenn Nielson cattle through the Two Dot herd on Blaine Meadows. As they debated how to avoid mixing the herds, Percy said quietly. "Just bring 'em on through, we'll keep 'em separated." And Martin watched the magic of a bullwhip, a dog, and a horse when directed by one very qualified cowboy. There was no cow that didn't go where he aimed, and nothing ever looked easier. "He and Jud were two of the best," Martin said.

Martin remembers others. Bill Duprey, the irrigator who could "make water run uphill just to get a dry spot covered." There was Jack Taggart, another brother, the mechanic who'd come back from California. There was Eddy Dorrance, a silent film actor according to Lucille Patrick, whose father had owned the Diamond Bar where Dorrance was cattle foreman before joining the Two Dot.

There was redheaded Elma Renner, Two Dot cook for eleven years and wife of cowboy Bill Renner; she kept a big garden. Martin often went home with boxes of produce that his mother had to quickly process, no matter the hour or her own schedule. Two Dot chore boy Frank Dobish was another wonderful gardener, Blackstone remembers.

Dobish also looked out for the wild turkeys that thrived

during the 1950s, often tossing them a shovelful of grain. The state even had a season on the turkeys: Wyoming Game and Fish allowed hunters to take fifty a year—if they could.

Blackstone also talked of Johnny Kirkpatrick, who lived just over the hill on his own place and worked for both the Trail Creek and the Two Dot in the earlier years. "He threw a great big loop," he said. "There's a picture of him in the Proud Cut Saloon still today riding a white horse with that great big loop. Johnny had a dog named 'Boy.'" For many years Kirkpatrick carried a flag in the Fourth of July parade. After his death, his little legacy would become part of the Two Dot, as well.

Blackstone had one final Two Dot story to tell. "I was living out at the Pat O'Hara cow camp and this particular day I was shoeing a horse," he said. "Suddenly there was a Jeep station wagon come into sight...The window was opened just a crack and a woman's voice calls out, 'Boy, hey boy, there's a bear back over there,' she said pointing emphatically." Blackstone decided to keep working and have some fun. The woman repeated her warning, and again the cowboy ignored it. "This time with the window wide open and the woman's head partially out the window she hollered, 'Boy, boy, there's a bear back up over there.'"

Blackstone dropped the horse's foot, straightened up and said, "Lady, I'll head right to the cabin and get my big ole slingshot and the leftover biscuits from breakfast and head on up there. Believe me that poor ole bear won't stand a chance against those biscuits of mine." With that the woman cranked up her window, hit the gas and left the cowboy in the dust.

• •

Nature went on a rampage the spring of 1955. Floods took out every bridge along Pat O'Hara except for the Sunlight bridge.

"All our gas floor furnaces quit as the water washed under the apartments," Verle remembered.

• •

Travel was always a challenge during the Taggart years, bad weather or no. As Mac put it, all roads led to Red Lodge; to get to Billings you had to drive around the mountain. Nobody even thought about going to town in those early years, one cowhand said, except maybe for the Cody Stampede on the Fourth of July.

Roads or the lack thereof made shopping difficult, but there were traveling salesmen eager to take the cowboys' money. Montgomery Ward and Sears Roebuck never catered to cowboys and ranchers. Instead, the Minnesota Woolen Mills salesman came every year in the early days, recalled Bob Richmond. "He'd always show up about noon, usually in the summer when the hay crew was there as well." He'd get invited for the noon dinner, then young Bob spent the afternoon helping him sort his samples: the pants, the shirts, the long johns, the socks, laying them all out for easy picking.

After supper with the crew, the salesman spent the evening taking orders for next year. He'd work late taking those orders, then have to stay for the night, eat breakfast with the crew the next morning and be off, aiming for the next ranch by noon. Just like the cowboys in winter, he had no expenses "riding the grub line" the way he did.

According to neighbor Georgia Close, who came to teach at the Paint Creek School in 1942 and stayed to marry rancher Harold Close, their road was difficult at best, and impassable when it was muddy. Despite efforts to work together and have picnics and barbecues once in awhile, communication just wasn't as good in those days. "The paved road put us all together," she said. Others called the new road from Cody to Belfry a superhighway. Now it was much easier to get produce to market—the Closes even sold cream to the Bridger Creamery.

"The Sand Coulee Road, too, it ran just below the ranch across Two Dot range to Powell, and was terrible, until it was designated a 'farm to market road,'" she said. Federal funds to build it and the county's agreement to maintain it broadened local ranchers' perspectives considerably.

Despite their remote location, Jud and Mac thought they'd maybe captured their fifteen minutes of fame when the ranch caught a *Saturday Evening Post* writer's eye. After the interviews and photo session at the Two Dot, both families imagined a full-page spread for their heroes.

When that issue finally appeared, it had a few paragraphs on the Two Dot in tiny print, and one small picture of the two men and their steeds. Hardly fame-building, the story would be fodder for humor that kept the two men chuckling in times of trial.

Neighboring came naturally to the Taggarts. Elaine Moncur, whose family ranch shares a fenceline with the Two Dot, recalled that "Hy Bischoff and Lloyd Taggart used to ride together and traded pieces of land along their fencelines." If Hy couldn't get a fence put in, they moved the boundary to make it feasible.

Elaine also remembers a cowboy named Shorty Edgmont, who worked mainly for Taggart Construction, helping out at the Two Dot as needed. "He died suddenly with no family that the Taggarts knew of. Well, Mac said that they couldn't bury him without a little fanfare so three of his family members volunteered to sing. They called themselves Shorty's Trio and nobody ever had a more beautiful send-off than Shorty did that day."

• •

Then the hour arrived, as it had for each owner, one that would change everything, proving once again that life is fluid. It was a sad day in 1963 when Mac called Jud insisting that he ride to town with him. Jud could tell it wasn't the time to refuse. As they drove Mac announced that the family had decided to sell the ranch. Jud was stunned. After eighteen years he had planned to retire at the Two Dot.

When they got to town Jud headed for a phone. He called Verle. "We're done," he said. "Taggarts are selling the Two Dot." Verle's confidence in her husband didn't waver. "I saw all sorts of opportunities in his future," she said. "I wasn't worried at all." Jud was less concerned about new opportunities than about losing what the Two Dot brought to him. For Mac, heavily involved in other aspects of the business, it may have been easier to walk away—or maybe not. Certainly the children would call their Two Dot years the best time of their lives. As for Lloyd, he would later invest in a sheep and Quarter Horse ranch in New Zealand, traveling back and forth several times each year.

Jud and his crew stayed on until the end, then Jud would remain for six months to guide the new owners. He went on to manage other outstanding ranches in the area: the Trail Creek, Nielsen's, and the Deseret.

Mac, too, went on to improve his community in myriad ways. After his death in December of 2000, the *Cody Enterprise* was filled with letters praising him as an "energetic community leader... authentic Western personality...a giant among many, one of the most kind and caring individuals...a selfless leader...one of the area's most steadfast supporters." A temporarily displaced Cody boy, Lieutenant Colonel Ward W. Severts, wrote, "His touch extended to so many corners of our community—scouting, health, education, government, church, business. I'd bet every person in Cody has reason to personally say 'thanks' to Mac."

Many had reason to thank all the Taggarts, whose twenty-nine years of ownership was the longest the Two Dot Ranch has seen. A letter from Jim Nichols of Oak Ridge, Tennessee, sums up the family's wide-ranging influence.

"When I was a back-east dude of about twenty, my granddad and I were at the Irma for lunch, and he introduced me to a guy that had 'rancher' written all over him.

"It was Mac Taggart, then of the Two Dot Ranch, the first Taggart I ever met. He was lean and tan, with a crewcut, cowboy shirt and Levi's. His clear eyes sparkled as we spoke, and I thought to myself, "He's the genuine article.

"I went right out and got a crewcut, and bought myself a similar cowboy wardrobe to outfit me for the balance of my summer visit, thinking it would prevent my looking like a dude.

"I didn't know him again until I moved there in 1992. He still had the sparkle and a smile for anyone who wanted one—that smile will be missed."

A Biography of Place

CHAPTER SIXTEEN

A Decade of Hemingway

*After the first snow plowing of the early spring on the road
from Red Lodge over Beartooth Pass to Yellowstone National Park.*
(Courtesy Beth Jobe Spears)

IT WASN'T LUXURY that drew Ernest Hemingway to claim the two-bedroom River Ranch cabin for his summer writing retreat that year. From the living room window he could observe the brookies leaping high, teasing the eagles that made their homes along the stream. The sights were not an encouragement to Hemingway's writing but he thrilled at the fishing opportunities.

The River Ranch house, long a part of the Two Dot, sits snugly in the curve of the confluence of the Clarks Fork River and Pat O'Hara Creek. One of the most breathtaking views on the Two Dot is there, where the Beartooth Mountains to the northwest meet the Absarokas running north and south of the Clarks Fork Canyon.

While neighbors knew the author was vacationing at the ranch house, then owned by the Frank G. Hopkins family from Florida, he was left to the peace he seemed to be seeking. Their respectful silence turned his short stay into lore that many considered fiction.

But Mac and Janet Taggart found proof while sorting through a box of memorabilia stored for a quarter of a century in that shoreside cabin. They blew dirt from covers of scrapbooks, papers, photos, and souvenirs. Then, in an old guest book, the Taggarts

One of the mule deer bucks the Two Dot is famous for.
(Courtesy Yves Burrus)

discovered the signature of Ernest Hemingway, making truth of the rumors. Not only had the famous author spent occasional summers into autumn in the Clarks Fork Valley from 1928 to 1939, he had vacationed on the Two Dot at least one summer.

In fact he had stayed at that very cabin. While Mac questioned the exaggerated weights of Hemingway's fish noted beside his name, neither he nor his wife doubted the authenticity of his signature.

The author's invitation had come from Frank Hopkins, an eastern industrialist with a home in Florida, where presumably the two men met. Hopkins used the six-hundred-acre ranch primarily as a vacation home and he welcomed visitors. He would have sold Hemingway on the privacy of the cabin—and its fishing opportunities.

Hemingway wrote in the morning, fished in the afternoon, and imbibed in the evening all through the summer. In late August when the Absaroka Range was already welcoming snow, he left the cabin to join hunts farther west—for elk, deer, bear, and antelope. He wrote little of this country and his neighbors were grateful.

Hemingway's talent could make famous a country, a war, a sport or a place, such as the city of Pamplona, Spain. Visiting there as an unknown in 1923, he witnessed the centuries-old Fiesta of San Fermin, with its running of the bulls through the streets. After he described it in his 1926 novel *The Sun Also Rises*, Pamplona's small-town festival would grow into one of the most famous events in the world.

Hemingway last visited there in 1959. Pamplona celebrated the hundredth anniversary of his birth on July 21, 1999, forty years later, and still the town was filled with Hemingway books, merchandise, and fans. His image was posted high above every street corner.

To Hemingway's credit, that didn't happen to the wilderness of northwest Wyoming. Despite a decade of visits to the Clarks Fork Valley, Hemingway wrote little of his stays. Maybe that part of "home" was too precious to publicize. While he wrote letters about his hunting experiences to a few friends and his publisher, he was vague as to location: "somewhere in northwest Wyoming" was the most he would offer. He finally mentioned the area by name in a short essay, "The Clarks Fork River Valley, Wyoming" for *Vogue* in 1939. In a 1934 *Esquire* article, he had also referred to his 1932 visit.

Instead, Hemingway depicted the area through characters such as Robert Jordan in his 1940 novel *For Whom the Bell Tolls*.

Hemingway has Jordan growing up in Red Lodge; another character battles a snowstorm similar to one Hemingway encountered on a hunting foray. A short story, "Wine of Wyoming," tells of a couple's efforts to produce wine for their café during Prohibition. In *Green Hills of Africa*, a 1935 nonfiction work, he compares tracking game on that continent of savannah and rough hills to "hunting at home" on Wyoming's Timber Creek and Pilot Peak. Many writers, editors, and critics believe that although he wrote little of the area, the landscape left an indelible mark on him as a writer.

Hemingway would reappear for a number of summers and several fall hunting trips during the thirties; his last visit was in 1939, though he passed through again in 1959. Not only was it a good place to write, fish, and hunt, but even during Prohibition he found all the liquor he wanted.

On his first trip, in 1928, Hemingway may have traveled mostly in the Bighorn Mountains and Sheridan, only discovering northwest Wyoming late in the season. Reports indicate he also drove to the east entrance of Yellowstone National Park during that visit.

Later Hemingway would disapprove of the construction of the Beartooth Highway, which was meant to encourage visitors to Yellowstone. The new road, across seemingly impenetrable mountains, was made possible through funding created by the Park Approach Act of 1931. According to biographer Carlos Baker, Hemingway believed that the highway northwest of the Two Dot would send all its wildlife into the park, compromising hunting opportunities on the ranch itself.

As Robert Hoskins noted in an article for *Wyoming Wildlife*, 1930 found Hemingway driving his Model T into the area with his second wife, Pauline, and son, Bumby. Suddenly the vehicle dropped, running-board deep, into a boggy stretch of swampland not far from the river. From then on the Hemingways were carless until the ground froze in the fall and it could be pulled out.

In the meantime Hemingway explored both the wilderness—a far cry from the African terrain he periodically treated himself to—and its people, such as hunting guide and dude ranch owner Lawrence Nordquist, whose family had been one of the first to settle in the area.

Jane Riddle Thompson remembers seeing Hemingway at her grandfather, Priestly Riddle's ranch in Sunlight Basin. He seemed huge from her preschool vantage point. In fact he was five-eleven, but barrel-chested, broad and deep, and the force of his personality heightened the impact of his physical presence even for adults.

He must be very nice, Jane thought—the smile, the hearty laugh—that would make him so. Photographer Jousuf Karsh, whose Hemingway portrait would become legendary, also noted his "wonderful smile—alive, kindly, and full of understanding."

Jane also remembers Hemingway relaxing with her grandfather in the grass by a creek in Sunlight Basin west of the Two Dot. They were enjoying a drink from the stash her grandfather kept hidden deep under the bank.

Two Dot Ranch crew around 1900 including Pres Riddle, relative of John Chapman, and Hardy Shull, an old Oregon friend along with unnamed crew.
(Courtesy Jane Riddle Thompson)

••

Hemingway seemed to rise to every challenge offered by this vast country, and surprisingly suffered only two accidents. As Neil Grauer later noted in *Cigar Aficionado* (another Hemingway passion), the writer "was wounded in wartime and accident prone in peace, suffering numerous concussions and the injuries were exacerbated by his alcoholism."

His first Wyoming mishap occurred when something spooked his horse as he rode upcountry to check some bear bait set by Nordquist. He found himself perched on an animal racing full bore through the forest, as if on a straightaway that didn't exist, branches slapping him and finally slicing across his face. A forest ranger working in the area found him and sent him to Cody in the care of the ranger's daughter. Dr. Trueblood, a well-known veterinarian turned human doctor, patched him up with bourbon and some pretty plain stitching.

The second event proved more serious—but it would also precipitate a short story, "The Gambler, the Nun, and the Radio."

At the end of the summer, Hemingway headed south for the winter with two companions. Floyd Allington, a Nordquist wrangler, was going fishing. John Dos Passos, writer and artist, had an agenda of his own, and Hemingway was going home. Bound for Florida, they turned their Ford roadster out of hunting camp onto the northern route out of Sunlight Basin.

When a law enforcement officer questioned how they ended up in a ditch on Highway 10 between Columbus and Park City, Montana, their answers varied. He was temporarily blinded by oncoming lights, Hemingway said. When he swerved to miss them, the vehicle landed in the ditch with the writer pinned under the car. Allington's variation had another car pulling onto the highway from a side road. Dos Passos' version, which admitted to some bootleg whiskey, shed a little more light on the debacle.

Obtaining liquor in those Prohibition days was only a little tricky, since law officers often ignored the use of bootleg whiskey. Still, it was a jailable offense and the trio didn't want to spend any time in the hoosegow: thus the lame excuses. The officer let them go; they already had trouble on their hands.

While his two comrades complained of a stiff neck and bruises, Hemingway was seriously hurt. His upper right arm was shattered: a spiral fracture of both bones about three inches above the elbow, requiring surgery.

Joe Allard, son of the late Dr. Lou Allard who was Hemingway's surgeon, remembers that "Dad said the bones were sheared and during the four-hour surgery he put them back together with kangaroo tendons." Hemingway must have been satisfied, as he later came to the Allards' for dinner. "He was such a big guy with this black beard and long hair. He was a little scary to me. I was only nine years old, and he looked like a pirate or mountain man," recalled Joe.

The nurses at the front desk, too, saw Hemingway's roughness when he first arrived at St. Vincent's Hospital in Billings. They wrote him off as a sheepherder minus his flock, just down from the mountains. Noting his unkempt beard, long scraggly hair, and mumbled answers to their questions, they entered his profession in the paperwork as "rider." Dr. Allard was the one, sitting down with his patient the next morning, who recognized the writer.

Hemingway proved a difficult patient, restless and frequently close to paranoia. Part of the surliness was due to his inability to write. While his wife offered to take dictation, Hemingway made it clear that the story in his head was not enough: he needed the action of pen against paper. That's where the work took shape. As his frustration deepened, he even accused a friend, poet Archibald MacLeish, who had traveled from the East to cheer him up, of coming to watch him die.

Apparently Hemingway found some solace in listening to sports events on the radio. He also observed others at the hospital and noted them well. As Jim Healey and Sue Hart of Montana State University discovered, two of those people appeared in Hemingway's 1933 short story "The Gambler, the Nun, and the Radio": the nurse was Sister Florence and the Mexican gambler was the patient across the hall from Hemingway. His convalescence lasted nearly three months, but another year would pass before his arm was healed enough for writing every morning. In the meantime his editor, Max Perkins, waited for Hemingway's nearly completed *Death in the Afternoon*.

While Hemingway has certainly left his mark on literature, he also left one on the neighbors, guides and fellow hunters and fisherman he pleasured with—and those looking for something to whet their whistle. Hemingway always had a stash, some even he forgot until found by cave explorers and stream bank travelers.

CHAPTER SEVENTEEN

Horseflesh and High Water: The Skoglund-Curtis Years

*Curtis cattle snake out along Highway 120 N pouring over Skull Creek Pass
and down into Two Dot pastures after the long railcar ride from Montana;
all under the watchful eye of Heart Mountain.*
(Photo by Jack Richard, courtesy Buffalo Bill Historical Center)

JUST AS MINNEAPOLIS financier Skog Skoglund picked up the pen to sign the contract forming a ranching union under the name of NOLACO in 1963, the pen froze in midair. Looking up at "CW" Curtis, his partner to be, he stated firmly, "The ranch has to pay or I don't want anything to do with it."

Under their partnership, the Two Dot would prosper, grow dramatically, and expand its focus, producing some fine racehorses and rodeo mounts in the process. CW—Charles W. Curtis, Sr.— provided the ranching talent, H. P. Skoglund the capital; he headed the North American Life and Casualty Insurance Company of Minneapolis and was an owner of the Minnesota Vikings football team. Curtis was named vice-president and general manager of the Two Dot Corporation, Skoglund president and majority stockholder, and his son John, secretary treasurer. The Curtises and a number of outsiders were invested as well.

Born in Blackfoot, Idaho in 1905, CW grew up in Greybull, Wyoming. His father, Alfred Curtis, had brought some of the area's first Percheron horses into the Big Horn Basin in the 1880s, as had Chapman in the northern lip of the basin a few years earlier. He was involved in construction and ranching along the Greybull River most of his life, except for six years in Idaho.

John Skoglund and CW Curtis wait for the unloading to start at the Cody Railroad Station after shipping cattle, horses and machinery intended for the Two Dot.
(Courtesy Buffalo Bill Historical Center)

Earl Curtis moving cattle through the sagebrush.
(Courtesy Steve Devenyns)

CW had already managed two outstanding Meeteetse-area ranches when he and Skoglund met. He was foreman of the Pitchfork from the fall of 1936 until 1941, when he broke his leg just before the ranch's split. Then, eager to be his own boss and tired of the really big outfits, he leased the historic W Bar from William K. Nelson for five years, a ranch now owned by the Wyoming Game and Fish Department.

When CW married Edith Hewett, her own rich pioneer heritage joined his. Her paternal grandparents had arrived in the Cokeville area of western Wyoming very early and her maternal grandparents settled near Greybull in 1897.

CW loved ranching, not only as his livelihood but as the only hobby he'd ever have, as he was quoted in *The Historical Encyclopedia of Wyoming*. He taught his three sons—Richard (Dick), Charles, Jr. (Chuck), and Earl—how to manage water and grasses, select and husband a cattle herd, and appreciate a good horse.

When the boys were all grown and starting their own families, Chuck realized that the Curtis clan could be a strong operation unto itself, but it would require a massive amount of land. Dick and Chuck joined their parents on the W Bar. Meanwhile, young Earl was operating a Caterpillar for a construction firm. "I learned from the main Cat skinner, Slim Brewer, on an old Seven. My legs were almost too short for my feet to reach the pedals when I started but Slim showed me how to run it." That training would later prove invaluable to the family for projects from ditches to reservoirs. Earl married ex-classmate Frances Hamby), an oilman's daughter, in 1951. They leased the Moon Ranch on Gooseberry Creek and settled there, but in two years, with their first daughter, they were ready to pack up and join the rest of the Curtises, now at Big Timber, Montana.

"That was short-lived," said Frances. "In another year we were off to Melville, Montana, to another ranch and spent five years there."

As a ranch foreman in Big Timber, CW worked for Maurice Knutson. Knutson owned two John Deere dealerships and a Packard auto dealership and managed the Montana operation for his in-laws. He is credited with introducing the deep-pocketed Skoglund to CW Curtis, a man with assets of his own.

"I had known Skog for years," said Knutson. "I had served on the St. Olaf College Board of Regents in Minnesota while he was president of that board. He knew I had interests in the West and let me know that he would like to invest out here.

"He was personable and in fact we became quite close. After having CW managing our ranch up in Montana, I knew he could handle the kind of operation Skoglund had in mind and introduced the two. In fact I invested in NOLACO myself," Knutson added.

Next, the Curtis clan purchased the Three C Bar Ranch at Browning, Montana, running three thousand cows for about five years, and forming the Three C Bar Corporation to encompass their other investments.

In 1963 Curtis and Skoglund received word that the Taggarts were selling the Two Dot. While CW had never worked there, he knew its reputation. The partnership purchased the ranch, put its Montana properties up for sale, and began the ticklish process of moving the operation from Browning to Cody.

On February 26, 1964 the *Cody Enterprise* noted, "A major cattle drive is expected to take place in the Cody country today. Approximately twenty-five hundred head of cattle are scheduled to arrive on a Burlington train this morning. They will be trailed north to the Two Dot Ranch."

"We had to rent a freight train to move the stock," Earl Curtis remembered. They were Herefords crossed with Black Angus bloodlines. "There were 2,027 mother cows, fifteen hundred yearlings, one hundred bulls and 250 horses that filled more than seventy box cars along with a number of flatbeds that held the farm machinery."

The train stopped just past the Cody Depot north of the Shoshone River. As the livestock spilled from the cars, cowboys held them together. As the riders "headed 'em up" north along Highway 120 toward the Two Dot, Frances' dad, Glen Hamby—who loved any excuse to mount up—was one of the most eager. While the depot had served for years as a livestock gathering place, the animals were usually boarding cars headed to market. Reversing the tide, the incoming herd was certainly the largest the depot had ever seen. It would also be one of the last. Before long, Two Dot market calves would be loaded onto eastbound semis, instead of being trailed to the rails at Cody or Billings as they had since Chapman's time.

The following week, on March 7, the newspaper carried a now-famous photo by Jack Richard on its front page. The *Enterprise* had to rotate the horizontal photo sideways to do it justice: Curtis cattle were strung out for several miles after their twenty-two hour train ride, headed for Skull Creek Pass where they would spill down into Two Dot headquarters, mixing with the Taggart cattle the partnership had purchased. The new cows learned from their peers the seasons of their rotation—always clockwise around the ranch's range. The cow-calf pairs ran through five pastures of thousands of acres each. "The Two Dot is a natural grass ranch," noted Earl. "With the genetics we used we had small birth weights that made for easy calving, then the calves gained fast. Once settled on the ranch we usually weaned in November at five-fifty to six hundred pounds."

For ten years in a row the Curtises shipped five hundred calves to an eastern cattle feeder at a five-dollar premium per head—long before premium was a ranching buzzword. The feeder paid extra because Two Dot calves were healthy and uniform. "You couldn't see an ounce of difference between any of them," Earl said. That "peas in a pod" look of their potential market steers was a big advantage.

Grazing almost year-round, the cows only needed feeding for a month around calving season and if bad weather caught them on Polecat Bench where they wintered from November 1 to March 20. Cowboys always provided vitamins A, D, and E with loose salt for them.

As for their winter drinking water, Earl bought it from the oil companies in the Polecat Bench area. But one year the water lines were cut when one of the companies failed to pay its bills. "No one told me that's what they were doing and I suddenly had no water for my cows," Earl said. "That meant that we had to trail cows home starting clear up at Bridger, Montana." The

*Dick, Edith, Betty Curtis, and trainer with Red Savage Sam at Centennial Race Track
on October 21, 1965.*
(Courtesy Curtis family)

mother cows came home to calve on grounds traditionally used for this purpose since Chapman's day. Curtises did not calve out heifers; they let them grow another year so they got some size and maturity. "We preferred to raise our own heifers with that genetic imprint that told them how to take care of themselves in this environment," Earl explained. Of course, what calves don't know instinctively mother cows can explain in a language all their own.

While Curtises got settled, Jud Richmond, the Taggart foreman, stayed on board for six months providing continuity and

Dick Curtis with Red Savage Sam after a win at Miles City, Montana.
(Courtesy Curtis family)

BILLINGS TRACK
7TH RACE MAY 30, 1965
WINNER: RED SAVAGE SAM
OWNER: TWO DOT CORP.
TRAINER: RICHARD CURTIS
JOCKEY: K. PULVER
DISTANCE: 250 YDS. TIME: 14:26
PLACE: EMBAR LEOLITA
SHOW: LOMELLA TROUBLE

It was a great day in 1965 when
all the Curtis cousins got to go to Billings to cheer
Red Savage Sam on to a win at the track there.
Front l-r: Bob, Doug, Stanley, Ann.
The second row is Dick, Joannie, Betty and Linda.
(Courtesy Curtis family)

to advise Earl, who would manage the cattle operation, just as he had for eighteen years. Jud was to shake his head later over Earl's appetite for work.

Percy Large also stayed on, preferring as always to cowboy by himself in the summer on Bald Ridge and in the winter out on Polecat Bench. Earl found him one of the best hands he'd ever had, and Frances found her own reasons to rave: "All the kids loved Percy, he was so good with them." Earl added, "The only time I got in trouble with Percy was one winter when I sent another cowboy out to Polecat to help him. That was a wreck."

Pete Moller, who had herded sheep for the Taggarts in the 1930s and irrigated for Jud Richmond a decade later, now worked for Chuck, who handled the farm and haying.

Meanwhile, Dick ran the registered horse operation from the Lower Two Dot, once owned by Healds. Gradually the ranch's changing focus would also change its name to the one that still slides off the locals' tongues most easily today—the horse ranch.

• •

The Curtises were all outstanding horsemen and rodeo competitors. Now they expanded their herd with Taggart horses and about fifty newly purchased ones, and developed a reputation herd through their breeding program. "We sold horses all over the country and Canada," Earl said, "especially to those associated with rodeo." CW boosted the program further when he purchased two studs from the King Ranch in Kingsville, Texas, foundation of Quarter Horse genetics. CW's pride was the racing stock. By then the family had disbanded the Three C Bar Corporation and formed the Two Bar, racing horses throughout the West under that banner, Centennial Race Track in Littleton, Colorado; Miles City, Billings, and more.

Three outstanding racers were Savage Bob, who ran 358 yards in 18.9 seconds; his full brother Red Sam—214 yards in 14.5 seconds—and Red Sam's half brother Red Savage Bar, who set a world record with two hundred yards in 10.2 seconds at Billings in 1965.

The only downside to the horse operation was that mountain lions loved the taste of the foals. "We lost about ten colts every year to the lions," Earl said.

While Earl enjoyed all aspects of rodeo, especially team roping, Dick thrived on the rough stock events and eventually became the stock contractor for Cody's famous summertime Nightly Rodeo, partnering with Lyle Ellis. Eventually all of Earl's children,

Young Stan Curtis at cow camp in 1968.
(Courtesy Curtis family)

Ann, Stan, Bob, and Linda, were rodeo competitors; later Bob's children would make that five generations.

Earl's favorite mount was a double-bred Joe Hancock gelding. "He was six years old and spoiled bad when I got him but when we finally got everything worked out, he could do anything I asked. I used him every day: rodeoed, team roped, rode him when called on to be a pickup man for the saddle bronc and bareback events for Dick. I managed to earn some pretty good money competing myself."

Earl brought home a trophy buckle from Montana's first dally team roping event, won at Birch Creek with Doug Taylor. One of his favorite team-roping partners was Frances's brother Gene Hamby. While they frequently won "day money," the Night Rodeo season would elude them. "It was just too hard every night to haul a horse into the rodeo, work for Dick, compete in the roping, haul my horse home, get to bed about one and then get up at two to start the day."

Indeed, during the summer Earl often rose in what most would consider the middle of the night, so both his crew and his animals could avoid the worst heat of the day. In winter he got up at about six to head for Polecat Bench. It might well be midnight before Frances saw him again.

• •

The Curtises' first year on the Two Dot was especially busy. There were houses to build for their extensive family, and 200,000 acres to get acquainted with. "You sit on your horse a lot on that ranch," explained Frances. "That was our life."

Tragedy struck that first summer. One day shortly after Earl starting moving the herd up onto Bald Ridge, he rode into what looked like a war zone. Dead cattle lay all over the hillside, more than

Nine-year-old Bob Curtis at a branding in 1965.
(Courtesy Curtis family)

a hundred of them. Larkspur was doing its deadly work.

Larkspur is a wild plant native to the Rocky Mountain region, a member of the buttercup family. In its domesticated form, known as delphinium, it fills flower gardens with gorgeous purple blooms. The story is different on the plains and mountain areas of the Rockies, where it is one of the first plants to provide grazing opportunities in the spring.

The three types of wild larkspur all carry toxic alkaloids, which cause fatal poisoning in cattle. Sheep and horses are rarely affected, and once other forage is available and larkspur reaches maturity in late June, it is no longer a problem.

Bald Ridge has been vital to the ranch ever since Chapman's arrival. Each operation has found its own way to deal with the larkspur problem. Earl had been advised that the danger might be overstated, but the mass death scene was a crushing lesson that the Curtises never forgot. "You had to run the ranch right on account of that poison. We did a lot of spraying to rid the pastures of much of it," said Earl. They ran cows and calves in the area the first two years, then switched to yearlings, who could better handle the poison.

Branding took place in June. "We usually did the gathering in the middle of the night to avoid the heat," recalled Earl. They placed about six hundred animals in a holding pasture. "Then we'd start branding as soon as it was light—about three hundred a day, do that two days, then go gather more on the third. It would take us about two weeks to get them all."

Curtises branded the old-fashioned way, roping and wrestling. "I usually gathered a batch of hungry kids from the night rodeo and had them come out to do the wrestling and we were done in an hour and a half to two hours each day. We didn't want to be wrestling those calves the middle of the day."

Earl's boys, Stan and Bob, were roping calves and dragging

The Curtis cabin was later remodeled by Scott McKinley during the Burrus era.
(Courtesy Curtis family)

them to the branding fire when they were barely big enough to sit a horse. Linda was in charge of the necessary vaccinations, and little Ann carried the Rocky Mountain oysters from calfside to the bucket where they were washed and stored for a barbecue later on.

Frances, who did most of the regular cooking, also provided a meal for each day's branding. "We usually fed forty to fifty people." How could she plan quantities for the fluctuating numbers? "I just cooked and they ate it all regardless of the numbers," she laughed. Earl added, "Those kids were just glad for a good meal."

Curtises chose not to ear tag their cattle during branding, as many operations do. As Earl explained it, "We just didn't need them. Just like no two people look alike, no two cows look alike either. We just knew our cows." Earl had a sense of which calves went with which cows. As far as he was concerned they had as much variation as human families.

Earl had always admired his dad's ability to ride into a herd, move his horse around quietly for about five minutes, then come back out and announce the number of strays. Strays were the animals that wandered into the Curtis herd, perhaps through a broken fence or a gate left open by trespassers. Likewise, their neighbors had to deal with Two Dot strays. Eventually Earl, too, could assess a herd with great accuracy.

"Everything I know I learned from my dad," Earl said.

• •

In 1964 the Curtises added the Daly Ranch, a composite of earlier homesteads also known as the Paint Creek Ranch. Later they would sell off some of the other property, smoothing out the boundaries. Gradually they cut their stock numbers by nearly a thousand in order to take some range out of production, reseeding pastures including much of Chapman Bench. They also burned the abandoned homesteads that could be death traps for animals.

Earl remembers visiting with a young Bureau of Land Management (BLM) employee who advised burning some brush. Earl had to explain that this brush, salt sage, was excellent spring feed, "the highest plant in protein, whether green or brown." Of course the youngster couldn't take him at his word, so he took a sample to the university for analysis. Earl was right.

Charles W. Curtis. (Courtesy Curtis family)

A Biography of Place

Two Dot lodge slung low against the hillside with dark clouds threatening stormy weather.
(Courtesy Yves Burrus)

While reseeding meant reducing stock numbers, Curtises made up for the loss with genetics that yielded higher quality and extra pounds. Eventually the numbers also recovered.

Water development was another key. Spreading cattle out by moving them away from riparian areas was a highly experimental approach then, but one that is certainly valued today. "We developed 150 springs on Bald Ridge," noted Earl. They took some of the kinks out of Pat O'Hara. The BLM built stock reservoirs at Slippery Ann Draw, a tributary of Curtis Draw, and on Bull Draw, a tributary of Little Sand Coulee.

The animals weren't the only thirsty ones. Water-users at headquarters were already rationing their needs because the old well that had provided for so many owners was giving out. "We didn't even have enough water for the Stone House," Earl said.

One day as Earl rode along Pat O'Hara Creek five miles above headquarters, he noticed a spring spilling into the stream. There had to be a way to pipe that flow over to headquarters, he thought.

Earl discussed it with CW. They turned to Skoglund, who brought a planeload of engineers to inspect the site. "Too much friction," the group mumbled, turning a thumbs-down after a short discussion. But their arguments didn't hold water with Earl. When the engineers flew home, he called a local plumber. Another no. Earl didn't believe him either.

Next he discovered that when you're through with all the experts from far away, maybe someone close to home can help. That man was neighbor Paul Stock, owner of Trail Creek Ranch.

Stock's history made him versatile. As a ten-year-old in his hometown of Florence, Colorado, he started his first business hauling Arkansas River driftwood by burro. He roughnecked in his father's Salt Creek oil fields and by 1914 was in business for himself. He moved to Cody to be part of the development of Oregon Basin and the Byron and Garland oil fields. When Earl called,

Stock would draw on his years of experience and innovation.

"I told him about my brainstorm and he came right up, seemed to be fascinated with the idea," Earl said. The men rode the grade from headquarters to the spring. Stock studied the spring entrance, calculated gallons of water per minute. Then he stared down the stream, analyzing every rise, every hill. Little was said as they rode back over the rough terrain where the pipe would be buried. Back at headquarters, Stock, who had been looking pretty serious, gave Earl a big grin and said, "It's doable!" At last Earl had the answer he was searching for.

The project would require larger pipe than anyone had anticipated. As they laid out the path from spring to ranch, Stock recommended air vents spaced along its length. The doubting plumber was brought back to install new lines in all the houses and barnyard facilities. These would bring the purest water, gravity-fed, to all the buildings as well as Skoglund's new lodge.

The day the system was finally in place, the plumber waved a flag from the lodge signaling Earl, down at headquarters, to open the valve. Earl cranked it about halfway. The plumber disappeared into the lodge. Out he came, shouting, "Crank it wide open, wide open!" Earl paused, giving him a chance to change his mind. "I want it wide open," the plumber yelled again. Earl opened the valve.

Back into the house went the plumber. Immediately he returned, this time at a run. "Shut it down! Shut it down!" he shouted. At two hundred pounds of pressure, the solders were bursting, and water was spraying wildly both inside and outside the lodge walls.

The water engineers went back to work. To relieve some of the pressure, they piped excess water back into the creek. That prevented further problems, although Earl admitted that they continued to replace damaged pipes for several years afterward.

Edith Hewitt Curtis.
(Courtesy Curtis family)

Skoglund/Curtis cow camp in 1969 before pack rats
drove them to give up the tent in favor of a cabin.
(Courtesy Curtis family)

Soon the families were taking that water for granted—until the morning in 1966 when they discovered it just wasn't there. That was the morning that Earl discovered a mistake or two the water system architects had made. It would be a learning experience.

• •

Work on Skoglund's lodge had started the very first winter of ownership. The project foreman was a man by the name of Ray— his last name forgotten, his expertise well remembered. Cody Lumber Company cut the trees Ray marked at Camp Creek. Skoglund sent out two log men from Minneapolis. Jack Braten worked with them for two winters; they were joined by two men from Shell, Wyoming, who peeled the logs, and Slim Waggoner, a Cody carpenter.

"All the log work was done by hand—slow, hard work," said Braten. "I was very much interested in the building and learned a lot—you can always learn if you keep your eyes open. They were just meticulous." The crew also laid the floors, drilled and doweled, with hardwood in random lengths and widths of three, five and seven inches. Skoglund had his own people build the fireplace. Braten explained, "Jets would fly supplies and materials in."

The building had been sited on a filled-in draw. While the lodge would settle, Ray had planned for that. All the logs were pinned together, even around windows and doors, so it could shift as a unit. Ray's plan saved the structure.

Finished in 1966, the lodge was rumored to have cost $600,000. Other rumors circulated as well. The 150 foot long structure seemed huge to the locals. Was Skoglund, who also owned the Minnesota Vikings, planning to use it as a summer camp for the team? And that unfinished basement—would that be a bowling alley for the players' recreation?

Skoglund's wife, Margaret, who remained in Minneapolis, missed out on all the gossip. Later she would tell caretakers Mary and Senius Nielsen that she had assumed from her husband's comments that he was building them a little cabin. She pictured a getaway place, maybe with a hot plate to cook on and a good view of the mountains, surrounded by tents filled with her children, John and Carol, and the grandchildren. When Margaret first saw the finished lodge she registered shock, then utter awe at its beauty.

While they did not live on the ranch year-round, the Skoglunds became active in the community. Skog was named to the Buffalo Bill Historical Center board and served several years on the executive board as well. Mary Nielsen remembers parties at the lodge celebrating gallery openings.

Earl Curtis with one of his favorite cowponies—Joe.
(Courtesy Curtis family)

Mary found the Skoglund family a bit "unpredictable." They might call from Denver, announcing their arrival—shortly. Could she have dinner on the table at such and such a time, for whatever number of guests, and could Senius pick them up at the Cody airport? "We had to keep the pantries and freezers full all the time, because you never knew when they might arrive."

··

Having lived all their lives in the West, the Curtises and the Nielsens were all familiar with worries of drought, which always led to concern about wildfires.

Late summer 1963 was dry like tinder. Fires broke out all across the mountains, one lightning strike after another. Martin Nielsen, Mary and Senius's son, was working for the Forest Service that summer. Now atop Pat O'Hara Mountain, Nielsen was part of the crew trying to complete a fire line before the next shift took over. Bill "Blackie" Blake recalled, "We had been sent in to clear a heliport while the rest were trying to fight the fire to no avail because of the treacherous terrain."

Another crewman, John Wyllie, said they had about a hundred yards to go when the wind came up. "The fire camp and command post was located right on top, so the helicopter picked us up on Monument Hill Road and ferried us into the camp. Bombers were dropping slurry on the north face and we were going along hitting the hot spots. We could hear the Forest Service guys on their radios...saying the fire would catch us if we tried to walk back to camp, but we were young and found that pretty hard to believe." Suddenly the fire was upon them. They quickly cleared a circle and lay down side by side, said Wyllie. "The fire burned right up to the circle, then held as the mist from the slurry, let go high above us, gradually settled over us. We were each kept busy watching the back of the guy next to us, picking embers as they exploded off the edge of the fire."

"Even with watchful teammates our clothing still caught on fire," Nielsen added. "We owed our lives to those two slurry bomber pilots who kept us wet down while the fire raged around us."

"That's about as hot as I ever want to be," admitted Wyllie.

When the fire was finally contained, the men headed back to

camp feeling pretty lucky as they picked their way across a shale slide.

"That wasn't the end," said Blake. "There were to my memory about 100 to 150 men trapped on the fire the next day but they, too, were freed, thanks to their teamwork and the aviation crews taking care of us.

"Three years later, it was a different natural disaster. In 1966 spring rains promised serious flooding. Mary Nielsen watched the torrents from the same window where Yves Burrus would study similar flooding more than thirty years later. "It rained for a month," she said. "Threatening though the possibilities were, it was fascinating to watch the sheets of water coming down across the canyon."

Eventually rain and snowmelt merged with a serious thunderstorm, overfilling the earthen dam and destroying the placid little lake Skoglund had created on Pat O'Hara below the lodge. The entire new springfed water system was uncoupled as well.

In retrospect, said Earl, "we should have buried the line from the spring to the headquarters along the road between the two sites rather than following the stream where we even crossed it back and forth several times," Like a basting thread, the pipeline criss-crossed the banks until "the force from all the trash and trees raging down the overflowing creek broke through the lines in several places."

This wasn't the first time the Nielsens had been out of water. Inconvenient, yes, devastating, no. "We grabbed five-gallon cream cans, still commonly available in those days, and placed them strategically at the corners of the eaves outside to catch the rainwater. Fortunately, at least for us, with our houseful of guests, it kept raining," Mary said. "When they were full we placed a cream can in each bathroom so guests could flush. If one can imagine praying that the very rainwater that had just destroyed the water system, fields, and structures keep coming, it seems questionable, but we did."

Soon the flood that had ripped its way through headquarters at about four in the morning, gathering mud, debris, tree trunks—anything it could devour—heaved itself completely out of Pat O'Hara's banks. The violent mass spewed its catch across the lower meadows between headquarters and the highway. Then the flooding mass passed on down the river, wreaking further havoc there.

"Those hay meadows, which ordinarily yielded five tons to the acre, could barely push enough plants through the silt to make a ton and a half that summer," recalled Earl. "That year we bought a lot of hay. Fortunately it was a good year for hay every place else and we went down to the Powell farmers and bought everything they had at a good price."

Back at headquarters, left behind in the ebbing water, a barn had been partially destroyed, but with saddles and tack still in place. When Earl got up that morning to wrangle horses in the dark, he discovered more by sense than sight that the footbridge was gone. He saw the devastation soon enough.

At about ten that morning Earl discovered that his daughter Linda's barrel horse had broken from his corral and attempted to cross the creek to the other horses. Earl found him in what was now Pat O'Hara River, tangled in woven wire and frozen in fear. Earl slipped the loops from both Bob and Stanley's ropes over his shoulders and they held tight as he waded in with his wire-cutters, speaking gently to calm the animal. "The horse seemed to understand that I was there to help and held steady until we could get him clear of the wire. Fortunately when the boys pulled me out and he followed he wasn't even hurt."

But nature's fury was not finished with them yet. Next the flood had raged toward the Horse Ranch, spilled out of its banks, then back in, having gobbled up the newly built horse barn. Finally, with its own weight as a battering ram, the water smashed the bridge over Pat O'Hara there, and nearly destroyed the Sunlight

Creek bridge as well, before its power was spent.

Not yet grasping the devastation, CW knew only that his house had no water that morning; something must be plugged up. He saddled his horse, despite Earl's warning to wait for him, and was off to check the spring. He did not come back.

Earl fretted as he worked, checking the time. Finally he saddled his own horse and headed out to find his dad. CW was fine. In the course of his ride he had begun to understand the damage, and to imagine the work ahead. It was going to be a long summer. The family buckled into the labor of cleaning, repairing, and rebuilding that took them well into fall.

None of the Curtises ever took a gentle rain for granted again. They watched the sky much more apprehensively, and Edith Curtis always rushed to her room to pack a bag when it started to pour.

• •

At about that time Glen E. Nielson, whose ranch was centered in Sunlight, offered Curtises the opportunity to purchase the Paint Creek Ranch property, which would fit nicely with the rest of the operation. Nielson kept the mountain leases, which the partnership did not want, and Curtises added the core ranch to their ever-expanding acres.

While all the Curtis cousins loved the ranch—both the work and the play—Earl's children counted the days every year until summer and moving to cow camp in Pat O'Hara Basin. In the early years they lived in tents all summer. The site had been a homestead, and there were still signs of the pioneers' foundations, corrals, and a partial shed.

Eventually bears became as enthused about the camp's cook-tent meals as the Curtises were. The family brought in a camper to suffice as their summer home after bears clawed through the tents.

Like all Two Dot ranchers, the Curtises have bear stories—and they usually involve a rope. When a story about young Bob and Stan roping a bear came to light, Frances was quick to lay the blame where it belonged. "It was Earl and Wayne Hodson, who worked for the ranch about two years, and who set the example for the boys," she said. In fact Earl remembered his son Bob had yelled at the two men, probably wise enough to realize the danger his dad could be in. It appears the roping was much easier than retrieving the rope for use another day.

"After that, the boys set a goal of roping every wildlife species on the ranch," Frances said. "To ensure that we would believe them they would take a notch from the animal's ear just like we did with domestic animals. It was their intention to show us what they'd roped, but what usually happened was that the specimen was stuffed in a pocket and forgotten as they aimed for the next species on the list." It wasn't until sorting the wash that Frances found proof of the boys' prowess.

"The boys never caught up with an antelope, one of the fastest animals in the world," Earl said. "And they never roped a grizzly, thank goodness, although I know they tried."

In 1970 the Curtises received a shock of a different color. One day as Earl unloaded salt from his pickup high in the mountains, preparing to pack it in to his grazing cattle, Forest Service staffers informed him that he was trespassing on wilderness, and was subject to a fine. Earl knew where the boundary was. But after a discussion, he was informed that the wilderness boundary had been moved without notice to the permittees. He reloaded his salt blocks and moved his cattle.

There were other omens of change in the wind in 1974. Cattle numbers were down. In a *Billings Gazette* article, Pierce Packing blamed "the dwindling supply of livestock in the Billings area" which caused one company to reduce its work force by about fifteen percent. The same article indicated that "only about twenty-five per cent of the capacity of Yellowstone Valley feedlots is now in use."

In the meantime work went on. "I don't know what I would have done without my boys, both summer and winter," Earl said. "And the girls worked right beside me, too." When the boys were in high school, Earl placed one of them on Pat O'Hara for the summer, and the other on Bald Ridge. "People really fussed at me but I saw them most every day and knew they could handle their jobs."

Then it happened. Once again the time came for another Two Dot partnership to dissolve. Each time Two Dot ownership reached this decision it always made economic sense. Yet when the corporation actually placed the ranch on the market in 1975 the emotional blow to the Curtis family was devastating.

The clan watched potential buyers tour the ranch. Even Jim Arness of *Gunsmoke* fame tried the idea on for size, watching Earl and the crew run cattle through the dipping vat, visiting with the kids. But it would be another partnership, Ken Rogge and Bob Hadley, who would take on the Two Dot next.

For CW the sale meant retirement and more involvement with groups such as the Shoshone Bank board of directors. He was also active in the Wyoming Stock Growers Association, American Angus Association, and American National Cattlemen's Association, today known as the National Cattlemen's Beef Association.

For Dick it provided a two-year hiatus at the small place he and his dad purchased, then a long-dreamed of move to Arizona and a continuation of his horse business. His wife Betty and his children, Douglas and Joannie, remain there today.

For Earl Curtis's family it was one thing to own a piece of it, another to try and gather it all up for their own family. Bob and Stan were both newly married and freshly established with their own families on the ranch. They were all eager to bring a new generation up on this historic and wonderful place. Much brainstorming and "what if-ing" went on before they gave up on the idea. Their strongest tie to their predecessors may have been that bond of disappointment felt at leave-taking.

While the Curtises all went their separate ways, Earl's family would return years later to help another newcomer, Mark McCarty, get started as his management firm took over the Two Dot. Stan would spend a great deal of time there and Earl was always available for a ready word of encouragement to the next generation.

A Biography of Place

C H A P T E R   E I G H T E E N

Built to Fit:
A Ranchland Patchwork

Mark McCarty and Randy Pond camping on top of Dry Fork in the summer of 1998.
(Courtesy Yves Burrus)

IN THE EARLY 1960s the Curtis-Skoglund partnership bought the Paint Creek Ranch and the Flying Diamond Ranch, now referred to as the Daly place, in separate transactions. They were all well north of ranch headquarters.

These two properties became the hub of the Two Dot farming operation. Paint Creek is so named for its red color at flood stage, when it picks up soil as it rages. Both had been known earlier as the Jack Higham (pronounced "Hime") place, for the man who homesteaded a 3,420-acre parcel there in the 1930s, then added more as pieces became available. Eventually Higham controlled much of the land north of the Two Dot—facilitated, no doubt, by the fact that his father owned the bank in Belfry.

Higham, who grew up south of Belfry, Montana, hadn't ventured far in his life, distance-wise. But traveling wasn't important to Jack; work was.

Taggart foreman Jud Richmond remembers Higham as a workaholic, made of sinew, gaunt and raw-boned. "He spent his honeymoon on Bald Ridge building fence," Jud said.

Jack and his hired man, "Post Hole Dave" Lindsay, were known for their quirky, heroic labors. Jud recalled another

Harold Davidson checking cattle on their summer pasture.
(Courtesy Harold Davidson)

fence-building episode. Cutting poles, Dave tried to keep up with his boss, but no matter how he sweated, Jack would be six or seven posts ahead of him at the end of the day. Later, while running the tractor-powered post hole digger, Dave got his bib overalls caught in the auger. As the fabric wound around the digger, pulling him tighter and tighter, Dave managed to hold himself away. But in the course of this slow-motion accident his overalls were completely ripped from his body, thus freeing him. He was Post Hole Dave ever after.

Harold Davidson, who hired on with Jack in 1948, found him a difficult boss, his work ethic so extreme he often ran from task to task. (Later, Davidson would turn part of the Higham place into the Paint Creek Ranch.) Davidson acknowledged, "He was a really smart man, had graduated from Montana State University—very capable. He was up to his reputation, I can tell you."

Jack was smart enough to build an electricity-generating water wheel on Paint Creek, the envy of neighbors still using coal oil lamps or light plants, "We were glad to see electricity come when it did," said Verle Richmond, "but Jack was way ahead of us."

The water wheel was to be housed in a small building whose design required a pillar of cement. The men mixed the cement on the site, pouring it by the wheelbarrow load. As the pillar grew, Jack realized they needed a ramp, so he angled some planks up to the pillar. But why stop there? A tractor was backed up to the site. Then Jack fastened a pulley at the ramp's upper end and fed a rope through it. One end he tied to the wheelbarrow, the other to the back of the tractor. Jack positioned himself with a load of wet cement at the base of the ramp. Seated on the tractor, Dave's job was to move forward, *carefully*, when Jack said the word. He got the first part right.

Jack gripped the wheelbarrow handles and yelled for Dave to go. The hired man shoved the tractor into gear and never looked back. Jack blanched at the speed, but had no choice: he followed the barrow up the plank, faster and faster. He had no time to look back, but then neither did Dave, so the tractor driver never saw the barrow rushing to the end of the ramp. When it hit the pulley at the top, Jack, wheelbarrow, and cement all flew into the air from this makeshift catapult, tumbling well over the pillar into Paint Creek below.

Eventually the water wheel was completed to Jack's satisfaction. Each subsequent resident marveled at his inventiveness.

Harold Davidson standing with Norman Dodd
watching Harold's younger brother, 10-year-old Edwin on his horse "Cocky."
(Courtesy Harold Davidson)

• •

Of the early homesteads Jack collected, he eventually sold four to the Daly family, who named the aggregate the Newmeyer Ranch, for the creek flowing through it. The Dalys also had a Forest Service sheep grazing permit for the Flat Iron area on the east side of Dead Indian, south of the Sunlight Road. Mary Helen Daly recalled, "The home ranch started at the forest boundary on the side of Bald Ridge and stretched to the county road, which at that time was called the Pig Trail."

The four homesteads comprising their ranch included Jim and Annie Hogans', who in 1904 had obtained water rights on the enlarged Paint Creek Ditch, and on Hogan Springs, a tributary of Newmeyer Creek. Another homestead had belonged to Fred Manning and included the Paint Creek schoolhouse. The third had a claimant named Shauger, and the fourth was the Brown place.

Mary Helen Daly had about as much history in her bones as any area resident. Born in 1913, Mary, like Janet Blackburn Taggart, was the daughter of a sheriff, Henry Dahlem. She often said of her childhood that she was "born in jail," but the family returned to ranching after her father's second term. Later, in 1925, one of Wyoming's Prohibition-era governors, Nellie Taylor Ross, threw Dahlem's replacement out and asked the ex-sheriff to fill out the unexpired term. Dahlem did, but when he ran for office at the end of that period it was Janet's father, Frank Blackburn, who won the election.

When Mary Helen married Roy Daly, they were to relive much of the region's history, buying a ranch on the Shoshone River below the Corbett Bridge. Their house had been the stage stop at Corbett Crossing in its pre-bridge days. The business developed there was considered the first of its kind in the Big Horn Basin.

The Dalys ran sheep, but by 1940 no more land was available

to lease for their ever-expanding flock. That was when they purchased what they called the Newmeyer Ranch. The family wintered at Corbett, lambing and shearing there before trailing the flock out for the summer. They skirted the east side of Heart Mountain, said Mary Helen, "to the Clark shearing pens located on the north side of the mountain, then down across Chapman Bench to the Clarks Fork River Bridge near the mouth of Pat O'Hara Creek.

"Then we followed the county road to Paint Creek and Newmeyer." Each fall the sheep were returned to the Cody depot stockyards after making an almost full circle of Heart Mountain. "There the lambs and cull ewes were cut out and sold, with the best ewe lambs kept for replacement ewes."

When much of Heart Mountain was opened for homesteading to World War II veterans, the Dalys could no longer drive their sheep through the area. So in 1948 they moved to their Newmeyer Ranch year-round.

In the winter of 1960 the Dalys added the adjacent Bosley Ranch, also on Paint Creek. Felix and Bessie Bosley Hoff had taken the property over from Bessie's parents, Alvin and Emma Bosley, area residents since 1917.

Thus the Daly properties encompass a sort of a "Who's Who" of area homesteaders. The Dalys then made the Hoff property their headquarters until 1964 when they sold to the Skoglund-Curtis partnership.

•   •

Higham continued to operate the rest of the land he'd laid claim to through the 1940s, following a practice established by the Homestead Act of 1862. The original law granted a tract of public domain land, no more than 160 acres, to any citizen—or documented would-be citizen—who was either the head of a family, twenty-one years old, or a veteran of fourteen days' active U.S. military service. Then they were required to "prove up" on the land, developing their homestead for five years.

In 1909, Congress enacted the Enlarged Homestead Act, which doubled the size of an initial grant to a half section, or 320 acres. The prove-up time was lowered to three years. Finally, in 1916, Congress passed the Stock Homestead Act, which granted a full section, 640 acres, in marginal areas suitable only for grazing.

Higham continued to gather these homesteads, one of which was the Gordon A. Kneisely place. It boasted the "Natural Corral," considered one of the most beautiful spots in the world by a later Two Dot owner, Yves Burrus. This keyhole-shaped, two hundred foot high canyon has a natural spring whose water, visitors say, is as blue as the Caribbean, and the fishing is great. There are only three narrow passages in and out: when you fence the three you have a tightly enclosed, though broad, meadow.

Shoshone Indians had used it as a buffalo jump. When they spotted buffalo on the hill, they chased them toward the corral, then over the edge. Again, according to one oldtimer, they descended into the corral to process the dead and dying buffalo, using every speck of the meat, fur, hide, and horn. Nothing was wasted.

While most of the Natural Corral is now owned by the Barrows family, it has been leased to homesteaders since early times. One of the first to use it was Gordon Kneisely.

Kneisely was a bachelor who rode into the country with two other men in the 1880s, bringing a large horse herd which he would later run in the Natural Corral. He also had dogs; Sunlight homesteader Norman Dodd told Davidson they were the best cattle dogs he had ever seen.

Kneisely worked alone. Dodd remembered him driving three hundred head of cattle to the top of Bald Ridge with only his dogs. Then he sent the dogs ahead with the herd down Dead Indian, while

Davidson cattle turned up the moutain toward summer pasture.
(Courtesy Harold Davidson)

he went back for pack horses and food. Dodd saw this demonstration more than once. Later when Kneisely caught up, the cattle were always bunched just as he'd left them, not a one wandered away. How did the man do it all by himself with no cowboys to help? That was remarkable enough, let alone turning the herd over to a couple of canines.

Several homesteaders applied for water rights during that time—Kneisely for Paint Creek tributaries under the name of Kneisely Pipe Line. Two different Schultzes were listed as appropriating water from area creeks as well. The Schultzes built their water line with a wooden pipe, laying it quite a distance from the creek to the homestead buildings.

While Harold Davidson was learning his ranching lessons in Wyoming—the outside of the cow— his father would bring his interior cattle experiences—meat cutting from the Midwest.
(Courtesy Harold Davidson)

The fourth homestead added to the ranch had been proved up by Milton Gorsuch. Then there was the fifth, Red Gulch Pete, who claimed 320 acres above the Schultzes where the creek exits the Natural Corral. He was a colorful character, better known for his moonshine making than for his agricultural endeavors. Those connoisseurs of liquor beat a proverbial path to his door, remote as it was.

Homesteaders believed in gardens and fruit-bearing bushes and trees. Frances Curtis and her family enjoyed picking apples and other fruits saying, "They sure made great pies and sauces." Earl Curtis recently learned that a current Two Dot cowboy, Randy Pond, had rediscovered a special crabapple tree that was a Curtis favorite. "Crabs are supposed to be bitter but this one was so sweet," Frances said. But when Randy rode up ready to do some picking, his horse kept shying away. Finally he took a serious look and discovered the pickers on the opposite side—a grizzly bear and her cubs were stuffing themselves with the delicious fruit. He rode away empty-handed.

Randy was another cowboy following the same trails his dad had—a second-generation Two Dot cowboy, "His dad worked for me," Earl explained.

The land surrounding the homesteads—several thousand acres—was owned by the Bureau of Land Management. There was also dry land school section number 16. It was without access to irrigation water. It became part of the Paint Creek Ranch permit when Harold Davidson and his father Earl joined forces, coming out of Ohio in 1949, to buy Higham's second place.

"Ungulate fever, a disease contracted from cows, was catching up with Jack," Davidson explained. "He needed to get someplace where he didn't have to work so hard and could rest when the bouts of fever came on, which they seemed to be doing more and more often."

After selling the ranch to the Davidsons, Higham moved to

Montana where he bought a little dry land farm. "He found one where he didn't have to irrigate or put up hay but still died a young man, in his early fifties," said Harold.

The Davidsons were tackling something new for all of them, except for Harold's one year of experience with Higham. "Dad had been a high school math teacher for seventeen years, but was also an experienced butcher and had sold meat retail. Now we'd learn how to grow it, that was the only part he didn't know," he remembered. "Dad was one of those jack-of-all-trades that really was quickly an expert at anything new.

"We were really blessed at our place," he went on. "Our headquarters were a mile above the county road and we always got twice the moisture that was received down country. Moisture-laden clouds come in from the northeast and pile up at a right angle against Heart Mountain, Pat O'Hara, and Monument Hill. No way to go around the mountains most of the time so Cody gets less moisture. At the same time the ranch has good winter range because the west winds quickly clear the snow in one to three days."

In 1960 Davidsons sold to another Earl—McConnell—who retained the ranch for three to four years. Jud Richmond remembers McConnell as a big stout scrapper best known in the neighborhood for his fisticuffs.

He, in turn, sold to Glen Nielson, who was after the high mountain deeded lands. Nielson split off the headquarters and farming land. This core would expand the Curtis-Skoglund Two Dot both in pasture—bringing the total operation to 250,000 acres—as well as in farm land to make them even more independent.

Even today trails leading to the homesteads create a spiderweb of tracks all over the Two Dot. Earl Curtis remembers finding several lonely graves, some marked with names, others without—reminders of hard work, big dreams, and sometimes goals unclaimed.

PART FIVE

A TWIST IN THE WIND

CHAPTER NINETEEN
The Pivotal Short-Timers: Rogge and Hadley

The gateway to the Two Dot Lodge.

It was Robert Hadley who dreamed of ranching the Two Dot, but Kenneth Rogge, a lumberman headquartered in Oregon, who signed on the deeded line in 1975. There in Wallowa, Oregon, rancher Hadley had leased land to Rogge on which he built a lumber mill, according to Rogge's daughter. Now Rogge had his eye on the rest of Hadley's timber-rich property. Hadley didn't want to sell his ranch—he wanted to trade. But first Rogge had to find something to trade with.

Ken Rogge was a high-energy, hard-working, astute businessman with lumber in his genes. His father had owned mill operations in Michigan and Wisconsin. He was a man of vision whose belief in taking advantage of every opportunity paralleled Hadley's way of thinking.

When Rogge attempted to join the service during World War II, he was declared 4-F due to a severe hearing impediment he had had all his life. Being aware of his background, the government implored him, in lieu of active duty, to expand a mill operation in Sitka, Alaska. He accepted the challenge.

After the war Rogge looked around for ideal opportunities and in 1952 chose Bandon, a small town on the Oregon coast, for the

Ken Rogge stands before his business sign, Rogge Lumber Inc.
(Courtesy Barbara Faulkner)

headquarters of his own lumber operation. His business interests eventually spread his mills across the state as Rogge Lumber, Inc.

In 1974 he turned to the far corner of his state as the optimum location for his next mill. That's when he met Hadley. When completed, the facility overlooked prime timber country—Hadley's.

The first step in the complicated ranch swap brought Bob and Mary Hadley and their seven children to Wyoming to manage the Two Dot Ranch for the new owner. Rogge was listed as the purchaser. Few knew of his plans to trade for the Hadleys' Oregon ranch later. He and his family never resided on the Two Dot during almost two years of ownership.

Rogge's daughter, Barbara Faulkner, who was a partner in her father's business for years, recalled that both her parents were fascinated with the Two Dot. "I know that Dad made several trips to the ranch during the time he owned it," she said. "Mom, who appreciated wonderful things, loved to describe the lodge, how beautiful it was, the setting—she even talked about the dishes, how they carried the Two Dot brand."

The Hadleys, although truly short-timers, found the Two Dot an exceptional ranch—and they had owned and managed several, in California, Nevada, and Oregon. Wyoming grabbed hold of each member of the family as they rode the Pat O'Hara, the Polecat and Bald Ridge.

While Rogge was purchasing the ranch, Hadley bought the cattle. "We ran yearlings on the Forest Service and Pat O'Hara Mountain, as well as the traditional cow-calf operation," Bob Hadley explained. They purchased about seventeen hundred head of "excellent breeding stock" from the Curtis family—outstanding cattlemen, according to Hadley.

He found the Two Dot to be an environment that had answers to any problem that developed. "As I remember, cattle prices weren't all that good while we were there, but we were still able to make some money." The first thing Hadley found out about the operation was that twelve months of grass were potentially available with no gap in the feed supply. "The winter range on Polecat Bench is very economical."

The one problem that did have to be faced every spring, as Earl Curtis, too, had discovered, was the giant larkspur on Bald Ridge. Chemical spray programs were expensive, so Hadley found the best bet was to let it dry and mature, then bring the cattle in. Like his predecessors, he learned that lesson the hard way, losing more cattle in one day than someone inexperienced with larkspur could imagine possible.

Bob Hadley did the farming while his children ran the cows. "We ran the yearlings on the Forest Service permit and on Pat O'Hara, too, starting in the foothills early in the spring." The ranch simply had no drawbacks except for the larkspur. "In fact," he said, "As I think about it, the Two Dot might have been the best ranch we've ever been on!"

But the final trade deal never materialized, and the curious continue to speculate on the reasons. Circumstances had changed for Rogge. First, environmentalists' efforts to save the spotted owl's old-growth habitat in the Northwest were making times difficult for anyone in the lumber business. Then there was also talk of economic concerns as Japan attempted to import cheap lumber. Here Rogge strode a faultline that began to gape as he watched nearly helpless as a prosperous industry dramatically downsized.

"Certainly the spotted owl was a factor," acknowledged Barbara Rogge Faulkner. "It will always be remembered as the bird chosen to save, but in truth the owl was only a figurehead to implement an environmental 'plan.'"

At the same time, an insect infestation was damaging timber. "And yes, there was a downturn in the market which further complicated the situation which we found financially draining," Barbara explained. "It was also when the industry was drifting from small independent companies like ours to large corporate giants."

Barbara joined her parents on their final journey to Cody. They savored a day at the ranch before they sat down with the lawyers and signed the papers that turned the operation over to the new owners. Then they flew home. "I still think of the Two Dot whenever a ranch is mentioned. That's the only definition of ranch I know."

And who were those new owners? The autumn before, the Hadley family had first introduced Yves Burrus to the Two Dot. "I liked them very much and in fact met them again after they returned to Wyoming later," Burrus said.

The Hadleys stayed long enough to complete the logistics, then returned to their Oregon operation. Even as they turned onto the road to Wallowa, Mary and Bob knew they were somehow hooked on Wyoming and the state would draw them back.

Eventually they returned to Cody, purchasing a smaller spread on the South Fork of the Shoshone River. When their children were grown and anxious to get into the business themselves, Hadley found a rich grass operation, the SY Ranch, in northeastern Wyoming near Sundance.

As for Rogge, he continued to represent the timber business during a decade that shook the industry to its roots. "Dad was so knowledgeable, he knew every facet of the industry and people trusted that if he made a promise he would make every effort to see that it happened," said Barbara.

Sadly, their timing with the Two Dot was unfortunate for the dreams of both men. In hindsight the Rogge-Hadley ownership provided the first signal that a new era was dawning at the ranch. The delicate balance of economics and environmental concerns would set new stewardship standards for a ranch that up to this time found weather and livestock prices the biggest challenges to its success.

PART SIX

The Environmental Era

A Biography of Place

CHAPTER TWENTY

An Environmental Revolution:
The Yves Burrus Years

*One of the cowboys holds horses while the rest gather cattle
off the road during blizzard conditions.*
(Jim Bama photo)

When Swiss investment banker and outdoorsman Yves Burrus first met investment manager Al Parker in Geneva, neither had heard of the Two Dot Ranch. But Burrus was interested in hard U.S. assets: "We were looking for an investment, not so much to make money, but to protect what we had. At that time, 1976, Russian tanks were still moving around Berlin, communists were a strong political force from Italy to Finland, and European families, having not forgotten World War II, were looking—just in case—for a safe place far away."

Later Parker toured the Two Dot, then up for sale by Ken Rogge. He still had no buyer in mind, yet the ranch intrigued him. While most ranches are a loose mosaic of properties, the Two Dot is a contiguous landmass. In John Chapman's time you could ride all day without crossing a property line—and the same is true today.

Parker measured a ranch with four investment criteria. It needed to be located in a "magnet" area with active air traffic. Cody, similar to Santa Fe or Jackson at the time, fit that description. Second, it needed to be a large operation priced as a working ranch, not as development property. By this time the Two Dot consisted of fifty-three thousand deeded acres along with two hundred thousand

*Al Parker, who introduced Yves Burrus to the Two Dot Ranch,
entertaining Yves Burrus's wife Marie Paule
and daughter Geraldine at the lodge piano.*
(Courtesy Yves Burrus)

in United States Forest Service, Bureau of Land Management, and Wyoming state leases.

Third, it had to produce income. Parker rated that potential as excellent. The water rights allowed Pat O'Hara, Paint, and Blaine Creeks to feed a thousand acres of irrigated farm lands, alfalfa, and meadows. Cattle wintered on Polecat Bench, where forage sufficed for an average cold season, thanks to its soil—it is the Big Horn Basin's only original sea-bed soil dating from an ancient ocean.

The fourth factor was natural beauty. Parker found the Two Dot breathtaking even by his high standards. Pat O'Hara Mountain, the high country, the creeks; all offered recreational opportunities. Deer, antelope, and a few moose wandered the ranch—so did a herd of two hundred elk, a species that would grow in numbers over the years and become the focal point for the new owners.

Most of all, Parker could feel the spirit of the place. "I've found that some properties breathe and others don't. The Two Dot Ranch is one that breathes."

When Yves Burrus arrived for a look, a winter storm prevented the aerial view that he would find so spectacular later. After a tour with Parker, he remembered, "They didn't tell us much about ranching and the cattle business in Wyoming but the projections showed nice returns on invested capital. Al Parker offered to manage the estate for the first two years so we said yes...the beauty of the place, the cowboy country, the adventure, plus the expected return—we agreed to purchase the Two Dot."

"I think in the beginning Yves bought the ranch for the investment more than anything, but a few trips later it would become the quality of life that he found himself wanting to be a part of," Parker said.

Burrus acknowledged, "For the first two years we came as tourists. What a beautiful country, what a scenic ranch! The summer we crossed the Atlantic with the whole family and discovered the

Yves Burrus with the mares 1992.
(Courtesy Yves Burrus)

rancher's life complete with real cowboys was unbelievable to us.

"We went all around, branding, moving cattle, breaking young horses and for sure walking and riding over the 150,000 acres. We slept in the cow camp with cattle all around and bears not too far away. We swam in icy cold lakes and enjoyed the summer evenings with coyotes barking. The children learned to eat marshmallows burned on the open fire, a new delicacy for them. We learned about deer, the tracks made, the songs of the birds and the hundreds of Wyoming flowers."

While Yves and his family celebrated this new way of life,

Scott McKinley helps his son, Brett, get ready to move cattle with his pony.
(Jim Bama photo)

Parker was hunting for a trustworthy ranch manager, and he found one in Texas: Ryan St. Clair. "I have three criteria for any manager's position and Ryan fit all three. He knew both farming and ranching, could manage people, and he was honest."

Parker and Burrus then made a decision to buy the resident cow herd. Ryan got his first taste of cattle ranching Wyoming style when Parker sent him to count the mother cows that autumn as they came off the mountain. He learned that Two Dot cattle follow an

A Biography of Place

A Two Dot cowboy nursing a broken foot leans against the horse barn wall.
(Jim Bama photo)

annual clockwise migratory cycle. As Spike Voyle described it, it starts in early spring at the calving fields, with first-calf heifers watched more closely at horse ranch headquarters. After the calves are branded in April, the cow-calf pairs are moved in May to Chapman Bench, where soon they are bawling at the gates for their next move to the Hill Pasture. In July they cross the Chief Joseph Highway into the Skull Creek pasture. They follow the green forage crawling up the mountain as they enter Pat O'Hara Basin, grazing their way through Ox Yoke, then Beef Trap; their natural instinct triggered by signs of autumn flurries, and a bit of cowboy nudging, points them back down to the shipping area west of headquarters. There the calves are weaned and shipped. Then two thousand cows are turned towards Polecat Bench, their home from November to February, when cowboys will start them toward the calving pastures once again.

"This was new country for us," explained Ryan's wife Teddie, "But we got lots of help from the cowboys and made up our minds to learn fast." Help came from cowhand Scott McKinley and his family at the Lower Two Dot (still called the Horse Ranch at the time), Jim and Annie Laverdure (Rogge-Hadley holdovers who stayed on at Paint Creek), and Spike Voyle, who brought his family to the ranch in 1979.

As Yves Burrus put it, "Ryan was the boss from Texas, Scott the one for the pictures and Spike, well, Spike was the mechanic who was able to repair machinery, yet could climb aboard a horse when needed."

The Laverdures, too, were essential, providing the glue for a smooth transition through Jim, still vigorous in his late sixties. His wife was known as "Paint Creek Annie":—no stranger had better wander around without permission and an explanation. Their children, including Kay and Tammi, also worked as ranch hands.

Scott McKinley, too, brought continuity to the Two Dot; he had cowboyed for both the Curtises and the Hadleys. Scott was very

Jim Laverdure, one of the Two Dot cowboys.

much taken with the Old West, and the remoteness of the Two Dot let him imagine himself there. He loved to ride across the vast land, show up at a neighbor's door miles away for a cup of coffee, listen to old-timers' stories, and offer help whenever needed.

Artist Jim Bama, who celebrates his own love of the earlier times in his paintings, became a good friend. He found in Scott the perfect cowboy model. "He was tall, better-looking than Kenny Rogers or Kris Kristofferson, but of that type." Meanwhile Scott was introducing the artist to the realities of ranching. Each loved the other's way of life.

In 1985 they both attended the opening of Jim's one-man exhibit at a gallery in New York City. "There was the painting of Scott in the exhibit, and there was Scott in his western gear, his hat— he was the hit of the show," Jim explained.

Bama's finest Two Dot hour came in a two day, ranch spanning cattle drive from Paint Creek to Trail Creek. "There was so much snow that it came belly up on the cows and the calves struggled in their mothers' tracks. There were about six hundred in the drive. At one point about fifty panicked and ended up on the Billings highway, then headed back across Monument Hill. They were tough to catch," he recalled. "Then when they got to their destination it still wasn't over—the cowboys got drifted in at Trail Creek. This was a

Ryan St. Clair, earlier ranch foreman, moves quietly uphill
towards two of the ranch mares, halter tucked out of sight behind him.
(Courtesy Yves Burrus)

According to Clarke Straight there was the sense of "wreck" in the air that morning as they realized there was too much snow and they'd have to ride from headquarters to pick up the cows and head for Trail Creek. When Straight got off his horse to open the gate, Smokey shied and took off down the gully breaking trail with every lurch.

It was before the new road had replaced the old and the cattle crossed the fence-line up onto the highway despite the best efforts of the cowboys who included upper left, Scott McKinley, upper right, Monte Huff, a cowboy out of Montana, and Kent Shroyer, who'd dismounted with his dogs. Eventually the cowboys were able to get the cattle turned and headed south. (Jim Bama photo) once-in-a-lifetime drive for me; they were the best models. They were real, and the weather was real, and so was the struggle to complete the job."

Todd Churchill, too, remembered drives so cold that "you had to dismount and walk to keep the circulation going...so cold you wanted to whine like a little pup," he laughed.

"That first spring and the following winter was a bugger," Teddie St. Clair chuckled. "It was the worst in ten years, according to the old timers. We fumbled through it, but having been raised in the desert and panhandle of Texas we were ill-equipped, except for the fact we had really good people more than willing to help us."

The next winter, 1978-1979, was the worst in twenty-five years, said those same old-timers. The crew calved in blizzards and if

Monte Huff attemps to turn back one of the strays still lingering in Cottonwood Creek Draw where the road starts up Monument Hill.
(Jim Bama photo)

Yves Burrus with the crew. (left to right) Larry Dodge, Rocky (last name unkown),
Scott McKinley, unknown, Yves Burrus, Mick McCarty, Jim Laverdure,
Paul Burling, Miles Dixon, Ryan St. Clair, and Keith Voyles.
(Courtesy Keith Voyles)

the snow stopped, the temperatures dropped to the point where calving became tragic.

Snowstorm intensified into blizzard; winds blew such huge rolling drifts that it always seemed to be snowing. "The snow crusted over and the animals couldn't dig through to reach any feed," Teddie explained. "If they tried to move across the drifts, they broke through the crust."

That was the year Travis Bullard, a Texas cowboy just out of high school, came to the north country. Others told him the winter

Branding with Jim Amsbury at the iron and Kent Shroyer on the right.
(Courtesy Keith Voyles)

winds on Polecat Bench always exposed forage for the cattle, but it just didn't happen that year, he said.

It was also the year the Cody Country Snowmobile Association saved the Two Dot herd—twice. But club member Stan Biesmeier recalled that first, the Two Dot crew had helped them in a tough situation of their own.

The snowmobilers were returning from their Christmas party at Cooke City, Montana, when the snow started, explained Bob Florida. "By the time we got about halfway down Bald Ridge in our vehicles the snow was drifting so high we simply couldn't move forward...we were going to spend the night on the mountainside.

After gathering up his horse, Clarke Straight plows through the snow to clear the draw and get around the cattle, moving them back on what should have been a trail. "The wind had caused avalanches across the trail in several places so it was easy for the cattle to lose their way. We seemed to be pushing them that morning more than we should, maybe it had something to do with being so cold."
(Jim Bama photo)

We were pretty well prepared with full tanks of gas and food. A couple of the guys decided to ride their snowmobiles onto the Two Dot to use the phone to call down to Cody to let everyone know where we were." When the crew at headquarters offered to plow the group out with the Caterpillar, they accepted. Off they went, with sixty-mile-an-hour winds filling in the road behind them. When they reached the stranded sportsmen, they lined up their vehicles behind the Cat, which plowed its way back down bite by bite.

"We of course told the cowboys if they ever needed our help, just come get us and that's just what they did," Stan explained. "One of them showed up at our very next meeting asking if we could help drive some cattle out of the area of the Powell Cutoff. We did so well there that they came later after the next blizzard...thirty-five head were holed up in the breaks on Polecat Bench. The ranch horses were all worn out and they needed help getting the cows home."

• •

Later that spring, Al Parker gave up his management lease on the ranch and Yves Burrus took over.

Burrus recalls Parker's decision. "In fact conditions were so harsh, the price of cattle so low, they never made the yield they had promised," he said. So now Yves Burrus would be "in charge of fifteen hundred mother cows, fifty-some horses, a bunch of yearlings and, for sure, the five cowboy families who came with them, as well as all the wildlife," he explained.

"Next to the stock market, which was our business, we now tried to understand the cattle market in order to be as smart as Willard Wilson, our friend, master of the western cattle business," Yves explained. Wilson was a respected Thermopolis-area cattleman himself as well as a cattle broker, one of Burrus' many mentors.

Now the St. Clairs reconsidered the herd's genetics. Teddie

With the sky clearing, Scott McKinley holds as the cattle move on by,
finally seeming to know their way.
(Jim Bama photo)

said, "These were the old-style Black Angus and we started immediately to streamline them through selection of the best Black Angus bulls we could find, doing the same with a number of Hereford bulls we needed for terminal crosses."

"We moved to maternal bloodlines to get the milk that would give us the weaning weights we were looking for...In no time at all, the order buyers were coming." That was when they got acquainted with Willard Wilson.

Wilson buys from producers across the Rocky Mountains and

Branding at Horse Ranch spring of 1998. In chaps, Mark McCarty, ranch manager. Branding, Todd Churchill and Jim Oudin. Vaccinations, Janice Churchill, Darlene McCarty. Castrator Dough Pierce. Others include Dee Oudin, John Severide (Horseback) and George and Randy Krier hold the calf being branded.

sells into Nebraska, Iowa, Colorado, and Kansas, generating a million dollars' worth of business a week during the peak fall months. He'd been buying Two Dot cattle for at least a quarter of a century. He and Burrus became friends, and even got together once in Switzerland.

The next step was to bring in massive paternal bulls like the Leonhardts bred at nearby Cowley; the American Breeders Service was distributing that breed's semen worldwide. Besides raising bulls for their own use, the Two Dot started selling some as well.

While St. Clairs were used to running cattle on a tight budget, Yves Burrus objected when the stock seemed ill-prepared for winter in his first few years in charge. Regardless of the cost, protein blocks were to be delivered daily to ensure the health and comfort of the animals. The issue of poor condition never arose again.

Earlier owners had fed out the ranch calves on site. St. Clairs weren't satisfied with the setup for carrying weanlings over the winter so the calves were shipped to a feedlot, then brought back home in the spring, turning them out on pasture as yearlings throughout the next summer.

Spike Voyle said that when he first came to the ranch in 1979, you claimed your horses and they were yours for the duration. "If we didn't ride 'em, no one did, but that's no longer true."

By the early 1980s St. Clairs were raising pinto horses, using twelve to sixteen mares. "Our cowboys broke the colts, then trained them during their work with the cattle."

Ranching is a team sport. Monte Jackson, resident manager of the Trail Creek Ranch for sixteen years, recalled good relations with St. Clair. "We were always spilling cattle in with each other...We shared a twenty-five to thirty-mile fenceline," Jackson said. "We had an unspoken agreement that we'd take care of each other when physically possible." By the mid-1980s Burrus had seen both good and not-so-good years. "We soon learned we could not reach the return expected, if any, and started more and more to see the Two Dot, not only as a cattle ranch, but as one of these places where you have to find an equilibrium between nature and man's will," he said. His friend Wilson explained what he had observed during this period. "Not only was Yves interested in becoming a top cattle rancher, his efforts included improvements in every facet of stewardship of the land, producing grass from a sunshine factory and caring for every blade."

Yves went on, "Yes, we had to raise cattle to pay the costs and made improvements accordingly, but at the same time...we became more and more concerned with deer, wapiti, bears, moose, even the marmots—all the living creatures. We came to understand that we were the stewards of all that as well as taking care of the streams, forests, and lakes."

• •

It was about this time that Ray and Lucille Krier were hired as lodge caretakers. They also cooked meals not only for Burrus and his guests, but for ranch events such as brandings. Ray recalls a varied crowd around the dinner table during the 1980s—well-known locals plate to plate with ranch cowboys and foreign visitors.

One of those cowboys was Clarke Straight, who joined the crew in 1982. Raised on a Hyattville ranch across the Big Horn Basin, he, too, defined the word "cowboy" in artist Jim Bama's eyes. As for Clarke, "I don't think there's a better ranch than the Two Dot in the state of Wyoming." He and his wife, Connie, would stay for six years.

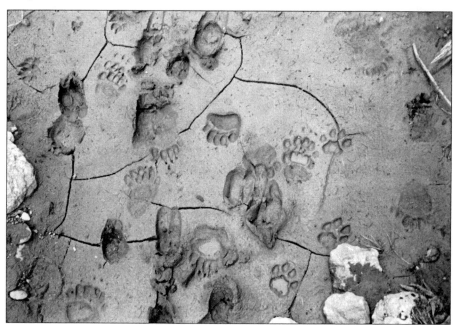

A cross section of footprints in the mud tells a story of the many species crossing paths on the Two Dot.
(Courtesy Jim Oudin)

Two Dot mares running in Beef Trap.
(Courtesy Wilderness Images by Carla Zerkie Wawak)

Another crisis struck in 1984—this one too big for horsepower. "A surprise fall storm hit us September 13 that year," said Teddie. "Forty-two inches of snow in about thirty hours in the high country—thirty-two inches at headquarters. It was a wreck! We still had cattle out on Pat O'Hara Mountain.

"We had to try to get the cattle headed our way, but there were no trails and no way to get them moving," she explained. "We took the horses and tried to pack a trail. First one cowboy would plow ahead, then the next. We were going forward inch by inch when there were miles to go . . . the horses were working so hard that they overheated and of course we ended up with sick animals.

"Finally, the same Mother Nature that had created havoc stepped in to save the cattle. Hunger started driving the elk herds

Two Dot cowboy and farm operator, Todd Churchill.

down off the mountain, just the way we wanted the cattle to go. They created the trails for the cows to follow."

With most of the herd down, Ryan rented a plane and flew Pat O'Hara, Ox Yoke, and Sunlight Basins looking for strays. Only when the last of those were back home did the Two Dot crew finally relax.

For Ray Krier the next September 13 was also significant. Krier doesn't know what took him to the window, at about five-thirty that evening, but "it was something to see," he said. "Three to four hundred elk were emerging from the trees, headed for

Yves Burrus children, Paul and Geraldine, explore the expanse of range on the Two Dot.

the alfalfa meadows, and there they stayed. Amazingly, they were there again on the same date the next year. I've been gone from the Two Dot for a long time now but I still wake up on September 13 every year breathing a little faster and with an excitement that it takes me a little while to explain. It's those elk. Will they be on time again this year?"

When the Kriers left, Mary Louis Wood joined the Two Dot crew. A Powell native, she lived in Laramie and returned several times a year to take care of Burrus and his guests.

"For twelve years Mary Lou was the soul of the lodge," said

Shipping cattle at Two Dot with Pat O'Hara in the background.
(Courtesy Darlene McCarty)

When a buck was shot while fighting with another buck,
though he fell, the battle continued.
(Courtesy Yves Burrus)

Burrus. "Preparing everything for our arrival, cooking hearty meals for hungry hunters, learning European recipes from our guests. She was always smiling, from the earliest hunters' breakfast to late-night dancing. She heard more hunting stories than anyone on the ranch." In turn, Mary Lou described Burrus as the quintessential refined European, one who definitely is used to the best, but can rough it up when he chooses.

While Mary Lou came and went according to Burrus' itinerary, others were drawn back through their fascination with the ranch.

Jim Oudin heads out across the Two Dot to check on wildlife.
(Courtesy Dee Oudin)

Elk calves on Pat O'Hara.
(Courtesy Yves Burrus)

Travis Bullard was on his second stint at the Two Dot the year the cowboys discovered a young, motherless black bear down in the meadows. The bear stayed around, and the guys got a kick out of watching the little orphan.

Then one day they heard shots, and soon a vehicle pulled into headquarters. Did they realize there was a bear between the highway and headquarters? The driver had shot at it but missed. The cowboys did as cowboys will do, they listened, pondered, and pretty much failed to answer. The vehicle took off.

"We decided that someone needed to get that bear out of the field before a better shot took care of him," Travis said. "There were three of us saddled our horses—Rod Eppling, Dave Hellyer, and me. We figured on roping him, putting him in a horse trailer and calling the Wyoming Game and Fish to come pick him up."

Well, even the first step in their plan failed; their ropes got caught in the high alfalfa. Determined, they threw ideas out. Aha,

Elk cows on Pat O'Hara. (Courtesy Yves Burrus)

they'd bulldog him. One of the riders would fling himself from a running mount just like in the rodeo, and throw the animal to the ground. How hard could it be?

"It took all three of us wrestling that bear, and even then he left us pretty well beat and battered by the time we finally had him in the horse trailer—with him still looking pretty good and us guys wiser and pretty bloody. Of course we went and got all the ranch kids

Turkeys graze like Black Angus cattle across Two Dot range after a planting project that Yves Burrus undertook to replace those that disappeared after the fifties.
(Courtesy Yves Burrus)

Trophy hunt.
(Courtesy Yves Burrus)

so they could see a bear up close," Travis added.

"When the Game and Fish specialist finally got there the guy just wasn't so easy on us. We pointed to the horse trailer, he pointed to his bear cage on a trailer behind his pickup. Then he pointed at us. 'You fellas were the ones that got him into the trailer, you're gonna be the ones who put him into the cage.'"

Whatever parts of their bodies weren't already bruised from the earlier tussle were now pounded by the final transfer to the cage.

"The Game and Fish people took him up to one of the canyons, threw scraps down for him regularly until winter set in. He was doing fine. In fact the last I heard he'd gone into hibernation somewhere up in there and by the next spring was gone."

Paul Burrus, son of Yves, and Mark McCarty, Two Dot foreman,
with the trophy elk Paul downed during a late fall hunt.
(Courtesy Yves Burrus)

• •

In early 1986 Ryan St. Clair, while not ready to admit it, had health problems. Norm Heath and his wife, Cindy, moved to the horse ranch during that period, becoming an integral part of the operation.

Two years later Todd and Janice Churchill came to the Two Dot to buy a horse; they would stay for ten years. As Ryan drove them to take a look at the animal—which they didn't buy—they passed a swather standing in a hayfield. Ryan complained of his need for someone to run it and Todd, a Powell farm boy, said he'd do it.

Todd and Janice hoped to hire on as a team, but St. Clair promised only Todd a seasonal job first. He then suggested Janice might help the other wives with the cooking. She turned the tables and offered to work a month as a cowhand for free; then Ryan could decide what she was worth. She was on the payroll making a man's wages in two weeks. "I learned later I wasn't the first female cowboy Ryan hired but I loved being one of them," Janice said. "Branding and shipping were always a lot of fun and we had some great crews and good times."

"We gathered the Beef Trap once, which is a reasonably small pasture, when the fog was so thick you couldn't see past the ears of your horse. You just worked by sound, keeping the bawling cattle in front of you...You could hear cowboys riding back and forth trying to figure out where they were. It was pretty comical. Admittedly it took us a little longer than usual, but when the fog lifted we had all the cattle at the pens."

One day they were gathering cows in Pat O'Hara Basin when Norm Heath, pointing up to the ridge, indicated Janice had missed a cow and calf. "I told him I didn't think so but sure enough, there were two black spots. I headed back up to check. The trail was steep and rocky so it took me quite awhile until I got in sight of this 'pair.'

It was a black bear sow and cub. I looked back down at Norm and he was still waving me on... So I rode into the bears and got them to run off a little. It was then that Norm figured out what they were and when I got back down to the bottom we both laughed."

The Churchills settled at the River Ranch, where Hemingway had also spent a summer. Todd, too, learned to keep his fly rod handy and Janice was always hard-pressed to provide a mealtime invitation that could surpass the call of the Clarks Fork and the flash of its trout.

The River Ranch's microclimate was remarkable, often twenty degrees warmer than at headquarters. "The main ranch might be reporting a foot of snow and we'd have maybe an inch," Todd said. And the mountainscape to the west—where the Clarks Fork knits the Beartooths to the Absarokas in a treacherous canyon that only Chief Joseph knew well enough to traverse safely—that view could stop them at the window or doorstep a dozen times a day. "We never got over the scene at hand," admitted Janice.

"The Two Dot has everything; it is one of the wildest places in the country," Todd said. Agreeing, Janice pointed to a photograph taken by Wyoming Game and Fish investigator Jim Oudin. It shows a damp patch of earth filled with hoof and paw prints, representing dozens of species that had crossed that Two Dot microcosm. "The ranch is a thoroughfare for every creature that calls this environment home," she said.

In earlier times, one of those creatures was the bison. In 1989, during some roadwork on the Chief Joseph Highway, remains of a buffalo jump were discovered. The ranch opened to archeologists, headed by Daniel H. Eakin and his staff at the University of Wyoming's Office of Archeology, who plotted the full extent of the prehistoric site.

Marie Paule Burrus with cattle dogs loaded in the pick-up and ready to ride.
(Courtesy Yves Burrus)

• •

St. Clair offered the Churchills a chance to take over the farm work as independent contractors in 1990. "We couldn't get to the bank fast enough to apply for the loan to buy machinery. This was tailor-made for our dreams. While we would work off-season for the ranch, we would live at the Paint Creek place and manage the farming operation as our own business," said Janice.

The Churchills farmed 860 acres and carried a full-time haying crew. They aimed to increase the hay harvest from a thousand tons a year to at least eighteen hundred. It was tough, but they had some success. Janice did almost all of the irrigation on Paint Creek, in steep, rocky meadows, Todd remembered. "The guy who pulled those ditches was a genius."

But the most meticulous irrigation can't save a hay crop from wind, especially one funneling through Clarks Fork Canyon during haying season. Wind can spell the difference between harvesting a crop and watching it disappear over the creek bank. It can roll the newly cut windrows into a ball or simply spray them into the air. So once the alfalfa passes through the swather there is no slowing down, because this kind of wind cannot be predicted.

"One time we watched eighty acres on Rocky Flats roll across the field gathering every new windrow as it grabbed the crop... It rolled a twenty-foot wall clear across the meadow right into Paint Creek, clearing the field," recalled Todd. There was no bringing it back.

As for the Paint Creek wildlife, "You didn't need entertainment up there, you just went outside," Janice said. There were bears and beavers aplenty, and nearly a dozen moose. Todd recalled, "One old girl had her calves down in the willows behind the Paint Creek house every year. She put the run on the dogs because she didn't mess with anyone."

Other critters were less welcome. Rattlers popped up everywhere; Todd saw nine in one day and was struck in the boot twice. "Snakes were the biggest cause for losing hired hands," he said. They had to be especially careful while irrigating, unrolling the plastic irrigation dams that were placed in the ditches. While the Churchills became tolerant of rattlers, their crew never did. After meeting up with one snake too many, employees often quit on the spot.

One night, the couple recalled, they woke to the alarming bark of their dog. They knew, even in that state between sleep and wakefulness that Tucker was warning them they had company. Janice hit the floor running, Todd grabbed his .22—which would prove useless—and Janice snatched a flashlight as they shouldered through the back door. The light blinked, then went out. Twice she shook the light; twice it flashed, then went dark. Again Janice shook it in the air, and the light finally held. As they peered down the beam toward the bark, the yellow circle illuminated an upright grizzly. It had apparently come down the creek looking for winterkill. The couple froze, then backed up in unison until they reached their pickup, jerked open the door and leapt in, scrambling to slam it before the bear reached them.

Impressively, Tucker, who had fought off grizzlies when Janice worked in hunting camps, stayed between the truck and the bear until the animal tired of the exercise and wandered off.

In the fall the couple often fell asleep outside listening to bull elk bugling. "In the spring we watched the cow elk with their newborn calves leaving the fields. They'd signal the babies with a quieter and shortened version of the bugle the bulls make, calling back and forth until they all got through the fences and then went on their way."

Todd and Janice cherished living in a place where each moment must be lived wide awake, where nature was part of their every move. The Churchills would stay for a decade and mourn their leave-taking when the time came.

• •

Yves Burrus took a transatlantic phone call from Ryan St. Clair late one night in September—bugling season in Wyoming. The Two Dot foreman "was looking through his window and yelling, 'Sir, we are not running a cattle ranch here anymore but an elk ranch. What should I do? They are everywhere.'"

Though the numbers were expanding, this was the same elk migration that Krier had reported a number of years before.

Teddie St. Clair, too, remembers that evening. "We counted as they jumped the fence, finally giving up when the number passed six hundred. Ryan suggested to Mr. Burrus that they were eating the alfalfa. Mr. Burrus said that was fine. When Ryan explained that they were getting into the haystacks, that, too, was 'fine'."

Almost at a loss for argument, Ryan declared it was time to either let more hunters in for elk, or sell down some cows to make room for them. "We sold cows," Yves explained. "Yes, Two Dot became not only a cattle ranch, but also a place where the wildlife was everywhere welcome, where nature was taken care of."

Back in 1881, when John Chapman's brother-in-law Henry hunted elk on the Stinking Water (now the Shoshone River), the animals roamed in bands of up to a thousand. Later, as cattle and sheep covered the range, the species declined. But today—thanks to Burrus—the Two Dot once again hosts a large resident elk herd as well as a migratory band that spills out of Yellowstone in late fall or winter depending upon the harshness of the weather.

As a boy, Swiss-born Burrus learned to track game in the footsteps of his French grandfather; later they hunted shoulder-to-shoulder worldwide; later still Burrus taught his own son. "Raised in northern Europe where big game has been for centuries protected and hunted under very strict rules, we brought new ideas to our American ranch," he said. "We also tried to develop some ethical attitudes in the way game should be hunted and respected, even after death. These ideas are now, nearly twenty-five years later, much more usual, if not always respected by the Western hunters."

As Todd Churchill saw it, the new owner "seemed to come from a different school where there was more appreciation for the wildlife. When friends and family came to hunt, Burrus had rules.

Each hunter would spend at least one day out on the hunt riding the horses, scoping the elk, but shooting nothing." They needed to absorb the environment first.

Soon after his arrival at the Two Dot, Yves met Jim Oudin, the Wyoming Game and Fish Department investigator who would support his efforts to improve wildlife habitat. Oudin also knew the history.

In the late 1800s the bison that ranged the region were fast disappearing—it is rumored that the last one was killed at the mouth of Newmeyer Canyon. Pat O'Hara Mountain was already familiar to big game hunters at that time. Said Oudin, "The ranch was historically home to trophy hunting through the late 1800s." The Two Dot was—and is again becoming—a miniature Yellowstone, with grizzly and black bear, mountain lion, pronghorn, moose, mule and white-tail deer, as well as elk. There are also coyote, fox, badger, raccoon, porcupine and beaver.

But by 1905, under the Allison-Bent partnership, even deer were newsworthy, judging from a May 10 item in the *Wyoming Stockgrower and Farmer*, "A bunch of thirty deer passed east from Pat O'Hara to Heart Mountain within a few rods of Mr. Bent's house after the recent snowstorm. One old buck went through the yard between the residence and bunkhouse."

Several decades later, Mac Taggart still noted the paucity of game. As in 1905, wildlife merited a note in the newspaper.

White-tailed deer remained scarce in the 1950s and 1960s, but they are now increasing throughout all the drainages, attracted by timber and willow. In the fall of 1977, when Burrus started exploring, "there really wasn't much wildlife, a few muleys here and there, elk nowhere but on top of Pat O'Hara." That would change.

As the wildlife increased, the ranch was turning into an international hunting camp for Burrus and his friends. "We didn't know how to hunt elk and yet the French hunters arrived every

November," admitted Teddie S. Clair. "Once again, though, we had good cowboys who knew where the elk were and how to hunt them."

Killing game has long been man's necessity, and still is for many Wyoming residents glad to have meat in the freezer. But for Burrus and his friends, it was also a great adventure. They followed smart mule deer for days and admired the grace of white-tailed deer in the wind. They shot wild pheasants and gray partridges, birds nearly too fast for their guns. Their early-morning patience might be rewarded by a big six pointer emerging from the mist. They worked hard to shoot from close enough to kill without pain, and they brought home magnificent trophies.

But others, too, coveted those trophies.

Poaching was an old problem at the Two Dot, as Earl Curtis could attest—his own horse had its nose creased by a bullet from the gun of a would-be poacher.

Still, even Earl could understand why those criminals were tempted to hunt illegally and off season. While Paul Stock owned Trail Creek Ranch, he developed a private wildlife preserve at the head of Trail Creek on Pat O'Hara Mountain. "There were elk up there with racks wider than this room," Earl explained from his dining room table.

Now one of Oudin's major assignments was investigating poaching. Burrus was concerned that on the Two Dot, "animals did not feel safe, and went elsewhere." Despite Oudin's efforts, a persistent phantom deer poacher was never caught. But his tenacity paid off in the case of "Growler." In 1990 Oudin found evidence of an illegal elk kill on the Two Dot. He would pursue the case for two years.

During those years, Oudin noted, a certain proud big-game hunter was entering and winning contest after contest featuring outstanding racks. One rack came from an elk he had dubbed Growler for his distinctive broken bugling voice. The Growler rack was a Pope and Young bull scoring 365 points... The Pope and Young Club is a place for archery hunters to submit outstanding racks for the record books. It won first place at the Bowhunters of Wyoming Big Game Awards, second at the Wyoming Outfitters Association Big Bull Contest, and third at the Rocky Mountain Elk Foundation Bull of the Woods Archery Unguided Contest.

Not only did the hunter brag, he showed photographs taken at the kill site. That would be his undoing. Unbeknownst to the hunter, Oudin had a similar photograph. The head, cape, and antlers were not there but the backdrop convinced a jury that the photos were taken at the same location. The man was convicted.

Regulating hunting on the Two Dot was a time-consuming task for ranch managers until Jim Oudin retired from the Wyoming Game and Fish in 1996 and took over the supervision. Each of the thirty-odd hunters gaining access to the ranch each season must be properly licensed and pay a trespass fee. Their Two Dot hunting permit spells out the rules. These include: Hunt on foot and horseback only, no off-road vehicles, no hunting in the meadows, and close all gates. "I know who's there every day and where they are supposed to be," Oudin said.

While mule deer hunting is forbidden, there is a limited antlerless white-tailed deer season on the creek bottoms.

Elk season is the main event. At this time Highway 120N and the Chief Joseph Highway are jammed with sightseers—hunters of another kind—watching the bulls bugling and collecting their harems. The Two Dot issues thirty permits for antlerless elk in September, to help reduce elk traffic on the hay meadows. The season is suspended in October and resumes in November, also an antlerless hunt to protect the bulls.

Oudin noted that partly due to the Two Dot's tightly regulated elk season, "There certainly are a lot of trophy bulls in the area, and the nice thing is that those hunting outside the perimeters of the Two Dot reap the benefits of the care taken of the wildlife within its borders."

When Burrus learned that wild turkeys had once roamed the property, he dreamed of returning the species to the ranch. The birds had disappeared, but the stories hadn't. Verle Richmond, from the Taggart and Curtis years, recalled the day she asked her son Robbie to get her a turkey before he went to school. He was remarkably lucky that morning. When he arrived back at the house he dropped three turkeys on the kitchen table, holding up a hand to forestall the questions. "I'm so sorry, Mom, it was an accident." He'd gotten all three with one shot. Verle didn't run out of meat for a while.

Coyotes plagued the first wild turkeys Burrus and Oudin reintroduced, but now the feathered creatures strut around headquarters in winter, and wander up Pat O'Hara Creek in summer. The year 2000 proved to be a very good one. "There's one old hen out there that hatched eleven chicks in early spring and she still had all of them late in the fall," Oudin said.

Wolves, too, have reappeared as they expand their Sunlight Basin territory to the west. After their reintroduction into Yellowstone Park in 1995, three packs were producing litters on the Two Dot by the summer of 2000.

The Two Dot is also home to pheasants, sage chickens, chukars, mallards, owls, Hungarian partridges, falcons, ruffed and blue grouse, hawks, and golden eagles. There are many types of smaller birds such as meadowlarks, blackbirds, robins, magpies, nuthatches, and chickadees. Seasonal residents include many migratory songbird species and bald eagles. The bald eagle's status recently graduated from endangered to threatened, as its numbers recover nationwide. In the meantime there are candidates for endangered species status: the sage grouse and the mountain plover, a bird with a historical link to bison and, now, to cattle. Plover like short-grazed grasslands, and they have been known to breed on Chapman Bench.

While Jim Oudin continues to oversee the hunting season, he credits Burrus with all the wildlife improvements on the ranch. "Let's face it, because of this man's vision, the wildlife have a pretty good life here on the Two Dot."

Burrus recalls his first Two Dot elk hunt, with a friend and a guide named Harvey. Starting at six in the morning, they climbed Pat O'Hara and finally, Burrus said, "at four in the afternoon, Harvey stopped short and said, 'There, I smell elk.' I was not used yet to smelling that strong scent, but he was there, two hundred yards away, in a clear cut.

"After all the work of cutting the meat and putting it on the horse, we headed back. Riding home I couldn't stay any more on my horse—ten hours' ride is crippling, so we had to walk, and in the valley the moon was rising over Heart Mountain, clear and bright... You know you are getting closer to home when you see a few lights in the valley, from the headquarters or maybe the lodge on top of the hill. Everything is so quiet. You just hear the horse's shoes clicking against the stones. Tired, your companions don't speak anymore. You feel the beauty, absorb the strength, the plentitude and you say, thank you."

• •

In 1995 with the deterioration of St. Clair's health, Yves Burrus needed to move ranch management in a new direction. Although diabetes had plagued Ryan for years, he was able to pretty much ignore it. But when he was diagnosed with cancer in March of 1996, the couple knew it was time to return to Texas after nineteen wonderful years.

When Yves arrived at the office of Mick McCarty, the man who would become his friend, lawyer, and pivotal force on the operation, the cattleman-attorney had no intention of wearing yet another hat. But at the close of their session, Mick was on board as Two Dot ranch manager.

At that time Mick and his son Mark, who had run their own ranch, formed McCarty Management, which took over the operation of the Two Dot. As on-site foreman, Mark brought new energy and historical perspective to the job. In turn, his explorations put Yves Burrus on horseback headed in new directions, seeing the ranch through fresh eyes. "The Two Dot has everything a ranch needs," said Mark. "Running this ranch is a dream come true for us." Both Yves and Mark hungered for a deeper understanding of the ranch's wild species, its ecological balances. Their interest was served by an unusual project, already approved by Ryan back in 1992.

The Two Dot Ranch became a vast science laboratory; its plant species were extensively mapped by Kaush Arha, a doctoral candidate at the University of California at Berkeley. Both the size and the biodiversity of the ranch suited it for the five-year project.

First Arha gathered satellite imagery using remote sensing at a resolution of thirty-meter pixels, about a hundred feet square. His geographic target included everything from Big Creek west of the Billings Highway to the Clarks Fork and south to the North Fork of the Shoshone River.

"The Two Dot is one of the most productive wildlife habitats in the whole of the Big Horn Basin both in size and production—big game, elk, mule deer, white-tailed deer, antelope, moose. They also have black and grizzly bear, mountain lion, upland game birds and waterfowl.

"In this era of subdivisions and housing developments, it is a time when one of the best friends of wildlife is a cow," he said.

Indeed, Burrus placed a high value on wildlife and provided year-round protection for fifteen hundred resident elk. He developed a double goal—to run a profitable livestock operation while providing as much elk habitat as possible.

Arha concluded his work in 1997, a year that would bring more weather extremes for the ranch.

One blizzard that winter was memorable, but not for its damage; instead, recalled Janice Churchill, "It was a beautiful storm, one that came straight down continuously for several days until there was three feet of snow stacked and balanced on the top of the fence posts. It was rare to see snow that was not moving horizontally."

A more violent storm descended on Todd as he hiked the upper reaches of Bald Ridge. It quickly took on whiteout proportions. But Todd knew the area: there was a cave nearby in Newmeyer Canyon. He crawled and stumbled, feeling his way to the rock that jutted from the entrance. The cave opened into a large room; once inside Todd built a fire, brewed some coffee with the grounds he'd stashed away another time and settled down to wait out the storm.

Each new management team experienced the same weather patterns in their own way. As the Curtises had learned years earlier, floods could be devastating. All had seen quiet, meandering creeks turn into maniacs of destruction, taking out bridges, tearing out trees and beaver dams, gathering the debris that shores up its own banks.

On an early June morning in 1997, Yves Burrus looked out on an easygoing drizzle, a typical early-summer rain. But before midnight he would find himself in a trial that could easily have become a tragedy.

Late in the afternoon Burrus paused by the living room window to enjoy the glory of the panoramic, misty view. The water in the little lake below the lodge appeared to be rising, but he went on about his work. As darkness settled over the lodge, the drizzle became a downpour. That downpour was a torrent at ranch headquarters. High on Pat O'Hara, rain was melting snowpack; rivulets wandered into trickles, these into tiny streams—and the rush to the river was on. Only the earthen dam on the lake below the lodge stood in the way of the oncoming tide.

Although the head of water was still hours from the dam, a flash flood was in the making. Yves must have remembered stories of the flood that he never saw in 1966, the one that destroyed the little lake below the lodge. Skoglund had never replaced it, and it took Yves three tries to rebuild the dam, restore the lake, and get the dam to hold.

It was nearly midnight when Todd Churchill picked up the phone at Paint Creek and heard Yves's urgent call for help. The water was running over the dam. Pressure was building. A decision needed to be made—would they let the dam burst or would they try to relieve the pressure by opening the floodgate below?

Todd jumped into his pickup and half-slid, half-drove the five slick miles of clay to the lodge. The men followed the mud-soaked path to the edge of the dam; they could hear it groan and feel it shudder as water roared over its crest. Todd would try to reach the wheel out there in the dark, about halfway across the dam. Now well under the water's surface, the wheel controlled the cover. If he could feel his way to it, he could crank it around, raising the cover over the opening at the base of the dam.

Burrus lit Todd's path with a flashlight as he stepped onto the crest of the dam. Soon the water was over his boots as he inched toward the middle of the dam, where it stood about fifteen feet high.

Resisting the tremendous current, he took smaller and smaller steps, time dragging to a stop. Finally he reached what he calculated to be the midpoint, twenty feet out. The wheel should be here—he hoped. The young cowboy reached deep, his arm sweeping, groping for the wheel, with no luck. Then he moved a step forward, repeating the process. Still no wheel. Todd's body shuddered along with the groaning dam.

On the third try his palm met metal. Todd planted his feet

and forced the wheel one full turn. He heard the muffled groan of the gate far below and the metallic crack of the wheel. The cold metal vibrated in his hands.

Now Yves was calling to him. "Todd, Todd, I believe what you are doing is quite dangerous," he was shouting over the roaring water. "It is not worth dying for. Please come back." As Todd turned to answer, he saw that Yves had stepped onto the dam crest himself, the better to light Todd's work. Todd cranked faster.

Finally the dam's gate was wide open. Standing up, Todd turned and slid one foot after the other, moving ever backward. Could it be that the water, which had reached his knees at one point, was already receding? He scolded himself—far too early to tell. As Todd inched toward solid ground, Yves stepped carefully backwards, determined to keep the light on Todd. When they reached the embankment both men grinned, letting out the lung-bursting breaths they'd been holding. "Then we just stood there in the pouring rain in the middle of the night and prayed," Todd recalled. Both men knew instinctively that they had just barely saved the dam. Later one expert would call it a miracle.

Despite its wet beginning, any future moisture seemed to have drowned with the flood. As the summer crawled into August, fire danger increased daily. "On the Two Dot, but even more on the Paint Creek Ranch, you learned to keep one eye peeled on the horizon over Bald Ridge, knowing that if it was burning right behind the ridge— the smoke told the story," Todd Churchill said. Crew members were always ready to grab gunnysacks and beat out small flares that could quickly become horrendous firewalls. (While Burrus often learned of these events after the fact, he took advantage of technological advances to keep in daily contact with his people on the Two Dot by cell phone and e-mail.)

Now the Churchills learned that lightning had started a blaze in the Clarks Fork Canyon and firefighters could no longer hold it. They were ordered to evacuate.

For the young couple, saving the business meant "everyone jumping on a piece of machinery, moving it out towards headquarters, trying to stay ahead of the fast-moving fire. It was burning so hot that the fire was making its own wind," Todd said. "As we drove away from the head of flame coming toward us, we suddenly saw the fire rear up, twisting back on itself. We shut down the tractors, heaving a big sigh of relief and watched as it seemed to be retracing the path furiously, hungry for new fuel. The relief was short-lived though, for in a few minutes, as fast as it had swung away, the fire reversed itself once again, coming back at us strong as ever for the second time."

The pattern repeated itself. Again the fire was stopped. Finally feeling safe at last, the Two Dot team returned the machinery to Paint Creek and took their blackened, smoky bodies home for a much-needed rest.

• •

And still the Two Dot family continues to evolve and revolve. As it had for his predecessors, the day came for Yves Burrus to move on. It was with a heavy heart, yet a sense of fate, that he placed the ranch on the market. He had cherished this jewel of the Clarks Fork floodplain for twenty-one years.

By January 2000 the Two Dot was in new hands—and it remained intact. That was an accomplishment the environmental and local community could celebrate with Yves Burrus, who is truly, as he often described himself, a citizen of Switzerland, France, and Wyoming.

As the airplane taking Yves away from Wyoming for the last time climbed into the cold winter sky, he was able to follow the familiar trails of the Two Dot—the variegated geography, the varying landscapes, snow-packed Pat O'Hara reaching up toward him, his beloved lodge just a speck. He recalled the words of Karen Blixen, known as Isak Dinesen, in her opening lines from *Out of Africa*, "I had a farm in Africa at the foot of the Ngong Hills."

Yves Burrus, too, had laid claim to a foreign land—and while the ownership papers had been exchanged, the ranch, so deeply embedded within his heart, would remain there always.

S O U R C E S

My guide throughout the research on this book was Yves Burrus, owner of the Two Dot from 1977 to 1999. The individual stories by the Park County Story Committee edited by Lucille N. Hicks in the *Park County Story*, a collection of general and family histories of Park County from prehistoric times through 1980, (Dallas, TX. Taylor Publishing, 1980) set me on my historical path. I kept T.A. Larson's *History of Wyoming* (Lincoln: University of Nebraska Press, 1990) close by throughout. Because there was a steady migration of cowboys, homesteaders and ranchers between the Two Dot and Clarks Fork area and the North Fork, I took advantage of Ester Johansson Murray, *A History of the Northfork of the Shoshone River* (Cody, Wyo.: Lone Eagle MultiMedia, 1996), both for the characters involved and the sense of the times.

Bob Edgar and Jack Turnell's, *Brand of a Legend*, (Cody, Wyo.: Stockade Publishing, 1978) provided much parallel information regarding the Chapman era, especially excerpts from the Otto Frank diary which is at the Buffalo Bill Historical Center's Harold McCracken Library.

I referred frequently to Jeannie Cook, Lynn Johnson Houze, Bob Edgar, and Paul Fees' *Buffalo Bill's Town in the Rockies: A Pictorial History of Cody, Wyoming* (Virginia Beach, VA: Donning Company Publishers, 1996); David J. Wasden's *From Beaver To Oil: A Century in the Development of Wyoming's Big Horn Basin* (Cheyenne, Wyo.: Pioneer Printing & Stationery Co., 1973); and John K. Rollinson's, *Pony Trails in Wyoming: Hoofprints of a Cowboy and U.S. Ranger* (Lincoln: University of Nebraska Press, 1941).

B. Byron Price's, *Cowboys of the American West* (Singapore: Key

Porter Books, 1996) gave me a flavor of the West through former Director of the Buffalo Bill Historical Center Price's richly worded text as well as the writings and principal photography of Dudley Witney. Also Lawrence M. Woods' *Wyoming's Big Horn Basin to 1901: A Late Frontier* (Spokane, Wash.: Arthur H. Clark Company, 1997); Leona Lampi's *At the Foot of the Beartooth Mountains: A History of the Finnish Community of Red Lodge, Montana* (Coeur d'Alene, Idaho: Bookage Press, 1998); David J. Wasden's, "Two Dot Ranch" and "Pat O'Hara Creek," (*Annals of Wyoming* 49, Fall 1977); and Art Kidwell's, *In the Shadow of the Beartooth:* Clark, Wyoming (Powell, Wyo.: Desert Moon Press, 2004) were also helpful.

Tabulation of Adjudicated Water Rights of the State of Wyoming provided names, dates and water development in the area of the Two Dot.

Local and regional newspapers published in the area including the *Northern Wyoming Herald, Park County Herald, Cody Enterprise* and *Red Lodge Picket*, provided much information, especially regular columns like Mary Say's, "Pat O'Hara" and "Beyond Bald Ridge." Simpson's column kept up with the "Paint Creek News." All three were found in the *Cody Enterprise*.

Information was also obtained from an untitled and unsourced fifty page Two Dot manuscript given to me by Yves Burrus. I also used Ellen Waggoner's "Cattle Pioneer Starts Two Dot Ranch," *Cody Enterprise*, December 15, 1999.

Besides past owners and employees, individuals who helped me track my work throughout the book include Oscar and Jane (Riddle) Thompson, Paul Phillips, Donald G. Tolman, Ester Johansson Murray, Elaine Moncur, Lucille Patrick and many others. Without Tina Martinez and Janice Churchill's early research, I would not have been so quick to start this project.

Ranch in Crisis, Tragedy and Celebration: An Introduction

The opening quote is taken from a speech by Robert Utley, former chief historian for the National Park Service, now retired, given at the dedication symposium for the Buffalo Bill Historical Center, Harold D. McCracken Library, Cody, Wyoming.

Chapter One: John Colter:
A Lewis and Clark Explorer in Two Dot Country

John Colter first came alive to me when I sat in on a program presented by Gene Bryan, then Wyoming Travel Commission head. He has a passion for Colter and knows him well, describing details I'd failed to discover. I returned to Bryan in late 2005 to confirm my findings.

In my own research I started with Dr. M.J. Smith's *John Colter* (Cody, Wyo.: Park County Chapter of the Wyoming Historical Society, 1957). While Colter only takes up the first eight pages in this booklet, Smith, too, brings passion to his knowledge of the explorer. Stephen E. Ambrose's, *Undaunted Courage* (New York: A Touchstone Book, Simon and Schuster, 1996) was useful. Facts regarding the Lewis and Clark Expedition with occasional mention of John Colter, whom Clark found in Pittsburgh, PA, led to research in Gary Moulton's *The Journals of Lewis and Clark* (Lincoln: University of Nebraska Press, 2002).

Information came from the chapter on John Colter in Dr. DeWitt Dominick and Mary Dominick Chivers', *Doctor Dewey: Stories from the Life and Career of Dr. DeWitt Dominick of Cody, Wyoming* (Cody: WordsWorth, 1996), 129-133. Dominick chaired the 150th Coulter celebration in 1957 while president of the Wyoming Historical Society. Thomas James *Three Years Among the Indian and Mexicans* (St. Louis: Keystone Western Americana Series, 1916) 57-58; David J. Wasden's, *From Beaver to Oil,* (Cheyenne: Pioneer Printing &

Stationery Co., 1973); Jim Chenoweth's, "Colter and Drouillard," (*Fence Post*, February 12 and 26th, 2001); and Burton Harris's, *The Original History of John Colter, His Years in the Rocky Mountains* (Basin, Wyo.: Big Horn Book Company, 1952, reprinted 1977) also provides information about Colter.

A note per historian, Ester Johannsen Murray "Fort Raymond was actually Fort Manuel Lisa 1807–1811, Fort Benton 1811–1824, Fort Cass 1832–1835 at mouth of Big Horn River" was also helpful.

Finally, thanks to an invitation from archeologist, Chris Finley, Colter came to life, "under my feet," as I stood watching his team carefully pulling Crow artifacts from their camp of many years ago. Located just above the Cody Canal about seven miles southwest of Cody it was amazing. I knew at that moment that Colter had stood in that very spot, I could almost feel his spirit encouraging that Crow band to trade with Manuel Lisa at Fort Raymond, better known then as Manuel's Fort.

Chapter Two: The Final War of the Nez Perce

There is much material available about the Nez Perce and Chief Joseph including Helen Addison Howard's *Saga of Chief Joseph* (Lincoln: University of Nebraska Press, 1978); Merrill D. Beal's, *"I Will Fight No More Forever:" Chief Joseph and the Nez Perce War* (Seattle: University of Washington Press, 1963); Jerome A. Greene's *Nez Perce Summer 1877: The U.S. Army and the Nee-Me Poo Crisis* (Helena: Montana Historical Society, 2000); and David Lavender's, *Let Me Be Free: The Nez Perce Tragedy,* (New York: Harper Collins Publishers, 1992). L. V. McWhorter's, *Hear Me My Chiefs: Nez Perce History and Legend,* (Caldwell, Idaho: The Caxton Printers Ltd. 1952).

Newspaper articles consulted included, "Long Road to Surrender," *Billings Gazette,* a series that ran from September 28, 2002 through October 7, 2002 on the flight of the Nez Perce Indians;

"125th Anniversary of the Nez Perce War of 1877," *Park News,* a special printing done by Yellowstone Park staff; "Montana Press Publishes New Volume on Chief Joseph," *Billings Gazette,* November 29, 2001; "Dead Indian Road to Be Fixed to Open Up Region," *Northern Wyoming Daily News,* June 1, 1961; "Cody Club Backs Clarks Fork Road Proposal," *Cody Enterprise,* November 17, 1966; "Commission Renames Sunlight Road," *Cody Enterprise,* November 23, 1988; "Chief Joseph Highway Funding 'tough to secure,' Wallop Explains," *Cody Enterprise,* June 12, 1989; "2 Million in 1990 Funding for Chief Joseph Road Sought," *Powell Tribune,* October 5, 1989; "Paving Nears Completion on Chief Joseph Highway," *Billings Gazette,* August 4, 1995; "Governor Coming to Chief Joe Dedication," *Cody Enterprise,* August 23, 1995; "Chief Joe Completion Honored," *Cody Enterprise,* September 6, 1995; and "Governor 'opens' Second Park Route," *Cody Enterprise,* September 13, 1995. Chuck Hassler's, "Riders Retrace Retreat of Nez Perce Tribe" *Powell Tribune,* n.d. also provided details.

Chapter Three: The Bennett Butte Battle

Time seems to have erased any evidence of the exact site of the Bennett Butte Battle although weather washes up evidence periodically. "Two bodies found," *Cody Enterprise,* July 16, 1953 describes the find by sons of Georgia Close, a Clarks Fork rancher, who I interviewed several times both by phone and in person. The skeletons were never completely identified. Kyle V. Walpole's "Bivouac of the Dead, The Battle of Bennett Butte (Miles' Fight on the Clarks Fork) Reexamined" (*Annals of Wyoming 71,* No. 1, Winter 1999); and Bob Meinecke's, "Cavalry Fought Bannock Indians in 1878 Near Clark," *Cody Enterprise* column "Tracks, Trails and Tidbits," May 5, 1999; were also helpful.

Chapter four: Pat O'Hara: The Elusive Mountain Man

Folklore concerning Pat O'Hara abounds, facts are harder to find. Eugene Sayre Topping's, *Chronicles of the Yellowstone*, originally published in 1888 by Pioneer Press Co. and reprinted by (Minneapolis: Ross & Haines, Inc., 1968), offers facts on O'Hara as does "Pat O'Hara 50 Years Ago," *Cody Enterprise,* June 22, 1961. I also consulted Dave Wasden's, "The Day Pat O'Hara…," *Cody Enterprise,* December 24, 1913; Mrs. M. R. Hoffman's, "Pat O'Hara, A True Pioneer," *Rotary Rangler*, n.d.; Walter R. Hoffman interview (Park County Historical Archives, July, 1914) and Jim Hoffman for an interview and manuscript review.

Chapter Five: John Chapman: Founder of the Two Dot Ranch

While Chapman was a quiet man who said little of himself over the years, others were more eager to tell his story. A six-page name by name genealogical history of the Riddle family, "the Riddle Family In Oregon" (provided by Jane Thompson) says that John Chapman was a grandson of William H. and Maximilla Riddle. John K. Rollinson's, *Pony Trails in Wyoming: Hoofprints of a Cowboy and U.S. Ranger*, edited by E.A Brininstool (Lincoln: University of Nebraska Press, first copyright 1941), and his "John W. Chapman-Pioneer Cattleman" *Wyoming Cattle Trails* (Caldwell, ID: Caxton Printers, Ltd, 1948), tells of a relationship that Rollinson treasured. An article "Sells His Great Ranch," *Cody Enterprise,* September 19, 1901, offers a look at Chapman as well.

See also "Funeral Throng Pays Respect to Chapman," *Red Lodge Picket Journal,* December 28, 1933, Sec. 1. Co-editors Shirley Zupan and Harry Owen's book *Red Lodge Saga of a Western Area* (Red Lodge, MT: Carbon County Historical Society, 1979) contained useful information. Kathryn Wright's "Long-time Red Lodge Resident

Recalls…," *Billings Gazette,* September 30, 1949; Tom Stout's *Montana: Its Story and Biography,* vol. 2 (American Historical Society, 1921); and a booklet, *Montana National Bank, Originally Banking House of Meyer and Chapman 1907-1975* (Montana National Bank) were also helpful.

The story of Sword Bearer appears in Frederick F. Hoxie's *Parading Through History: The Making of the Crow Nation in America 1805-1935* (New York: Cambridge University Press 1995)

I also relied upon David Wasden, (*Annals of Wyoming* 49 No. 2, Fall 1977) for information. Other sources consulted include the *Billings Herald,* June 21, 1884; *Stinking Water Prospector,* June 24, 1891; "John Chapman," *Annals of Wyoming* 19; *Red Lodge Picket,* 1891; and *Red Lodge Picket,* June 16, 1894. "Mrs. John W. Chapman W.P.A." Montana Livestock History Project (MHS Library, Microfilm #250, Reel 15, Spring 1941) provided information as did Park County Historical Society *What Ranches Existed Before 1900 in Region of Park County.* Additional newspapers consulted were "Sells His Great Ranch," *Park County Herald,* September 19, 1901; and "Two Dot Ranch History, Looking at Agriculture," *Powell Tribune,* May 31, 1977.

"Chapman loses horses in Yellowstone Park in 1904. One survived winter with saddle still on and bonded with elk," (*Wyoming Stockman and Farmer,* September 27, 1905). "Former Douglas County Man Dead From Medford," story of John W. Chapman's stepfather's death, (Unknown publication, n.d) gave information.

See also "John Chapman a Covered Wagon Emigrant on Old Oregon Trail," *Red Lodge Picket,* December 21, 1933; "John William Chapman is Dead Was Pioneer Stockman, Banker," *Red Lodge Picket,* December 21, 1933; and "Mrs. John Chapman Dies This Morning" *Red Lodge Picket,* February 14, 1950.

In regards to the Butch Cassidy saga, much is written including Richard Patterson's, *Butch Cassidy: A Biography* (Lincoln: A Bison

Book, University of Nebraska Press, 1998); Doris Platts, *Incident of 1892* (Wilson, Wyo., self-published, n.d.); Chip Carlson's, "Train Robbery Involves Butch Cassidy," *Wyoming Livestock Roundup* (June 5, 1999).

"Information" and trial papers on Butch Casssidy, (Fremont County Courthouse, August 28, 1891; June 19, 23 & 24, 1892; November 13 & 17, 1893; June 39, 1894). "Watch Out, Little Train the Wild Bunch'll Get You," *Billings Gazette,* May 26, 1962; and Anne Goddard Charter's *Cowboys Don't Walk: A Tale of Two* (Billings, Montana: Western Organization of Resource Councils, 1999).

Chapter Six: The Stone House

A Two Dot tour paper written by David Wasden quotes Ray Prante in a September 28, 1985, oral interview, concerning the building of the Stone House (Park County Historical Archives). O.C. Bevelhymer, a construction worker on the Stone House, "Just a Breeze From Writer," *Cody Enterprise,* March 11, 1956, provided information. Interviews with Mac Taggart, Teddy St. Clair, Jackie Keesler, Jo Holmes, Cheryl Wright, Darlene McCarty, Jane Thompson and Frances Curtis were very helpful. I also perused "Chapmans Built Large House in 1902 for $6,500," *Red Lodge Picket,* n.d.

Chapter Seven: John Allison and the Elusive E. M. Bent

Photos and biographical information on John Perry Allison were provided by Daniel P. Truckey, Curator, Sioux City Public Museum. The materials included *Sioux City Journal,* November 6, 1908; July 15, 1910; July 18, 1910; October 23, 1911; and October 23, 1911. "First National Bank Grew From Little Tin Box Brought Here in 1855 For Service as Strongbox," *Sioux City Tribune,* April 5, 1940; J. K. Calkins, "Model Mountain Home of Allison-Bent Ranch,"

Wyoming Stockgrower and Farmer (n.d.). I also relied upon John D. Adams, *Three Quarters of a Century of Progress, Sioux City* (Sioux City: Verategen Printing Co., 1923); Arthur F. Allen's, *Northwestern Iowa: Its History and Tradition 1804-1926* (Sioux City: S.J. Clarke Publishing Co. 1927, 3 volumes); and *History of the Counties of Woodbury and Plymouth, Iowa* (Chicago: A Warner & Co. n.d.)

I am especially grateful for the work of Alice Spaulding of the Martha Washington Chapter of D.A.R. in Sioux City.

I studied *Wyoming Stockgrower* and *Farmer* issues including (August 9, 1905), telling of E.M. Bent preparing to put a track and car into his coal mine on Pat O'Hara. *The Northern Wyoming News*. September 19, 1901, explained Chapman's sale of the ranch to Allison. "Pioneer Banker S.C. Parks Dies," *Cody Enterprise*, 2003, describes Parks connection to the Shoshone National Bank with original stockholders E.M. Bent, J.S. Allison, and S.S. Newton. See also Fremont County Courthouse records.

Social activities and events were gathered by Art Kidwell recording newspapers *Free Press*, Bridger, MT; *Wyoming Stockgrower and Farmer*; and *Park County Enterprise* issues from 1903 through early 1906. Eleanor Buzalsky, Bozeman Museum, provided information on Mrs. E. Myron Ferris (Fannie) daughter of J.P. Allison. David Wasden in a 1977 paper prepared for the Wyoming State Historical Society trek of Two Dot area included information on Allison death (Gallatin County Historical Society).

Chapter Eight: Ganguet and Barth: A Young Immigrant's Opportunity

I consulted the *Northern Wyoming Herald*, August 20, 1915, for information. James Drummond's, *Montana Sheep Trails: A Century of Progress* (Helena: Montana Wool Growers Association, 1983) also provided information for me. "Gus Barth Buys Big Park County Ranch," *Cody Enterprise*, March 29, 1916; and two Pat O'Hara columns regarding the Barth Ranch, *Cody Enterprise*, August 6 and 8, 1916, both offered a look at Barth as well.

    A *Park County History* travel narrative prepared for a Wyoming Historical Society trek July 17, 1977, contained useful information. An interview with Jacqueline Fournier Benning, granddaughter of Ganguet (April 2000) provided important details and later photographs. An interview with Mrs. Peter (Victoria) Rachou was also helpful. Other sources included "Two Dot Middle Years Saw Sheep Operation," (*Looking at Agriculture*, une 28, 1977); A. H. Barth obituary, *Billings Gazette*, March 26, 1920; "A. H. Barth Funeral to be Held Tuesday," *Billings Gazette*, March 27, 1920; *Cody Enterprise*, regarding telephone lines 1922 and the *Park County Herald*, March 29, 1921 and May 28, 1924, added insight.

Chapter Nine: Their Own Kind of Partnership: The Jobe Brothers

    My research started with editor Lucille N. Hicks, *The Park County Story*, where several pieces on the Jobes came together. Ester Johansson Murray's *A History of the Northfork of the Shoshone River* provided much overlapping of Two Dot/Northfork resident names. I was also fortunate to interview both John T. and Rena Jobe's sons: John Jr. and his brother Glenn, before their deaths. Beth Jobe Spears, daughter of John Jr. provided photographs and plumped out details for me.

Chapter Ten: Evolution of a Homestead: The Heald Operation

    I obtained useful information during interviews with Paul Phillips, a close friend of George Heald, Jr. John K. Rollinson's *Pony Trails in Wyoming* (pg. 341) indicates that Andy Chapman, Affie Chapman's brother, too owned the Pat O'Hara ranch, probably he and Henry purchased it when James Weaver needed to leave the area due to poor health. See also "Chapman, Henry," a paper (Cody: Park County Historical Archives), and Clarence Stewart Peterson, Editor, *Men of Wyoming* (Chicago: A.W. Bowen & Co., 1903).

Chapter Eleven Frank Hudson

While the family remains prominent in the Hudson, Wyo., area little is documented of Frank Hudson's later life. I interviewed Bruce Finley who in turn asked the questions of his mother, Ellen Finley, and I reached Dan Szczpanski a cousin, as well. (June 20, 2001).

District Court, Dec. 15, 1921, Hudson had defaulted on his note. The Barth estate was finally closed May 14, 1923.

Chapter Twelve: James McKnight

McKnight research information received from Art Kidwell February 27, 2006. James N. McKnight born in 1889 and died 1967. Alice Elizabeth Davis, his wife 1892 to 1975. Jack, who grew up on the Two Dot was born in 1921 and lived in Texas until 1975 with his wife, Wilma. I interviewed Clytie Williams, a Clark native, who as a youngster knew the family.

The McKnights were mentioned frequently in the local papers of the day. For example, the *Cody Enterprise*, August 29, 1923, in the Pat O'Hara column regarding the Barth Ranch.

In the *Park County Herald* there was frequent mention from 1924 through 1926 including: two articles on, April 2, 1924, pp. 6 & 8; April 9, 1924, p. 8; May 7, 1924, on Holthouse, p. 3. The McKnights brought in "5,000 choice ewes" according to the May 29, 1924 piece, p. 4. Word of their neighboring was shared on October 1, 1924, p. 3; and information on their latest hunting trip was described, October 8, 1924, p. 6.

Notes on November 12, 1924, p. 3; November 19 and 26,

1924, as well as, January 14, 1925, p. 6; all give a sense of life on the ranch as well as trips to Texas. On January 21, 1925, p. 2, and February 7, 1925, there were two notes on digging coal on Pat O'Hara. More mention of McKnight on, July 15, 1925, p.3, October 21, 1925, p. 3, and, May 12, 1926, p. 4.

From then on the McKnights spent more time in Texas and were mentioned less frequently. Then on August 7, 1935, news of the end of their Two Dot ranching was announced and finalized, at least according to the *Park County Herald,* August 12, 1936, p. 4.

Courthouse records, Mortgage Book 67 page 129 describes McKnight activities as well.

Chapter Thirteen: The Walters Inn: Travelers' Rest

Mary Nielsen interview and manuscript, Elaine Rhoads handwritten manuscript provided by Mary Nielsen, and "Walters Inn is Bald Ridge Social Centre," *Cody Enterprise,* n.d.

Chapter Fourteen: Prohibition

Interviews with Carl Royal, Spicer relative (Dec. 10, 1999). Park County Historical Society, Ray Prante (Sept. 28, 1985) were useful. See also Ester Johannson Murray's, *A History of the Northfork of the Shoshone River.*

Chapter Fifteen: The Golden Age of Expansion: The Taggart Years

I appreciated the direction Mac Taggart provided in my early research starting on October 15, 1998. Also Daniel M. Davis, University of Wyoming American Heritage Center, in finding and gathering information on the Two Dot and the Taggarts from the Wyoming Stock Growers Association collection, which gave me additional insight.

I found a Lloyd Taggart, Sr. biography in a compendium of well-known Wyoming citizens, *The Historical Encyclopedia of Wyoming* (Dallas, Texas: Wyoming Historical Institute, n.d.) John Rolfe Burroughs "On the Upbeat" *Guardian of the Grasslands* (Cheyenne, Wyo.: Pioneer Printing and Stationery Co., 1971, p. 341). Lloyd Taggart took advantage of every form of communication to beat the drums of the Wyoming Stock Growers Association issues as its president in "Stockgrowers Assoc. President Taggart Attacks Union Power, Federal Spending," *Wyoming State Journal*, June 5, 1952. "Taggart Outlines Need for Stock Improvement" and "Lloyd W. Taggart writes an open letter to Senator Gale W. McGee" both published in the *Cody Enterprise*, April 29, 1963. "Taggart Attacks Controls in Address to Cattlemen," *Casper Tribune-Herald*, June 4, 1952.

The Taggart family is written about in the Park County Story mentioned earlier. Finally "Lloyd Taggart Dies Monday," *Cody Enterprise*, Feb. 20, 1974.

Chapter Sixteen: Hemingway—Famous Visitor Treated Like Neighbor

There is much written by Ernest Hemingway about his life, little of his life on the Two Dot and in Sunlight. He addresses some in Ernest Hemingway "The Wine of Wyoming," Scribner, (Aug. 30, 1931). Again he looks at "The Clark's Fork Valley, Wyoming," (*The Look of the West*, n.d.). I also used Carlos Baker's, *Ernest Hemingway: A Life Story* (New York: Charles Scribner's Sons, 1969).

Articles include, "History of the Beartooth Highway," *Billings Gazette*, June 29, 2003; "Chief Joseph," *Cooke City*, n.d., says that "while visiting here, Ernest Hemingway conceived and wrote the mountain part of *For Whom the Bell Tolls*. Dennis Davis, "Hemingway Found Wyoming of 1930s to His Liking," *Powell*

Tribune, Feb. 7, 1991. "Signature Recalls Hemingway," *Powell Tribune*, Dec. 6, 1990.

Hemingway's concerns about the already talked of "Beartooth Highway" addressed in "History of the Beartooth Highway" *Billings Gazette,* June 29, 2003, and again in Bruce H. Blevins book, *Beartooth Highway Experience* (Powell, Wyo.: WIM Marketing, 2003).

Other articles undated include "Portrait of the Author as a Young Man," (*Smithsonian Magazine,* Smithsonian Highlights*)*; Jim Fisher, "Ernest Hemingway and The Kansas City Star," *Kansas City Star,* July 10, 1999. "Hemingway Still Revered at Running of the Bulls," *Associated Press,* July 11, 1999; and Dan Burkhart's "Hemingway in Billings," *Billings Gazette*, February 22, 1998.

Robert Hoskins writes of Hemingway in "Paradise Lost" in *Wyoming Wildlife* (January 1997), and "Hemingway Books Sold Have Billings Connection" *Billings Gazette*, December 15, 2001.

Chapter Seventeen: Ranchland Patchwork

Research started with Park and Big Horn County records. *The Park County Story*, much used, and *Sisters of the Sage: Histories of Cody Country Ranch Women* (Worland, Wyo.: Serlkay Printing, 1998) expanded the story, especially regarding features on Mary Helen Dahlem Daly and Evelyn Braten Martin. Finally interviews with Mac Taggart, Jud and Verle Richmond, Harold Davidson, Lila Daly Siggins, Felix Hoff, Earl Curtis, Jack Braten, Georgia Close and Yves Burrus brought realism to the patchwork ranches and homesteads that make up such a part of the Two Dot.

"Paul Stock: Grand Old Man of Oil Production" *Cody Enterprise,* n.d.

Chapter Eighteen: Skoglund-Curtis

Interviews with Earl and Frances Curtis, Maurice Knutson, Betty Curtis, Jack Braten.

Horizontal photo by Jack Richard of Skoglund/Curtis cattle being moved from railway to Two Dot, *Cody Enterprise*, March 7, 1963.

Martin Nielsen, John Wyllie, Bill Blake interviews regarding fire fighting on Pat O'Hara.

*Chapter Nineteen: The Pivotal Short-Timers
Rogge and Hadley*

Interviews with Bob and Mary Hadley and Barbara Rogge Faulkner, daughter of Ken Rogge.

*Chapter Twenty: An Environmental Revolution
The Yves Burrus Years*

Interviews starting with Yves Burrus, with one-time employees, friends and neighbors including Al Parker, Teddie St. Clair, Kaush Arha, Jim Laverdure, Travis Bullard, Bob Florida, Mrs Scott (Pat) McKinly, Monte Jackson, Georgia Close, Willard V. Wilson, Clarke Straight, Jim Bama, Spike Voyle, Todd and Janice Churchill, Ray Krier, Mary Lou Wood, Jim Oudin, Mick and Mark McCarty, Chris Finley and Elaine Moncur among others.

"Purchase of Two Dot" *Denver Post*, Feb. 23, 1997. Daniel H. Eakin "A Prehistoric Stone Line Complex From Northwest Wyoming" (*The Wyoming Archaeologist*, 1997).

Lynn Burkhead "Deer Scoring: Numbers Add up for Big Bucks," *Outdoors*.

INDEX

Printed in the United States
151317LV00004B/1/P